WRITING

CREATIVE

WRITING

WRITING
CREATIVE
WRITING

Essays from the Field

edited by

RISHMA DUNLOP
DANIEL SCOTT TYSDAL
PRISCILA UPPAL

DUNDURN
TORONTO

Cover images: © Shutterstock.com/Keep Calm and Vector
Printer: Webcom

Library and Archives Canada Cataloguing in Publication

Writing creative writing : essays from the field / Rishma Dunlop, Daniel Scott Tysdal, Priscila Uppal, editors.

Includes bibliographical references.
Issued in print and electronic formats.
ISBN 978-1-4597-4169-0 (softcover).--ISBN 978-1-4597-4170-6 (PDF).--ISBN 978-1-4597-4171-3 (EPUB)

    1. Creative writing. 2. Authorship. I. Dunlop, Rishma, 1956-2016, editor II. Tysdal, Daniel Scott, 1978-, editor III. Uppal, Priscila, editor

PN145.W77 2018   808.02   C2017-907344-3
C2017-907345-1

1 2 3 4 5   22 21 20 19 18

 Conseil des Arts du Canada / Canada Council for the Arts   Canadä    ONTARIO ARTS COUNCIL / CONSEIL DES ARTS DE L'ONTARIO / an Ontario government agency / un organisme du gouvernement de l'Ontario

We acknowledge the support of the **Canada Council for the Arts**, which last year invested $153 million to bring the arts to Canadians throughout the country, and the **Ontario Arts Council** for our publishing program. We also acknowledge the financial support of the **Government of Ontario**, through the **Ontario Book Publishing Tax Credit** and the **Ontario Media Development Corporation**, and the **Government of Canada**.

Nous remercions le **Conseil des arts du Canada** de son soutien. L'an dernier, le Conseil a investi 153 millions de dollars pour mettre de l'art dans la vie des Canadiennes et des Canadiens de tout le pays.

Care has been taken to trace the ownership of copyright material used in this book. The author and the publisher welcome any information enabling them to rectify any references or credits in subsequent editions.
— *J. Kirk Howard, President*

The publisher is not responsible for websites or their content unless they are owned by the publisher.

VISIT US AT

 dundurn.com | @dundurnpress | dundurnpress | dundurnpress

Dundurn
3 Church Street, Suite 500
Toronto, Ontario, Canada
M5E 1M2

In Memory of Rishma Dunlop
(1956–2016)

Table of Contents

INTRODUCTION

Writing Creative Writing: A Student, a Teacher, and a Genre Walk into a Classroom and into Endless Possibilities

Rishma Dunlop, Daniel Scott Tysdal, and Priscila Uppal

The creative writing classroom is a joke. Or, at least, when speaking of the range of the identities of the participants, it has the makings of a joke: a student, a teacher, and a genre walk into a classroom. This is just one possible setup. Each of these individual figures, in truth, contains multiple identities.

The student alone could warrant a setup: *a student with a degree or diploma (at a university or college) or work and family duties (in continuing education or community courses), a burgeoning writer, and a human anxious about sharing one's most private meanings and tender experiences with strangers* walks into a classroom.

The same goes for the teacher: *an instructor, a professional writer, or a member of a department, organization, or community group* walks into a classroom. For those responsible for running creative writing programs, these identities expand: an instructor, writer, department member, administrator, program designer, promoter, extracurricular event organizer, funding solicitor, and more.

On the topic of the writing itself, the classroom fills up just as quickly. Whether a multi-genre introductory course or an advanced, genre-specific class, the material is many-layered, too: *the elements of craft of the genre or genres, the traditions and communities included in the course, and the traditions and communities a given course leaves out* walk into the classroom.

Instead of further embellishing the "setups" of these crowded classrooms or attempting to manufacture a punchline, we will share what is for us the crucial implication of these setups. Not only does a lot of work go into planning, running, and taking part in a creative writing assignment, class, and program, but also many different types of work go into building a successful assignment, class, program, and polished written product. What this implication lacks in humour, then, it makes up for by characterizing one of the key features that makes the creative writing classroom and the creative writing instructor's job so frightening and inspiring, exhausting and sustaining, and challenging and rewarding: the multi-faceted labour of the instructor, the multiple needs of the student, the various layers of craft and creation, and the many demands of the institutions, communities, and professional organizations in which creative writing and the teaching of creative writing take place.

The writing gathered in *Writing Creative Writing: Essays from the Field* encounters these many different types of work — documenting the difficulties, exploring the possibilities, reflecting on experiences, analyzing inner workings, and advising on design and action. Furthermore, these writers — diverse in terms of everything from genre to ethnicity to region — offer a wide range of unique perspectives on the practice of creative writing and the profession. Yet, crucially, what links this variety of essays and authors is their focus on a specific type or aspect of the work of teaching and producing creative writing, ranging from the particular creative writing assignment to the larger national, economic, and cultural contexts in which writing, publishing, and creative writing instruction take place. To this end, the collection is divided into four sections: "Writing Creative Writing Pedagogy" (which is, in turn, subdivided — "By Genre(s)," "By Approach," and "By Classroom"); "Re-Writing the Creative Writing Tradition"; "Writing the Creative Writing Professor"; and "Writing Creative Writing Programs."

"Writing Creative Writing Pedagogy" is our longest section for a reason: for a long time the hottest debate among those in the field was whether or not creative writing *can* be taught. While that debate hasn't entirely been demolished by the weight of sheer numbers of creative writing courses, it has been swept aside as more and more approaches to teaching creative writing have emerged. These not only develop best practices but also simply share different types of best practices — or what may be best practices under certain circumstances, or in the light of shifting demographics and shifting trends.

The subdivision "By Genre" is, traditionally, the way creative writing has been categorized. It still serves us as a useful category, since the vast majority of creative writing courses and creative writing products are still defined by genre. (And, arguably, all the essays in this collection discuss elements of genre.) However, the types of creative writing courses offered in any given program have shifted and expanded over the years beyond the staple poetry and fiction courses, and so this subsection highlights the ways in which teaching those traditional genres has changed radically. Wanda Campbell examines the tensions and satisfactions inherent in teaching fixed forms versus free verse; Daniel Scott Tysdal demonstrates how to use student-friendly modern technology to teach and create innovative poetry; while Nicole Markotić and Suzette Mayr delve pen first into the taboo topic of how to write and discuss sex in fiction. This subsection also offers invaluable pedagogical primers from pioneers in the field of such in-demand courses as screenwriting, with Peggy Thompson, and comic books/graphic novels, with Mary Schendlinger.

The next subdivision, "By Approach," moves beyond generic categories to suggest ways that creative writing can benefit from cross-genre writing as well as cross-discipline approaches: Rishma Dunlop advocates for how life-writing can be understood as research creation; Louis Cabri demonstrates how linguistics can offer new entry points for discussing creative language; Jennifer Duncan postulates whether or not creative writing curricula ought to be radically rethought according to a postmodern textual culture approach; while Priscila Uppal explores the benefits of adaptation as a nearly limitless creative strategy.

The last subdivision, "By Classroom," examines the challenges of teaching creative writing outside the model of the small literary seminar class — a significant growth area at many institutions, now becoming the norm rather than the exception. In that spirit Kathy Mac gives very practical advice on how to structure smaller workgroups as a strategy for maximizing learning potential in large classes; Gülayşe Koçak suggests ways to unlock the creative blocks students may have when accustomed to educational systems that value memorization over originality; and Kathryn Kuitenbrouwer offers structure and methodology to the increasingly popular and global context of teaching creative writing online.

"Re-Writing the Creative Writing Tradition" centres on ways of thinking about creative production in a postmodern and complex world where for some the avant-garde are writers who seek to divest themselves of any identity-markers, and for others the act of visibility constitutes both personal and professional bravery in an environment hostile to inclusivity and cultural diversity. Here a manifesto on the tenets of Uncreative Writing by one of its most famous founders, Christian Bök, sits alongside poems from Renaissance England that David Goldstein argues can be seen as precursors to much avant-garde poetics. Here also we find the brave trailblazers, such as Andrea Thompson, who examines why the highly popular spoken word phenomenon has been forced to fight for academic legitimacy; and why one of Canada's most respected theatre artists, Yvette Nolan, has faced death threats as she continues to tell the tales of her people even among those who wish they would disappear.

"Writing the Creative Writing Professor" is a section of self-reflexive pieces on the transformative power of language and creativity from the viewpoint of the professor or instructor. Some of these writers have more than several decades of teaching, publishing, and performing experience to draw on. Included are Aritha van Herk's lyrical meditation on differing teacher and student desires, and Judith Thompson's empowering yet sometimes explosive strategies on how to tap one's most urgent and emotionally difficult material; Stephanie Bolster writes about the learning curve of teaching creative writing within an academic institution, with all the politics and committee work involved; and Lorri Neilsen Glenn discusses confronting her own biases as she attempted to create safe writing spaces for women of diverse backgrounds.

The final section, "Writing Creative Writing Programs," takes a step back from the ins and outs of creative writing classrooms and the desks and computers of individual writers to consider the vast machinery of the creative writing program degree — and what might even be termed the creative writing economy. While Lori A. May details how and why low-residency programs are recruiting support from institutional bodies and international students alike, Catherine Bush invites us into the administrative and pedagogical underpinnings behind a successful MFA program. Darryl Whetter tackles one of the most controversial and fiercely debated divides in creative writing administration — whether or not English departments are benevolent homes for creative writing courses; and thom vernon offers a philosophical discussion of the meaning of burgeoning creativity in an increasingly capitalist society.

If one of the defining, valuable features of *Writing Creative Writing* is that it is a collection of diversely authored essays that explores all phases of the work of the creative writer and creative writing instructor with intelligence, rigour, individual flare, and imagination, then a related significant feature is the number of distinct readers for whom this collection serves as essential reading. This is a book for current creative writing instructors looking to deepen their understanding of their multi-faceted teaching labour, to expand the horizons of their practice, and to engage in this exchange of ideas and opportunities. This is a book that will provide the same opportunities to understand, expand, and engage with administrators, coordinators, and creators of creative writing programs, organizations, and communities. And ... this is also a book for students in graduate-level creative writing programs — developing writers and already established writers — eager to learn more about their craft and their profession. These essays provide practical insights into the craft of writing, an exploration of different forms and styles of writing, and a detailed introduction to teaching, a growing area of employment for creative writing professionals. This is a book, then, designed to get these interconnected but sometimes disconnected members of the creative writing community to enter into a shared conversation through the shared material of these essays.

Another trait, linked to these others, that makes *Writing Creative Writing* essential reading is that it is the first resource of its kind written fundamentally in the Canadian context, gathering together the experiences, analyses, and ideas of Canadian writers. This returns us again to the question of audience. The Canadian-centric quality of the collection makes it required reading for writers teaching in Canada; it reveals not a unified vision but the variety of practices, problems, and prospects that characterize this diverse community. The collection will equally reward creative writing instructors and creative writers from other countries and regions. Many insights into creative writing pedagogy and program design, and many reflections on the writing teacher's life, will transcend national boundaries. In fact, a number of the essays foreground the international nature of this conversation, reaching beyond Canadian borders to explore everything from Ancient Greek poetry to experiences teaching in Turkey. On the flipside of this, in those instances where national boundaries create differences, these insights and experiences may potentially raise new questions or help expose unrecognized issues and opportunities.

Perhaps the best way to summarize the indispensability and fertile potential of *Writing Creative Writing* is to return to our opening conceit. Within and around these pages gather a collection of insightful essays written by a variety of dynamic experts, a varied group of readers, and a distinct cultural-historical moment. Together, essay, reader, and world encounter the past, connecting to what we have learned and where we have failed. They inhabit the present, testing and questioning, answering and practising. And they look to the future, where book and life converge in a new view on the world and our work, a map to the paths up ahead, a glimpse of the points to strike off from in new directions. We are keen to hear from all who walk into the classroom. Who turns to the page to compose? What do they do there to thrive?

As with a good joke, then, *Writing Creative Writing* aims to create an experience of collective bonding, one that we hope, like a good joke also, prompts a response, spurs a little collegial one-upmanship, and lends itself to continuing the conversation by building on and beyond the ideas it shares, way on into the night.

PART I

WRITING CREATIVE WRITING PEDAGOGY

A. By Genre(s)

Raid, Warp, Push:
The Pedagogy of Poetic Form

Wanda Campbell

In the MTV television show *Pimp My Ride*, people convince the host that their dilapidated old cars should be whisked off to a custom body shop to be restored, personalized, and generally jazzed up with new paint and shiny accessories ranging from the practical to the outrageous. The verb *pimp* means "to customize or modify so as to be more stylish, ostentatious, or flashy" (*Oxford English Dictionary*) in relation to the conspicuous wealth associated with pimps, but may also be connected to the French verb *pimper* meaning "to adorn or attire." So why, a century after Ezra Pound's Imagist Manifesto called for "direct treatment," "absolutely no word that does not contribute," and "the musical phrase [over] the metronome" (3), would a poet want to adorn a poem with rhyme, metre, or any number of complex patterns and embellishments? The analogy between pimping a ride and pimping a poem may be imperfect, in that the former means taking an old car and making it new and the latter appears to mean taking a new thought and making it old, and yet the enduring desire to trick out the unvarnished image with inherited chrome challenges us to reconsider the value of writing in fixed forms.

When I enrolled in my first creative writing class as an undergraduate, convinced that formal rhyming poetry was a thing of the past, imagine my surprise when our professor handed us a list of traditional forms to tackle throughout the semester. I soon realized that writing in form is not about afterthought and adornment, but rather about forethought and fusion. It is not about the outside in, but rather the inside out. As Mark Strand argues, "All poetry is formal in that it exists within limits, limits that are either inherited by tradition or limits that language itself imposes" (69).

Though I rarely still write in the fixed forms I attempted in that first creative writing course, it was essential to convey my craft "into its own roots," as Walt Whitman puts it in his discussion of "the profit of rhyme" in his 1855 preface to *Leaves of Grass* (11). Because those early efforts still bear subtle fruit in my own work, I have made writing in traditional forms a part of my creative writing pedagogy for over twenty years, and though students are not always satisfied with the product, they are, without exception, positive about the process. The student feedback I have incorporated into the discussion that follows confirms that students agree that writing in traditional forms is a vital and rewarding component of a poetic apprenticeship. According to Annie Finch, one of New Formalism's most eloquent advocates, "aspiring poets and creative writing students need to learn the full range of English prosodic possibilities. They will gain fluency and resourcefulness as writers, flexibility and sophistication as readers, from learning to hear the many different metrical patterns in English and the rhythmical variation on those patterns" (121).

Dana Gioia's "My Confessional Sestina" begins with the line "Let me confess. I'm sick of these sestinas / written by youngsters in poetry workshops...." The practice of forcing creative writing students to write in traditional patterns is often mocked and rightly so. Former student and now published poet Christine McNair explains why it can be risky, even dangerous: "Dangerous if students are only taught with classic examples. It can change their voice and make them creaky-sounding, often Victorian. Dangerous if there's no exposure to other poetics, hybrids, mutant forms (those who have warped the form/broken the rules/re-written them). Dangerous if students are taught that form work is the only acceptable way of writing poetry and that anything freeform or different is incompetent or lazy." Richard Wilbur goes as far as to say, "Disgusting idea that someone should sit down with a determination to write in some form or other before he conceives of what the hell he's going to say" (Cummins 133), and yet throughout the last century and into this one, there have been many poets who have returned to fixed forms with memorable results. By encouraging students to explore the full range of poetic possibilities — to invent, reinvent, and experiment — we seek a lively dialogue between the best of past and present. This is not about nostalgia but about making it new. Ken Babstock argues, "At times this seems to me to be a function of being a Canadian poet; performing these backward raids into larger, more powerful traditions; warping them slightly to suit experience and vernacular, and pushing them up against asymmetrical subject matter." Babstock's dynamic troika of verbs — raid, warp, push — provides a useful way to incorporate fixed form into poetic pedagogy in a contemporary and kinetic way.

RAID: CONTINUITY

The notion of a raid suggests an inroad or incursion made by those who are outside. It also suggests there is treasure, something we want and need, on the other side of the wall. This is not mere guerilla warfare but rather taking advantage of our freedom to glean the best from the fiefdom. And now, for inhabitants of the global village, both past and present traditions are wider and richer than they once were in that we can draw on not only the established forms of Europe but also those of the whole world. Former student Tegan Zimmerman argues that working with fixed forms "can teach the historical 'progression' of poetry's history and movements so the student has a solid understanding" of the roots of contemporary poetry. Though it seems to be the goal of each generation to break with the past, the benefits of continuity should not be underestimated. Mary Oliver reminds us that "five hundred years and more of such labor, such choice thought within choice expression, lies within the realm of metrical poetry. Without it, one is uneducated, and one is mentally poor" (ix).

Through these backward raids, we become connected with the community of poets that has come before us, the strong shoulders upon which we stand, with the treasures of past poetic practice, and even with the fundamental human rhythms of our own bodies. In his *Preface to the Lyrical Ballads* (1800), William Wordsworth speaks of the "complex feeling of delight" generated by "the music of harmonious metrical language, the sense of difficulty overcome" (317). Nearly two centuries later, Frederick Turner and Ernst Pöppel argue that human information processing is, among other things, rhythmic, reflexive, and hemispherically specialized: "Poetry, as we have seen, enforces cooperation between left-brain temporal organization and right-brain spatial organization and helps to bring about that integrated stereoscopic view that we call true understanding" (247). Even Keith Mallard, who questions some of their conclusions and the science behind them, admits that the article "The Neural Lyre: Poetic Meter, the Brain, and Time" is "a fascinating read" (58). Turner and Pöppel suggest that "our species' special adaption may in fact be to expect more order and meaning in the world than it can deliver" (248), and that our efforts to seek them in poetry and elsewhere may be one of our most effective survival strategies. "We now know more of the linkages which connect any art to human function," writes Louise Bogan, "and this knowledge should make us take more pleasure, rather than less, in form" (213). Former student Jen Huizen puts it this way: "These traditional forms still exist for a reason. They appeal on some level to our mind, how we perceive words, or quite possibly simply stimulate distant memories of more ancient days, when the primary way of obtaining knowledge was through oral tradition."

WARP: CONSTRAINT

Accustomed to the more intuitive and organic practice of free verse, some students resist attempting fixed forms, but according to Oliver, "Trying on such forms needn't be like putting on a straitjacket. In fact, if you've never had to make creative use of language to fit a formal requirement, you're in for a pleasant surprise. Yes, it's challenging and often difficult, but may well send you down interesting paths you wouldn't have taken otherwise" (140). The key for poets is to rise to the challenge of constraint in a way that is conducive to discovery. Babstock compares writing in form to running an obstacle course. By being forced to scramble through tires or over walls, we are more likely to encounter interesting insights than if we merely make a beeline straight to the finish. He expands on the benefits of constraint in a discussion of writing sonnets:

> I am attracted to its no-holds challenge to composition. It says, "Here's a squarish block of text on a white field in which something or, more likely, nothing will occur. Are you up to it?" It gets strange here as, obviously, there is no real "block of text" anywhere present before one writes a

sonnet — except perhaps there is; a blast shadow from history, a kind of dimly perceived "dark matter"-sonnet that can serve as a vessel or threat or foil…. There's a game or risk or pressure inherent in knowing the end is on its way. Which is to say constraint does appeal to me, as does history; and perhaps more so the volta.

In contemporary practice we are likely to warp the traditions "slightly to suit experience and vernacular." (Babstock), to bend both ourselves and the form with intriguing results. Former student Corey Liu explains it this way: "A lot of the students in class were able to write sonnets well because they were able to adapt to the form better than I could. But the form also adapted to them, if that makes any sense." In his discussion of the constraints of the Oulipo [*ouvroir de littérature potentielle*] Movement, Christopher Beha writes, "It may be obvious why a poetic form as austere as the sonnet qualifies as an Oulipian constraint. Less obvious may be the extent to which *any* literary form — the very effort, in fact, to express oneself in words — limits, in often arbitrary ways, what a writer might express and how she might express it." Beha goes on to explain that "constraints can be used for giving words a kind of examination, for pushing away the extraneous jazz to see the beating heart within." In keeping with this musical metaphor, former student Abby Whidden argues that "fixed forms could be compared to scales, etudes, or the twelve bar blues. Musicians spend hours on these areas and that close attention to technique helps them in freer forms of music." W.B. Yeats once claimed he "would be full of self-contempt because of [his] egotism and indiscretion and foresee the boredom of [his] reader" if he wrote in free verse "unchanged, amid all its accidence" (522), and contemporary writers like Catherine Wagner still speak of the positive impact of constraint: "We may find, too, that meter can at times valuably caution us, in the manner of a resistantly honest friend or spouse, against hasty, ill-considered, or arbitrary speech. And we may realize that meter often has a magical, magnetic power to attract to our poems words and thoughts truer and better than those that normally come to mind." Female poets, in particular, speak of the power of constraints to allow the writer to cope with emotionally challenging subject matter. Adrienne Rich, in her essay "When We Dead Awaken," puts it this way: "In those years formalism was part of the strategy —

like asbestos glove, it allowed me to handle materials I couldn't pick up bare-handed" (18). Molly Peacock states it even more simply: "Formal verse often makes impossible emotions possible" (71). We can descend the dark staircase with the handrail of form to steady our step. Ironically, just as years of musical discipline can prepare the way for improvisation, what feels like work can actually open the way for play. As former student Amy James explains, "The best assistance of a fixed form for me is simply that you do not have a choice but to be ruthless in word choice and number…. I have found it refines and strengthens the poem, and allows new opportunities for play; play on words, on repetition, on line length, on the system itself." Eavan Boland describes a similar epiphany emerging from a personal encounter with form: "I begin to see how it would be to be able to work with the line by working against it, pushing the music of dailyness against the customary shapes of the centuries. Suddenly I see how these contrasting forces make language plastic. And how exciting it is to find that a poetic language will liberate and not constrain" (xxix).

PUSH: CONNECTION

The push and shove between classical symmetrical forms and contemporary asymmetrical subject matter and expression creates a new kind of flame, a firing across the synapses of understanding. So we have Sylvia Plath's sonnet "To Eva" beginning "All right, let's say you could take a skull and break it / The way you'd crack a clock;" (304). That opening "All right" catches fire in us by its very casual presence in an elegant symmetrical form. Kim Addonizio's sonnets about love as phenylethylamine or touching tattoos on naked skin, or Satan as earth's new CEO, strike us as particularly contemporary and compelling. Similarly, Babstock delivers a Shakespearean sonnet in the voice of a hockey player in the penalty box, and Anne Simpson shapes an entire corona of sonnets by juxtaposing Breughel paintings with scenes of 9/11 and the collapse of the Twin Towers. In "The Music of Poetry" T.S. Eliot writes, "I believe that the tendency to return to set, and even elaborate patterns is permanent" (36), and in "Reflections on *Vers Libre*" he explains why: "It is this contrast between fixity and flux, this unperceived evasion of monotony, which is the very life of verse" (185). Former student Rose Grieder writes, "I encourage curiosity in that which is foreign to you." If students habitually write in fixed forms they should be challenged to attempt free verse, and vice versa.

As human beings we are drawn to structure. When there is stone and wood, we build with these things. If we are beyond the tree line we build with snow. André Gide advises: "Pay attention only to the form; emotion will come spontaneously to inhabit it. A perfect dwelling always finds an inhabitant" (299). Using structures imposed upon us, Julia Alvarez argues, makes us Scheherazade in the Sultan's room: "I use structures to survive and triumph" (17). For the female poet, the journey through fixed forms of the past can be particularly vexed. "I wanted to go in that heavily mined and male labyrinth with the string of my own voice. I wanted to explore and explode it too" (17). Rita Dove asks, "Can't form also be a talisman against disintegration? The sonnet defends itself against the vicissitudes of fortune by its charmed structure, its beautiful bubble. All the while, though, chaos is lurking outside the gate" (57). To keep poetic forms contemporary and compelling, we cannot, indeed must not, lose sight of the world around us, the world that presses on the perimeters of our created structures. We must be constantly forging connections between outside and in. Oliver again: "Assimilating the experiences and the references of the poetry of the past *requires* that our relationship with the physical world be fresh, forceful, and firsthand" (73). Only then can writing in forms be a surprising and sustaining gesture.

Students lacking a technical vocabulary often resort to the word *flow* in commenting on the work of their peers. "Whatever else may be happening within the prosody of a poem, the student is sure that it makes the poem 'flow.' As a teacher, exasperated, I have forbidden students to use the word 'flow.' But I will use it here. In some textbooks the poetic stanza is presented as a fixed pattern, a static shape to be replicated…. I prefer to think of the poetic stanza as a dynamic shape, a kind of river channel through which the syntax of the poem, with all its pent-up kinetic energy, all its forward momentum, must find a way, despite swerves and obstruction, to *flow*" (Adams 71). The metaphor of the river channel is particularly apt in revealing how the contemporary and kinetic use of classic patterns can help propel modern poetry through ancient stone. As we raid, warp, and push, the results of our labours can be full of movement, music, and if the muses are kind, magic.

According to Keith Mallard, "The enemy is not someone who writes differently from you. The enemy is the same old enemy who has always been around: someone who tries to tell you that there is only one way to write" (68). Or as Miller Williams argues in his introduction to *Patterns of Poetry*, "The freedom not to wear a tie is an illusion unless there is also freedom to wear one" (10). The word *formal* brings to mind uncomfortable and constricting ball gowns and tuxedos designed to impress, but Patricia Monaghan reminds us that the word actually derives "from a proletarian source, the molds used by potters" (Sellers 329). In this expansive era, we can both use the moulds and break them, as long as we do so with intelligence and imagination. Sometimes the way back can be the way forward.

WORKS CITED

Adams, Stephen. *Poetic Designs: An Introduction to Meters, Verse Forms and Figures of Speech.* Peterborough: Broadview, 1997. Print.

Alvarez, Julia. "Housekeeping Cages." *A Formal Feeling Comes: Poem in Form by Contemporary Women.* Brownsville, OR: Story Line, 1994. 16–18. Print.

Babstock, Ken. "Suspension, Evasion, and Inversion: A Conversation with Ken Babstock." By Sina Queyras. *Harriet.* Poetry Foundation, 23 Mar. 2010. Web. 20 Jul. 2012.

Beha, Christopher. "Oulipo Ends Where the Work Begins." *The Believer,* Sep. 2006. Web. 20 Jul. 2012.

Bogan, Louise. "The Pleasures of Formal Poetry." *The Poet's Work.* Ed. Reginald Gibbons. Boston: Houghton Mifflin, 1979. 203–14. Print.

Boland, Eavan. "Poetic Form: A Personal Encounter." *The Making of a Poem: A Norton Anthology of Poetic Forms.* New York: Norton, 2000. xxv–xxix. Print.

Cummins, James. "Calliope Music: Notes on the Sestina." *After New Formalism: Poets on Form, Narrative and Tradition.* Ashland, OR: Story Line, 1999. 133–43. Print.

Dove, Rita. "An Intact World." *A Formal Feeling Comes: Poems in Form by Contemporary Women.* Brownsville, OR: Story Line, 1994. 57–58. Print.

Eliot, T.S. "The Music of Poetry." 1942. *On Poetry and Poets.* London: Faber and Faber, 1957. 26–38. Print.

———. "Reflections on *Vers Libre*." 1917. *To Criticize the Critic.* New York: Farrar, Straus and Giroux, 1970. 183–89. Print.

Finch, Annie. "Metrical Diversity: A Defense of the Non-Iambic Meters." *After New Formalism: Poets on Form, Narrative and Tradition.* Ashland, OR: Story Line, 1999. 117–22. Print.

Gide, André. *Pretexts: Reflections on Literature and Morality.* 1959. New Brunswick, NJ: Transaction, 2011. Print.

Gioia, Dana. "My Confessional Sestina." *Poetry Magazine.* Poetry Foundation, Oct. 1983. Web. 7 Aug. 2013.

Grieder, Rose. "Re: Poetic Form." Message to author. 13 Feb. 2012. Email.

Huizen, Jennifer. "Re: Help." Message to author. 17 Jan. 2012. Email.

James, Amy. "Re: Help." Message to author. 13 Feb. 2012. Email.

Liu, Corey. "Re: Poetic Form." Message to author. 18 Jul. 2011. Email.

Mallard, Keith. "The New Formalism and the Return of Prosody." *New Expansive Poetry: Theory Criticism, History.* Ed. R.S. Gwynn. Ashland, OR: Story Line, 1999. 52–71. Print.

McNair, Christine. "Re: Fixed Form." Message to author. 1 Sep. 2011. Email.

Oliver, Mary. *Rules for the Dance: A Handbook for Writing and Reading Metrical Verse.* Boston: Houghton Mifflin, 1998. Print.

Peacock, Molly. "From Gilded Cage to Rib Cage." *After New Formalism: Poets on Form, Narrative and Tradition.* Ashland, OR: Story Line, 1999. 70–78. Print.

Plath, Sylvia. *The Collected Poems.* Ed. Ted Hughes. New York: Harper, 1981. Print.

Pound, Ezra. "A Retrospect." *Literary Essays of Ezra Pound.* Ed. T.S. Eliot. 1954. London: Faber and Faber, 1974. 3–14. Print.

Rich, Adrienne. *Arts of the Possible: Essays and Conversations.* New York: Norton, 2002. Print.

Sellers, Heather. *The Practice of Creative Writing.* Boston: Bedford, 2008. Print.

Strand, Mark. *The Weather of Words.* New York: Knopf, 2000. Print.

Turner, Frederick, and Ernst Pöppel. "The Neural Lyre: Poetic Meter, the Brain, and Time." *Expansive Poetry.* Ed. Frederick Feirstein. Santa Cruz: Story Line, 1989. 209–54. Print.

Whidden, Abby. "Re: Fixed Form." Message to author. 4 Sep. 2011. Email.

Whitman, Walt. *Complete Poetry and Collected Prose.* New York: Library of America, 1982. Print.

Willliams, Miller. *Patterns of Poetry: An Encyclopedia of Forms.* Baton Rouge: Louisiana State U, 1986. Print.

Wordsworth, William. Preface to *Lyrical Ballads.* 1800. *Criticism: The Major Statements.* Ed. Charles Kaplan. New York: St. Martin's, 1975. 301–20. Print.

Yeats, W.B. *Essays and Introductions.* New York: Collier. 1961. Print.

Zimmerman, Tegan. "Re: Poetry Forms." Message to author. 1 Sep. 2011. Email.

Beginning at the Edge: Teaching Poetry Through Comic Book Panels and Internet Comment Threads

Daniel Scott Tysdal

Burgeoning writers are often moved to enrol in introductory creative writing courses by the same problem. They want to write X (a genre film, say, or a YA — young adults — novel), but they do not know where to start. In the introductory poetry workshop, this problem tends to take the following form: the students lack an awareness of poetic traditions (past and present) and they are better versed in other, apparently "non-poetic" mediums and media, from comics to film, from magazines and textbooks to the World Wide Web.

In this context, I find myself, as a poetry teacher, faced with a two-fold responsibility: to introduce students to the tools used by poets past and present, and to encourage them to experiment with the media of their contemporary moment. In realizing this responsibility, one method I have had success with is meeting the student halfway, by, so to speak, beginning at the edge, the boundary that divides and unites varying mediums and forms. I have developed a series of hands-on exercises that encourage students to explore these regions where the poem and these other apparently "non-poetic" mediums and media* meet. In this essay, I will introduce you

---

* I find it useful to distinguish between the two plurals *media* and *mediums*. For modes of communication (especially electronic communication), *media* serves well: the news media, social media, films, TV, and so forth. But I prefer to use *mediums* for the different category that includes modes of expression and artistic genres: poetry, prose, literature in general, the visual arts, video games, performance arts, and others.

to the general horizon of my approach, lead you through four specific exercises (encouraging you, I hope, to begin some poems of your own), and conclude with some remarks on the benefits of exploring the convergence between the poem and the "non-poetic" medium.

I. METHOD: WRITING MOMENTS AND THE TWO MAIN MEDIUMS

There are two central elements to this process of beginning at the edge; they can be considered in terms of form and content. The form the process takes is the writing moment, while its content or subject is the presentation of the "non-poetic" as two general mediums (which I discuss below) from which we can move to different particular mediums.

Writing moments are micro-writing exercises that invite students to try their respective hands at the topic under discussion. I call these short exercises writing moments because of the helpful double meaning of *moment*. These writing moments are *moments* because they only take a moment to complete and because, when you undertake them, you will be "having a moment," experiencing this break from the day-to-day that is more than likely common practice for you already as a writer: turning from a dinner table conversation or from a chat in transit or from a mindless stroll to your notebook to scribble down the line or the form or the vision that struck you.

Writing moments are designed with two goals in mind. The first is to immerse students in the meeting of life and art by coupling active practice with abstract explanation; their reading process becomes their writing process. The second is to initiate students into two of the extreme poles of the poetic practice: the work (the writing routine, the daily grind, the practice that becomes habit or possibly an addiction), and the inspiration (the burst of insight or feeling from which a poem often begins). Writing moments take place within the purview of both poles, nurturing habit and stimulating the composition of new work.

Regarding the turn to the "non-poetic," the two general mediums I encourage students to explore when beginning at the edge are two that have long been the companions of poets: other artistic mediums and modes of communication. The rich tradition of ekphrastic poems about paintings is an example of the former, while an example of the latter is the capacity of different social media to link poets to other poets and new audiences. One way to explore these mediums as poets, then, is to approach specific artistic and communication mediums as a means of generating new poems and as a means of reworking the form of the poem as such. There are four different areas in which these resonances can be investigated: content, theme, form, and dissemination.

In the following sections, we will explore comic books as an example of an artistic medium, and Internet comment threads as an example of a medium of communication, in relation to three of the areas of resonance: content, theme, and form. The particular encounters we stage between poetry and comics, and poetry and comment threads, respectively, are designed to inspire students and to provide them with some new tools to test out. Students should, however, also be invited to undertake this same approach to the artistic mediums they are most passionate about (whether sculptures, movies, or video games) and to the communication technologies they are most involved in or most anxious about (whether Facebook, Twitter, YouTube, or those not yet invented at the time of this writing).

Now, as we undertake the process of "beginning at the edge," I want to shift gears in terms of address and approach. The following sections are addressed to "you" the student, and rather than simply discussing the practice, these sections offer the practice in action. The following material is aimed at students who have been introduced to some of the basic tools and concepts of poetry (imagery, free verse, blank verse, and couplet), but are by no means experts. If you are game, you will want to grab a super-hero comic (in print or online) and load up a favourite comment thread, as we take our first steps with our companion mediums into the regions of content and theme.

2. COMICS, COMMENTS, CONTENT, AND THEME

With your comic in hand and your comment thread loaded, give them both a careful perusal: read, glance, flip, stare, and scroll. Become intimate with the life and language of the pages and posts.

Writing Moment #1

- Write a three- to four-line free verse stanza about your comic book (any aspect that you see fit).
- Write a couplet about your comment thread (any aspect you see fit). For the sake of practice, compose in blank verse or, simply, ten-syllable lines.

End of writing moment.

This is the most common approach to other mediums, taking the medium as the content or subject of your poem. To say this approach is the most common, though, is not to diminish it. In fact, this practice is both complex and essential. For one, composing with a specific medial content invigorates your form. Can you find the ways in which this happened in your first writing moment? If not, can you think of ways in which you could revise your work to encourage this influence? Three elements to consider are word choice, imagery, and voice.

In relation to your comic book, you could take on the diction of the heroes or villains, or you could employ the distinctive sound effects (for example, a fire-rendered *BWKSSSSSS* for a Bat Plane–fired missile), or the shared symbolia (the icons comics use to represent different states, such as a light bulb for an idea or bubbles for drunkenness). Attending to words could also prompt some play with puns; for example, you could riff on the link between Spider-Man's web and the Latin root of the word *text* (*textus*), which means *web*. The lush colours and energetic shapes might influence your imagery or, on this same front, you may employ the visceral and iconic forms and actions of the heroes and villains who fight it out in the frames. Finally, regarding voice, comic books are easily teamed with personas. You could speak in the voice of a specific hero or villain, or explore their thoughts in a poetic register.

The same methodological invigoration occurs when poetry is paired with the comment thread. If the thread is specialized you can borrow its specific jargon; even if the thread is more general, you could still mimic the community's use of Internet-speak. Imagery-wise, you could advance both literally or figuratively, drawing inspiration either from images in the posts and ads or from the (potentially "poetic") imagery generated by commenters (clichés, perhaps, but clichés you can renew). The persona could also rouse some original work in this context as well. The Internet troll, the white knight, and all of the other comment thread regulars are ripe for lampooning or revealing unique views on what is beautiful or good or true.

As this remark on the true and good suggests, composing a poem about an artistic medium or a medium of communication can allow you to think about the timeless themes — ideas we have long struggled with or in which we have found solace — in a new way. Superhero comics, for example, lend themselves to meditations on topics such as justice, power, and the nature of evil. As a poet, though, working always with the aim of looking awry, you might not want to proceed so directly. Perhaps you could write a poem about Superman in which you reflect on weakness, or a poem about Batman in which forgiveness is the theme. Superhero catchphrases could also serve as fertile material. Take Spider-Man's lesson (via Voltaire): "With great power comes great responsibility," and explore its opposite: "With great weakness comes great irresponsibility." Poems about comment threads could act as vehicles for mediations on communication, community, and freedom, or on silence, isolation, and oppression.

3. THE GUTTER AND THE LEAP BETWEEN LINES

Comic books can also help you develop your practice, expanding your range of compositional strategies, whether or not you are writing about a comic book. For example, the comic book can serve as a model for how you transition from one line to the next. This exercise is beneficial on three fronts, insofar as it helps you nurture three interconnected traits that often characterize a high-quality poem: concision, originality, and the leap (concerning the structure or development of a poem — a surprising, illuminating, defamiliarizing, stirring, and/or unbalancing shift in attention from one sentence to the next). In order to understand how this exercise works, though, we must first step away from poetry for a moment and turn to the gutter.

The gutter is comic book terminology for the gap between panels. It most often takes the form of white space between two black borders. The gutter divides panels, but it just as forcefully connects moments, providing the pause needed to create a distinct transition between panels rather than a senseless blur. Put another way, the gutter joins action in one panel to the action in the next, forming a sort of comic book sentence. Take a look at one page from your comic book, ideally a page that has a few gutters. How does the action transition from one panel to the next? How little or how much do we move in space and time? How does the new panel shift our attention? What is the new focus in terms of subject, proximity, and angle? These are the sorts of questions you can ask about the comic book page to, in a sense, spur it to shape your own practice. Once you have asked and answered enough of them, the next question to ask is: How can shifts between panels manifest in my poem in the shifts between sentences?

There is no right or wrong way to turn your answers to this question into practice, so I do not want to give you too many preconceived notions. However, my own endeavours with this exercise have suggested that there are two tips worth sharing. First, whether you are revising a poem or composing a new poem, employ a relational word to help you conceive of the relationship between your poem and the comic book page. In other words, work in concert or conflict with the comic, or aim to amplify or diminish the labour of its gutters. Second, make two separate attempts, employing two different comic book pages, to bring the benefits of this exercise into relief. You might even end up combining sections from the two very different results. To really gain from this second tip, use comic book pages created

Writing Moment #2

- Return to the three-or-four-line free verse stanza you composed for the previous writing moment.
- Revise this piece in concert with your comic book page.
- Do not be afraid to significantly revise lines or cut them entirely. Also, feel free to add new lines.

End of writing moment.

by different artists or, even better, by artists from different eras. The hodge-podge panel-construction of Golden Age comics (1930s and 40s) contrasts sharply (and, for our purposes, nicely) with the slick, integrated design of recent artists (see J.H. Williams III for the apex example).

There are a number of ways to undertake this exercise. If you are a big comic book fan, select a page from three of your favourite comics. Next, summon up a strong memory of an encounter with comic books or popular culture, and compose a three-stanza poem, with each stanza working in concert with one of the three pages. If you are not a comic book fan, you could write a three-stanza poem about a topic of your choice, and work in conflict with pages from three different eras of comics. Another productive approach is to rewrite a famous poem using a variation of either of these approaches.

As I've suggested, the central benefits to this exercise are threefold. Greater concision often results as the comic encourages you to remove lines that fill the "gutters" of your poem, cramming the effective blanks with unneeded information, superfluous words, and conventional digressions. Furthermore, we all fall into ruts when it comes to ordering our poems. This exercise helps shake you out of your habitual developmental logics. Not only does it challenge your usual organizational patterns, but it may also inspire you to refine new patterns. These new structures, coupled with concision, will combine to fill your poems with leaps and jumps between lines that surprise and challenge your reader.

4. THE REPLY AND THE SWERVE

You can undertake the same generative exercise in concert (or in conflict) with the comment thread. Here, though, the reply replaces the gutter as the active element.

Once again, you want to employ different relational words to help conceive of your relationship (in other words, work in concert or in conflict, heighten the influence of the thread or diminish it). Your work will gain depth from revising or attempting the same poem twice in combination with two different comment threads.

The questions we ask of the reply and the comment thread differ slightly from the questions asked of the gutter and the comic book page. For example, you want to consider the voice of the reply. What is the poster's motivation and persona? Composing lines in combination with different posters would give your poem a thrilling choral effect. Attend also to the language of the replies: sentence structure, word choice, speech acts. You could even quote replies. For example, borrow a question from the thread and then answer it in your poem. Ignoring all the replies that come in between, ask: What is the logic that connects an original comment to its most distant reply? Can you compose two lines of poetry bound by this same logic? Add to the comment thread and see what type of new replies and, in turn, new potential material, your contribution generates.

Writing Moment #3

- Return to your couplet about your comment thread.
- Revise this couplet in concert with your comment thread.
- Do not feel obliged to stick to the metrical or syllabic restriction established in the earlier writing moment.

End of writing moment.

Concision might not result from this exercise. However, as with our encounter with the gutter, companioning with the reply breaks your habits of order and organization and nurtures the leap. In this instance, the leap comes from the unusual swerve, the surprising jump in thought, shift in attention, or striking image.

5. COMICS, COMMENTS, AND LAYOUT

What if we went one step further in the meeting between poetic and non-poetic forms? What if, to perhaps stretch the metaphor too far, we, as poets, hopped onto these mediums' respective backs and created poems that were comic books and comment threads?

In terms of the act of composition, this is one of the most exhilarating, challenging, and border-bending ways we can write with a combination of image and text. In a way, this practice involves composing with a new pen and responding to a new speaker. New speakers are those who favour such hybrid works: comics, websites, graphic literature, and so on. Our new pens are technological devices, such as laptops and phones, and accompanying programs, such as Photoshop and InDesign, which allow us to bring innovative poems to life.

We undertake this practice in the same manner as our two earlier encounters with comics and comments. Only now, instead of attending to one element, we attend to all possible elements, in particular the physical, visible appearance of the medium. In others words, you transform the material appearance of the poem by adopting the layout conventions of your chosen medium as the layout conventions for your poem. Compose a poem about a comic that is itself a comic. Create a comment thread poem that is a comment thread.

The means of proceeding are many. The high- and low-tech are both options: utilize the authenticity gained with a laptop and its programs or go with old-fashioned pen and paper. While designing the layout, you could take the opportunity to draw in your readers further by making them active participants. Ink your poem into word balloons but leave the panels blank for your reader to fill, figuratively or literally. Leave blank comment boxes for the same purpose. You may also go "right to the source" in both cases. Digitally or manually remove the words from an actual comic book page and add your own. Post your poem on the comment thread of your blog, one comment box for each line, so your friends and readers can add to the poem with their replies. With these possibilities in mind, undertake the following writing moment.

Writing Moment #4

- What are two or three different ways that you could transform your poem about a comic book into a poem that is also a comic book?
- What are two or three different ways that you could transform your poem about comment threads into a poem that is also a comment thread?

End of writing moment.

This concludes the final example of "beginning at the edge." I hope it takes us far from conventional practice, and demonstrates the benefits of leaping away from conformity with convention and swerving from the uniformity of tradition. In fact, this pair of companion mediums inflects the word *uniformity*, suggesting the need to, every now and then, break with uniformity (work with a single form) and test out some hybrid, mongrel, and Frankensteinian forms.

6. CONCLUSION: THE BENEFITS OF WRITING MOMENTS AND BEGINNING AT THE EDGE

In employing these tiered, writing moment–filled assignments and encouraging students to experiment with the meeting between the poem and the supposedly non-poetic medium, I have discovered a number of benefits. Beginning students in particular value them for two reasons. First, a number have suggested that these writing moments take the pressure off by encouraging the act of writing without requesting a completed poem. Second, they seem to like the way in which, more often than not, practice precedes abstraction in these writing moments. In other words, they are practising with the tool or technique in concert with learning its abstract definition and structure.

It is worth adding that I follow up a collection of tiered writing moments with exercises designed to encourage the creation of complete poems. First, I invite students to return to the material they created during their writing moments and to compose one or two new poems. In the current case, they might compose a poem in the language of comics or comment threads, or compose a poem employing a comic book character or an Internet commenter as a persona. I also provide three- or four-tool/technique-relevant writing exercises. For example, I suggest students translate a famous poem into a comic book. This may involve making an actual comic or writing a lyrical description of the poem cum comic. Or students may compose a comment thread for a famous poem. They could people the comment thread with other famous poets, with critics, with a series of less distinct poetic voices, with the usual band of Internet commenters, or with some combination of all of them.

The benefits of "beginning at the edge" are multiple, too. For one, this practice offers a unique way of introducing students to core tools, techniques, and traditions, showing them the creative value of tending artfully and carefully to the tools of the trade. I have developed similarly structured exercises that cover everything from metaphor to metre to layout, and I lead students to compose in concert with everything from memes to textbooks to the art gallery. While grounding students in core tools and techniques, these meetings between poem and non-poem also encourage them to compose original, innovative, and timely works. Finally, "beginning at the edge" pushes students to reflect on the territory they share (or could potentially share) with other creators and makers, providing them with maps for exploring these boundaries that link as much as they divide.

The Comics Connection

Mary Schendlinger

Comics is a new art form in North America. It is only about a hundred years since the Yellow Kid, a cartoon boy from the other side of the tracks (created by Richard Outcault), debuted in a comic strip published in the *New York World* and became an instant hit with adults. The first book-length comic, a collection of short strips first published in newspapers, came along in 1933. As Jillian Tamaki, co-author of the graphic novel *Skim,* says, "Even how to read comics, even that basic, fundamental thing is something that a lot of people are still learning."

In fact, the form is so new that we don't yet know what to call it. Over the last twenty years there has been an explosion in the production of books, zines, booklets, and online series, with a spectacular variety of subject matter, style, and production values; but to most of us, "comic" still refers to a cheap, disposable, 6½ x 10 inch, twenty-four-page newsprint booklet with a thin, shiny cover and ads for sea monkeys in the back, about superheroes or talking animals. "Graphic novel" has caught on, but it leaves out everything that isn't a novel; "graphic album," "sequential art," and "drawn book" are interesting but obscure; "graphica" sounds high-toned. And not all "comics" are comical, which is why Art Spiegelman, author of *Maus,* a graphic memoir of his parents' years in Nazi concentration camps, prefers "comix." The conversation about terminology is more speculative than contentious: makers, readers, buyers, sellers, and teachers of comics agree that we need a good portmanteau word, as French and Belgian comics have *bédé,* which comes from *bande dessinée* (literally, "drawn strip").

By any name, the form has taken hold in North America. Readers, writers, artists, publishers, booksellers, and book buyers are taking it seriously. They are coming to understand comics as a medium rather than a genre, much as film and television are different media, and print publications are categorically different from online products, even when they have the same content. We comprehend comics in a different way than text, mainly because of the integral presence of images that must be "read" to understand the heart of the work, rather than experienced as accompanying illustrations. Because film and television require the same kind of "reading," the transition of comics from page to screen tends to be less arduous than the transition of written text to screen, and adaptations for film and TV have ranged from *Batman* (starting in 1943), *Wonder Woman,* and *Justice League of America,* to *Archie* and *Richie Rich,* to Bryan Lee O'Malley's teen-angst story *Scott Pilgrim vs. the World* and Daniel Clowes's cerebral *Ghost World,* and to *The Perils of Gwendoline in the Land of the Yik-Yak.*

The graphic novel is one of the few areas of book publishing whose market is expanding. In Europe, Central and South America, some Asian countries and other parts of the world, comics have long been a respected cultural form. Europeans treat well-produced book-length comics as works of art and literature, to be kept (and kept in print), rather than as cheap, low-art ephemera to be consumed and thrown away. In Japan, there is a long, rich tradition of manga (comics) in many categories, from genre fiction to be read on the train and tossed, to expensive, beautifully rendered volumes with hand-painted silk covers, to instruction manuals that come in the box with your new smartphone.

North American comics started as funny papers, and in the public imagination they stayed there — fun, but trivial. Superhero comics roared into popularity during the war years of the 1940s. These were followed, in the Cold War years, by science fiction and horror comics (*Tales from the Crypt*), romance (*Young Love*), and humour and satire (*Mad, Cracked*). Comics in general were attacked in the 1950s by right-wing politicians, doctors, and scholars, who claimed they would induce violence, suicide, and juvenile delinquency in children. Then, in the 1960s and 70s, came "underground comics," in which nothing was taboo — sex, drugs, crime, violence, explicit everything. The comics of the next wave, in the 1980s, were also provocative, but more thoughtful than deliberately shocking. In the early 1990s, Art Spiegelman won the Pulitzer Prize for *Maus*, and Scott McCloud published *Understanding Comics*, becoming the first English-language comics semiotician. Thanks to new printing, publishing, and communication technologies, comics proliferated in print and online, and North American readers feasted on comics from Japan, Western Europe, and points in between. Teachers brought comics and manga into the classroom, because even "reluctant readers" like to read comics. Courses on reading and comprehending comics sprang up in secondary and post-secondary schools all across the continent.

Teaching people to *write* comics, though, is more recent. Resources were few and far between in 2008, when I developed Writing for Graphic Forms, a workshop course for the University of British Columbia's Creative Writing Program. I knew the territory, though — I had been teaching writing and publishing courses for ten years. I had also been reading, writing, and drawing comics all my life as an avocation, had been publishing short comics in periodicals and anthologies for fifteen years (under the pseudonym Eve Corbel), and was underway with a book-length graphic novel. And I served as comics editor for *Geist* magazine, a literary quarterly co-founded in 1990 by my partner and me.

In a way, teaching comics writing is like teaching any other kind of writing. In comics, as in other forms, there are genres that come with their own formulas or conventions. In comics, as in written forms, the work must have a shape. In comics, as in film and other visual forms, the writer writes with images, or with images and words combined. When comics are done well, the words and images work together symbiotically, although there is friction between them: if either one is taken away, the piece is meaningless.

EXPLORING THE COMICS LANDSCAPE

Writing for Graphic Forms, the workshop course at the University of British Columbia, runs for one term and consists of fourteen weekly meetings, each two hours long. About half the students are skilled, confident, new writers. Three or four people have well-developed visual art skills. Everyone in the room has, or remembers having, a great fondness for comics of some kind, and a residual sense of guilty pleasure (more evidence of the lowbrow reputation of comics).

Teaching time is precious, especially when most of the students are new to the comics medium as a writing form. Our first two sessions are devoted to a concentrated introduction to writing comics, with copious examples by outstanding comics writers and artists, and informal discussion.

I start the course by saying that you don't have to be an accomplished visual artist to write wonderful comics, just as you don't have to be a cinematographer to write a wonderful film. Students are awed (not always in a good way) by the work of their artistically proficient colleagues — work that can seem much more realized than theirs whether or not the writing is solid. Gorgeous artwork is a great asset in comics, but it doesn't make a good comic, any more than proper spelling, punctuation, and grammar makes good writing. The American comics writer Joe Matt (*Peepshow*), for instance, is a talented visual artist whose exhibitionism, self-absorption, and addiction to pornography are his shtick, as well as the subjects of his work. He has his fans, but his daily self-loathing and "procrasturbation," regardless of how well drawn, can also be described as simply boring. *Susceptible,* by Geneviève Castrée, tells the story (apparently based on her own) of a gothic childhood in a family for whom "dysfunctional" is an understatement. Her drawings and page composition are sensitive and exquisite, but the protagonist is two-dimensional in her endless victimization ("a cartoon character," as some would say). A comic with strong writing and less technically proficient artwork is much more successful than the reverse. For example, the kindest word for the artwork in *Cancer Made Me a Shallower Person,* a memoir by the late Miriam Engelberg, is "naive," but the simple drawings are wonderfully expressive, actually enhancing her laconic, unsentimental text. *Longshot Comics* by Shane Simmons, which consists of 3,840 tiny panels in which two dots converse, is as vivid and clear as "real" artwork.

We go on to talk about the possibilities of the comics medium. As with other forms, a comic can be narrative (*Unterzakhn,* a memoir by Leela Corman), persuasive writing (*Palestine* by Joe Sacco), expository/how-to (*Drawing Comics Is Easy! Except When It's Hard* by Alexa Kitchen), personal essay (*Where I'm Coming From* by Barbara Brandon-Croft), or a combination (the short comic "Milgaard and Me" in *Portraits from Life* by David Collier). It can be any genre: superhero (*Watchmen* by Alan Moore), romance (*Blankets* by Craig Thompson), humour/satire (*The Essential Dykes to Watch Out For* by Alison Bechdel), children's (*Diary of a Wimpy Kid* by

Jeff Kinney), science fiction/fantasy (*Boston Metaphysical Society*, a steampunk Web comic by Madeleine Holly-Rosing), detective/noir (*City of Glass* by Paul Auster, Paul Karasik, and David Mazzucchelli), thriller/horror (*Vampirella* by Warren Ellis), true crime (*The Borden Tragedy* by Rick Geary), classics (*Remembrance of Things Past* by Marcel Proust and Stéphane Heuet), history/politics (*Exit Wounds* by Rutu Modan), or biography/autobiography (*Persepolis* by Marjane Satrapi). And a comic can be presented in just about any format: zine, classic comic book, folded slip of paper, tiny book, oversize book, or even in multiple formats. *Building Stories*, a comic by Chris Ware, is a box containing pamphlets, bound books, broadsheets, accordion-folded strips, and a game board. A comic can be digital or hybrid, an app, a comics/gaming combination, an all-digital pastiche of cheesy clip art or personal photographs (*fumetti* or a *photo-roman*), and so on.

Images in comics can be more or less "cartoony" or "arty," ranging from simple black-and-white line drawings to miniature works of art, but all employ the conventions of cartooning:

- *Simple lines:* In cartooning, less is more — a very few lines convey a lot of information. The simpler and more iconic the drawing, the greater the impact.
- *Exaggeration:* People, things, and effects are drawn so that they seem larger, louder, more extreme, or more intense than in real life. A crying cartoon baby has an enormous open mouth with a prominent uvula; a man's eyes pop out of their sockets when he gets a big surprise.
- *Cartoon language:* Simple but evocative symbols convey a sight, a sound, a feeling, a movement, and more — things that we *experience* but cannot actually *see:* a light bulb over the head of a character with an idea, short lines radiating from the sun to indicate heat, a talk bubble full of words hanging over a character's head.

We then talk about process and craft. In comics, as in other forms, the writer uses tools, techniques, and literary devices to tell a story, give information, make an argument, ponder a subject, or some combination. But there are two ways in which comics and other forms are very different — the rendering of space and time:

- *Space:* In comics, there is a "grammar" of space as well as a grammar of language. Working with a series of still images, or a series of symbiotically linked images and words (talking, thinking, "voice-over" narration, sound), the writer arranges the elements on a page or screen so that the order and placement itself becomes another visual component. When a comic is well composed, these combined elements are experienced as one unit by the reader, who (unlike a film viewer) is in control of what she sees, in what order, and at what speed. It is up to the writer to direct the reader's eye where she wants it to go.

- *Time:* In comics, the past and the present (and sometimes the future as well) coexist as they do in life, in the territory of hopes, fears, dreams, and memories. Readers feel a pace and infer time whether or not the writer intends it. As Scott McCloud points out, much of the actual motion in a comic occurs between panels. In a process he calls "closure," the reader subconsciously fills in all of the moments that are not pictured.

DRAFTING AND COMPOSING

Each student completes four major assignments during the term: a draft of a short comic (two pages or equivalent), a draft of a longer comic (four pages or equivalent), and a substantial revision of each comic. "Or equivalent" refers to the depth of the writing as well as the volume of visual material. Most comics are arranged in a series of panels, placed side by side in tiers that stack up to make a page, conforming to a pattern or grid; but a page can also consist of a single image without panel borders that incorporates the content of multiple panels. Marjane Satrapi, author of *Persepolis*, a memoir of growing up in Iran during the Islamic Revolution, works with a grid of rectangular panels and tiers of consistent size and shape, with the occasional splash panel (larger frame) for emphasis or dramatic impact. Joe Sacco, who writes "comics journalism" set in Palestine, Bosnia, and other volatile places, composes many pages with swirling lines rather than window-like panels, so that one image comprises multiple scenes, subtly separated by a stretch of barbed wire, a machine gun, or a woman's long skirt.

For either assignment, a student may submit an original comic that runs to the required length, or a sequence from a longer work-in-progress, as long as its content and shape can be comprehended and critiqued without explanation. Some students who are underway with long projects in some other form — poetry, fiction, creative non-fiction, children's literature — continue their work in the comics course. One student will write the next chapter or stanza as a comic, another will find a new entrance to a problematic passage by adapting it to the comics form, another might discover that her written novella works better as a digital graphic narrative with some gaming twists.

As soon as we finish the introductory talk (two sessions), students begin drafting their comics. Like the experts, they work with some combination of the following drafting stages, any of which may be done on paper or onscreen:

- *Script:* a written script, similar to a screenplay, with dialogue, narration, and notes on what will be pictured.
- *Thumbnails:* small, rough drawings or schematics showing the basic composition of panels and pages.
- *Pencils:* a first draft of the comic with drawings and text pencilled in.
- *Revised pencils* (as many as needed).
- *Inks:* drawings and words rendered in ink.
- *Finished colour:* all text and visuals with colour added.

Some writers draft the comic in words, writing a script that looks like a screenplay. Then they work on images and page composition, and redistribute the workload of words, images, and composition as the three elements coalesce. (In large companies that specialize in superhero comics and other products for a mass audience, a writer writes a script, an editor refines the script, an artist pencils the drawings, another inks the pencil drawings, a letterer pencils in the written text, another letterer inks the text, yet another technician adds colour, and so on.)

Other writers begin with images. David Collier's book *Chimo,* his memoir of re-enlisting in the army at age forty, incorporates a lot of text, but he began this book as he begins any comic, by sketching images and waiting to "hear" the words. Chris Ware describes his realization that "I was relying way too much on words and using words as a way of accounting for the deficits in my drawing, and vice versa, illustrating my words rather than actually telling stories in words and pictures."

The next step is composing, consistent with the spatial "grammar" of comics. A panel can be compared to a phrase or clause, a tier to a sentence, a page (or a spread — two facing pages) to a paragraph, and so on. So, like the lines and stanzas of a poem, these elements have deliberate starts, ends, and intersections, not arbitrary ones. The student presents the content graphically, on paper or screen, starting with thumbnails or going right to a full-size page, roughly sketching images and text into panels, tiers, and pages. The post-thumbnail draft, called "pencils," is usually done in pencil, so that it can be continually revised. "This is where your page takes on a composition," says Jessica Abel, author of *La Perdida*, "where you enrich the words with deeper meaning in the images, where you make what you're doing into comics."

Words, like everything else in a comic, are visual elements consistent with all the other visual elements. So the writer decides on the appearance of the lettering for text blocks — narration and dialogue "bubbles" (also called "balloons"): it may be loose, handwritten, and deliberately eccentric; or precisely calligraphed, letter by letter; or typeset in a "comics" font and added digitally later. Students are encouraged to try things, and also to let things happen. A student may find, upon drafting a comic, that no text at all is needed, or that it is best to place the text in separate, strategically located panels rather than combining it with images in panels — much the way text was presented in the silent films. A writer may also respond to a pragmatic prompt. When an interviewer asked Posy Simmonds about her decision to combine handwritten and typeset text in her book *Gemma Bovery*, she said, "I was going to handwrite it, and I began to and I thought, 'God, you're bonkers doing this hand-lettering.'"

We also look at the elements of visual composition: how to use panel size for emphasis or pauses; how to speed up the pace (as for a swordfight) or slow it down (as for a rising sun); how to establish point of view, foreground, middle ground, and background in a panel; how to use light, shadow, and texture to create a focal point or a sense of depth; and so on. We also look at special effects unique to the comics medium, such as an episode of "Little Sammy Sneeze," by Winsor McCay (1869–1934), in which Sammy sneezes so hard that the panel falls into shards as if it were a sheet of breaking glass.

STRENGTHENING THE INFRASTRUCTURE

The required text for the course is *Making Comics: Storytelling Secrets of Comics, Manga and Graphic Novels* by Scott McCloud (author of *Understanding Comics*). McCloud's text identifies the building blocks of comics and gives practical advice on choosing what to put in, what to leave out, and how to present it — all with vivid explanations and examples.

McCloud lists five basic types of choices to be made in creating comics:

- *Choice of moment:* Of all the moments that occur when a being takes a step, which will be shown?
- *Choice of frame:* For each panel or view, will the being be shown from a point far away or close by? From above the head or from the ground near the feet? Straight up, or at an angle?
- *Choice of image:* What characters, objects, and surroundings will be shown?
- *Choice of word:* In each panel, what word(s) will work best to convey talking and/or thinking in the panel or off-panel, as well as sound and text in the environment (signs, brand names, etc.)?
- *Choice of flow:* How will elements be arranged so that the reader's eye moves along where, when, and at what pace the writer wants it to?

These five choices are invaluable for comics writers (and readers) in many respects, but I am cautious in recommending a study of them. No writer should embark on a draft by following instructions. Nevertheless, McCloud's five choices are effective tools for comprehending the special demands of the comics form.

Throughout the course, we study exemplary work by established comics writers and artists. I use a data projector to show sample pages of finished work, as well as draft scripts, thumbnails, rough pencils, refined pencils, and any other in-progress examples I can find. These invaluable process documents are reproduced in various books and webpages on how to make comics (*The Complete Idiot's Guide to Creating a Graphic Novel* by Nat Gertler and Steve Lieber; *Comics and Sequential Art* by Will Eisner; *You Can Do a Graphic Novel* by Barbara Slate; or Jessica Abel and Matt Madden's *Drawing Words and Writing Pictures*). Students can even watch a professional comics artist create a set of roughs on video (*Drawing Roughs for Comics* by Troy Roberts). As we look at finished comics or work-in-progress, I ask the students pointed questions: Why did the writer use three panels to convey this moment instead of one? What is the effect of the extreme closeup, the size and style of the sound word *ch-ch-ch-ch*, the character's hand breaking through the "fourth wall"? To the extent that it is possible when studying short excerpts, I ask students to explore larger questions: How would you describe the tone or mood of the work? What is the compelling theme or story at its heart?

There is always disagreement in the group, which gives us all fresh opportunities to examine and articulate our responses. Craig Thompson's book *Habibi,* for example, tells the story of two child slaves, a girl and a boy, who become separated, grow up, and are reunited, in a fictitious, vaguely Middle Eastern world. Upon seeing passages from it, some students are drawn to the exoticism and suspense of the story, enhanced by Thompson's fluid artwork and his references to Islamist and Christian art and thought; others are offended by what they feel is his "racist" representation of Muslim characters and his sexualization of rape. And, in response to a page or two of *The Job Thing* by Carol Tyler, whose style is loose and uninhibited, some students are inspired to emulate her uninhibited exuberance; others are confused by her inconsistent portrayal of characters and her unorthodox arrangement of panels.

Our work with the textbook and examples of finished comics by experts is complemented by other infrastructure activities, including guest presentations by published comics writers, in-class exercises, students' analysis of comics they admire, workshop sessions in which they critique each other's work, and hands-on experimentation with various drawing materials. By the end of the course, students comprehend the special demands of comics: how "writing" in still images for page or screen differs from other kinds of writing, and how images and words in comics are uniquely entangled, being neither illustrated text nor captioned images. They know how labour intensive the form is, even with the assistance of software to set up grids, streamline the lettering process, and manipulate images. They are aware of the growing interest in comics among teachers, librarians, and trade publishing companies; and they grasp the differences in audience and production process between independent book publishers and large, multinational manga and super-hero comics producers. They also perceive the expanding market for short comics — for example, in mainstream and specialty magazines that have only recently begun to include comics, and on the Internet as a personal blog or series, or as part of a group or online periodical. Most of all, they understand the comics medium and its potential to enhance their writing work in any form, via reading comics, making comics, or both.

WORKS CITED

Abel, Jessica. *La Perdida.* New York: Pantheon, 2008. Print.

Abel, Jessica, and Matt Madden. *Drawing Words and Writing Pictures.* New York: First Second, 2008. Print.

Auster, Paul, Paul Karasik, and David Mazzucchelli. *City of Glass.* New York: Picador, 2004. Print.

Bechdel, Alison. *The Essential Dykes to Watch Out For.* New York: Houghton Mifflin Harcourt, 2008. Print.

Brandon-Croft, Barbara. *Where I'm Coming From.* Syndicated comic, 1991–2005. Print.

Castrée, Geneviève. *Susceptible.* Montreal: Drawn & Quarterly, 2013. Print.

Clowes, Daniel. *Ghost World.* Seattle: Fantagraphics, 2004. Print.

Collier, David. *Chimo.* Wolfville, NS: Conundrum, 2011. Print.

———. "Milgaard and Me." *Portraits from Life.* Montreal: Drawn & Quarterly, 2002. Print.

Corman, Leela. *Unterzakhn.* New York: Schocken, 2012. Print.

Eisner, Will. *Comics and Sequential Art.* Tamarac, FL: Poorhouse Press, 1985. Print.

Ellis, Warren. *Vampirella.* Mt. Laurel, NJ: Dynamite Entertainment, 2010. Print.

Engelberg, Miriam. *Cancer Made Me a Shallower Person.* New York: HarperCollins, 2006. Print.

Geary, Rick. *The Borden Tragedy.* New York: NBM, 1997. Print.

Gertler, Nat, and Steve Lieber. *The Complete Idiot's Guide to Creating a Graphic Novel.* New York: Penguin, 2004. Print.

Holly-Rosing, Madeleine. *Boston Metaphysical Society.* E-books, 2012–13. Web.

Kinney, Jeff. *Diary of a Wimpy Kid.* New York: Penguin, 2007. Print.

Kitchen, Alexa. *Drawing Comics Is Easy! Except When It's Hard.* Amherst, MA: Denis Kitchen, 2006. Print.

Matt, Joe. *Peepshow.* Montreal: Drawn & Quarterly, 2003. Print.

McCay, Winsor. "Little Sammy Sneeze." *New York Herald,* 1904–06. Print.

McCloud, Scott. *Making Comics.* New York: HarperCollins, 2006. Print.

———. *Understanding Comics.* New York: Avon/HarperCollins, 1994. Print.

Modan, Rutu. *Exit Wounds.* Montreal: Drawn & Quarterly, 2007. Print.

Moore, Alan. *Watchmen.* New York: DC Comics, 1987. Print.

O'Malley, Bryan Lee. *Scott Pilgrim,* vols. 1–6. Portland: Oni Press, 2004–10. Print.

Proust, Marcel, and Stéphane Heuet. *Remembrance of Things Past.* New York: NBM, 2001. Print.

Roberts, Troy. "Drawing Roughs for Comics." *Vimeo,* 18 Feb. 2012. Web.

Sacco, Joe. *Palestine Collection.* Seattle: Fantagraphics, 2001. Print.

———. *Safe Area Gorazde.* Seattle: Fantagraphics, 2002. Print.

Satrapi, Marjane. *Persepolis: The Story of a Childhood.* New York: Pantheon, 2004. Print.

Simmonds, Posy. *Gemma Bovery.* London: Jonathan Cape, 2001. Print.

Simmons, Shane. *Longshot Comics.* San Jose: Slave Labor Graphics, 1995. Print.

Slate, Barbara. *You Can Do a Graphic Novel.* New York: Penguin, 2009. Print.

Spiegelman, Art. *Maus I and II.* New York: Pantheon, 1993. Print.

Tamaki, Jillian, and Mariko Tamaki. *Skim.* Toronto: Groundwood, 2010. Print.

Thompson, Craig. *Blankets.* Marietta, GA: Top Shelf, 2004. Print.

———. *Habibi.* New York: Pantheon, 2011. Print.

Tyler, Carol. *The Job Thing.* Seattle: Fantagraphics, 2002. Print.

Ware, Chris. *Building Stories.* New York: Pantheon, 2012. Print.

It's All About Structure: The Craft of Screenwriting

Peggy Thompson

FADE IN

Studying screenwriting is, to my way of thinking, a great way for a writer in any genre to get comfortable with plot and story.

As a guiding principle, we follow the professional model as closely as possible in my workshop. And I don't mean the professional model of sitting around in your pajamas at home — a legitimate professional model as far I'm concerned, but we have to make compromises for the university. So we gather in a classroom and do what people do in the world of screen-based media: pitch, outline, write a first draft, polish, and then pitch again. And we discuss how our pitches have evolved. By the end of term, the screenwriters have completed all of these steps with one or more projects.

In my undergrad classes, writers tend to work with the short film form (we get a good number of film production undergrads who are shooting their screenplays); in grad screen classes they work on anything from television to webisodes, shorts or features.

We diverge in our practice from fiction workshops, where discussion of the material takes place without the writer speaking until the end. In my workshops we work as we would in an ideal writers' room, with the writer clarifying and others questioning. And we always read at least some of the script out loud — perhaps the most effective way of helping students figure out what isn't working in a script, because they hear problems immediately.

Teaching screenwriting to creative writing majors is like coaching elite athletes in literary cross-training. Athletes cross-train by working in different sports with the goal of improving overall performance: a basketball player might train in distance running and tennis to sharpen her game. While images of elite athletic training may seem incongruous in our small, dusty enclave where the main activity is sitting in a building where the cleaning code is Benign Neglect, nonetheless, that's what we do. So when novelists, stage writers, poets, and graphic novel students come to screenwriting, to continue the cross-training metaphor, they find that by working in the area they don't usually work in, their overall skill set improves.

The element of story that gets most student novelists and short fiction writers stuck, and most screenwriting students, too, is plot. The joy and the horror of writing for screen is that screen is nothing but plot, action, and form. And plot. All right, it's other things as well — characters, image, theme, dialogue, conflict and thwarted desires, secrets, climaxes, reversals, and more climaxes. Screenwriting is a story-eating beastie that needs constant feeding.

Here's an old saying about the difference between story and plot, attributed to E.M. Forster:

> The king died and then the queen died (story).
> The king died and then the queen died of grief (plot).

That doesn't sound like a plot to me. In fact, with that plot, one may well end up with the "Passive Protagonist" problem, which challenges all screenwriters at one time or another. So let's try it again, as story and movie plot:

> The king died and then the queen died (story).
> The king was murdered and then the queen tracked down the perpetrators, killed each and every one, and became a beloved monarch to her whole country (movie plot).

And, of course, studying screenwriting also prepares students for a life of writing in screen-based media, a goal of many writers-in-training. When serious screenwriters go on to work in film, television, and Web-based media, their writing is strengthened by cross-training in fiction, graphic forms, radio, non-fiction, and poetry.

The challenge with the cross-training and multi-genre approach is that in any workshop there may be students who have made films, often a number of very successful films, working alongside students who have never written a word for screen — and, for that matter, seldom see a film. We meet this challenge by allowing everyone to work at their own pace, but we all follow the same steps, starting with The Pitch.

THE PITCH: WHY IT WORKS

A major part of the work of creating a screenplay is conceptualizing the film, which means thinking about the story, the characters, the setting, and so on. It also requires research, such as identifying an audience or demographic. What's the genre, or genres? Who pays to see a film in that genre? How does it do in the marketplace? What's the theoretical budget (revenue and expenses)? Is this a film for festivals? If it's a feature, do you hope for a theatrical release? I like to get screenwriters thinking like filmmakers.

Some students are determined to write for the LA market. Others are very interested in the low- or no-budget categories of Canadian independent film, and some fall in between. All of these are fine — as long as the students do their research.

Then I ask students to pitch.

THE PITCH: WHAT IT IS

The pitch is a short, persuasive verbal sales talk tossed out at producers, funders, and distributors — and, after the film is done, the press. So the writer or filmmaker may be pitching a project before it exists, or long after it's done, or both. Most pitches are short. In our workshops we bring them in at three minutes, about the time you'd have to pitch someone at a film festival or a market such as the Toronto International Film Festival or the Banff International Television Festival.

THE PITCH: HOW IT'S STRUCTURED

- Compliment the person you're pitching on their work (do your homework).

- Introduce yourself.
- Say why you're passionate about this story and how it began for you.
- Give a brief overview of the story: beginning, middle, end.
- Describe the tone. For television, what Canadian network would this show be on? For theatrical release, which distributor would it best suit?
- Say how this project would benefit the person you're pitching.
- Name the key people on your team to date.
- Finish by giving the person a way to follow up.

Once we've all pitched — and regardless of class size, we do all the pitches in one two-hour class — we move on to cards or outline.

CARDS/BEAT SHEET/OUTLINE/TREATMENT

I prefer *cards*. I have the student put a header on each card, such as EXT. FOREST DAY, and what happens in each scene in the screenplay, which is still being visualized. There is no dialogue, and the action is boiled down to a sentence or two. The student presents the cards in class out on a table, and the rest of us stand around and look. If we feel it helps, we move the cards around and add more of our own.

A *beat sheet* is similar. It has numbers and a brief description of each scene, but it's written in note/text on paper. A beat sheet tracks the emotional moments of each scene and is extremely useful. A *treatment* is more detailed and is written out as prose.

What's difficult about this phase is that the student has to try to work out the overall arc of a film story. Many writers, myself included, prefer to work organically and let the story and the characters work it out. But in the professional world of screen-based media, or trans-media, deadlines are assigned and kept, and begun with cards, or a beat sheet, or an outline, or a treatment. This is particularly true in television, where speed is the order of the day, every day.

When a student lays down cards, she reads out what happens in each scene. If she has written prose, the class will read it out while the student listens, going around the table with each person reading a few sentences out loud. Reading out loud resolves much student/writer resistance to revising. Once a writer hears her work, she hears many of its problems.

FIRST DRAFT

I've been teaching screenwriting since 1995. Before that, I was a screen-writer of short films, two feature films (*The Lotus Eaters* and *Better Than Chocolate*), and television programs (*The Beachcombers, Weird Homes, Da Vinci's Inquest,* and others). I've worked in both documentary and fiction. I'm also a producer and have written for the stage, radio, and print. I've also acted and directed. I still do most of these things. In my various work-shops at the University of British Columbia, I teach writing short films, writing feature films, and writing television scripts — both original to the student and specs. (A spec script is a screenplay for an existing series written within the storylines of the current season.) For each genre I give different advice.

Short Film

Ten to twelve pages is often the ideal length for a short film in a festival. If your idea is strong enough, you will be able to describe the dramatic story-line and provide vivid descriptions of your characters in two or three sen-tences. Choose a situation and a story that can be told entirely within about twelve minutes. You must be very selective with the topic to make it fit. Get to the heart of the characters as quickly as possible. This is a major key to a successful short film. The film must have a hook, or (for lack of a better word) a gimmick — an interesting and unique element, ideally a visual one. There must be a twist/reversal at the end.

Television — Original or Spec Script

I advise my students to write a show or spec script for a current or recent half-hour program, such as *Parks and Recreation, 30 Rock,* or *Community*. Hour-longs and originals are also acceptable, but students who write a spec script have a better chance of finishing it in one semester.

It may seem counterintuitive, but they will experience great break-throughs in their writing when they write for a show with characters they know and formats they're familiar with. Freed from the work of creating a whole universe, they can apply their ideas to an existing infrastructure, mir-roring the show and discovering how plots are put together.

In this class, too, we begin with the pitch, and then cards, beat sheets, or outlines, which must be prepared in the format the show uses. Students have to analyze the series they're writing for, and identify and count the scenes in each act. Is there a teaser at the beginning? Is there a kicker at the end? Suddenly the form cracks open and is no longer mysterious. Because the characters are familiar and strong, students can focus on plot and form. And they tend to have breakthroughs in those areas, which are the most complex to teach and learn.

Feature Film

The student who undertakes a feature-length screenplay faces the ultimate challenge: three-act structure. It may take her a few years to finish a screenplay, or the work may go much more quickly. I could easily write an entire chapter on three-act structure, whose complexities never cease to delight and challenge.

In teaching it, I use a template I've put together over the years, a combination of approaches inspired by Emma Thompson, Aristotle, Margaret Mehring, John Yorke, and various blogs and videos (John August, BAFTA, and others), and the granddaddy of all structure goodness, Lajos Egri. A word of warning about Lajos Egri: his book *The Art of Dramatic Writing* was written for the theatre and took me ten years to read. However, it is used by many in the industry. His analysis of how to build a dramatic climax is both brilliant and correct — with a dash of Blake Snyder and Robert McKee.

In my lecture classes, I screen a film and discuss the story points in my template as we go. The films I use include *Babe*, *The Sixth Sense*, *Juno*, and even, in one lengthy class, *Star Wars*.

- **Act 1:** Inciting Incident — approximately 1–5 minutes in. An event that kicks off the story. The First Turning Point occurs approximately 17–25 minutes in. The story is under way. We have met our main characters, including the antagonist(s), we understand the premise of the story and film, and an action happens that spins us into …
- **Act 2:** Stakes and conflict continue to build. Halfway through Act 2 (50–60 pages in), about halfway through the film, the stakes get even higher and the conflict with the antagonist(s) intensifies further. Action then builds to the Second Act Climax or Second Act Turning

Point, a reveal of information that leads to a crisis for the protagonist, out of which the protagonist takes action, and we spin into …

- **Act 3:** In the Third Act Climax, another reveal of information creates a crisis for the protagonist, out of which the protagonist again takes action — usually face to face with the antagonist, who has had their own reveal of information.
- Resolution (can be very brief).
- Obligatory Scene reiterating the theme of the story, either visually or in language (can be anywhere in Act 3).
- Final Image.

To demonstrate the Three-Act Structure, I use the movie *Babe* for several reasons. It's a film for both children and adults, it's funny, it was nominated for seven Oscars, including Best Adapted Screenplay, and it has a wonderful structure.

In Act 1 a narrator tells us the theme: "This is a tale about an unprejudiced heart and how it changed our valley forever. There was a time, not so long ago, when pigs were afforded no respect, except by other pigs. They lived their whole lives in a cruel and sunless world." *Babe*, like most comedies, is a film about changing the social order: a pig can be a sheep dog. Act 1 establishes the theme — the plot — the main character, and the style of the film. It presents the main character with a problem that he will spend the entire film solving.

Near the beginning is the Inciting Incident, the event that sets the story in motion. In *Babe* this occurs when Babe is taken to the fair and won by Farmer Hoggett … and then taken home to Hoggett's farm where he learns that every animal has a place in the social order. And his place is in the barn. And his job is to eat.

The First Turning Point occurs at the end of the first act. It begins when Babe and Ferdinand the duck do not heed the command to never go inside the house. They do.

In Act 2 there are several key points — the Mid-Point, the Hidden Information, the Crisis, a.k.a. the Second Turning Point (or plot point). What drives Act 2 is conflict — conflict between characters and the situations they find themselves in. These conflicts stem from the themes, dilemmas, and desires established in the first act.

Babe and Ferdinand enter the house so that Ferdinand can steal the alarm clock that has usurped his position on the farm as a kind of rooster who wakes the farm every morning. The alarm clock renders Ferdinand obsolete and thus condemns him to the dinner table. Babe and Ferdinand are caught, of course, and Babe, too, seems doomed to be dinner sooner than planned. The first half of Act 2 of *Babe* centres on the theme of the film: Babe's destiny, his place in the social order as food. Through a wily trick of Farmer Hoggett's, Babe is saved from being eaten at Christmas. And then on Christmas Day Babe unwittingly points the way to his own salvation.

By opening the gate so Ferdinand can escape his fate and the farm, Babe receives what the mythologist Joseph Campbell calls "the call to adventure." Babe slips out into the sheep pasture and saves a number of sheep from being stolen. This gives Farmer Hoggett the idea that Babe could be something other than food. He could be a sheep dog, or a sheep pig, as it were. And this leads us directly to the Mid-Point.

Halfway through the second act comes the Mid-Point: the time in the film when the story crystallizes. Nothing new will be introduced after this point; everything will complicate, develop, and complete. The Mid-Point is a sequence of extreme intensity. At the Mid-Point of *Babe*, after Babe has saved the sheep, Farmer Hoggett takes him out into the sheep pasture to begin his "training and initiation," again, steps from Campbell's *Hero's Journey*. There, Babe takes the first steps toward becoming a "sheep pig."

The second half of Act 2 builds to a series of developments, conflicts, and crises, which lead to the climax. In *Babe* these include Rex the head dog sliding into viciousness and depression over Babe taking over his job. When a vet sedates Rex, the problem becomes further exacerbated. Now he can no longer do his job at all, thus opening the door for Babe to become even more of a sheep pig. This sequence contains both conflict and complications.

A further complication develops when wild dogs attack the sheep and Farmer Hoggett thinks that Babe has killed one of his sheep. Babe is saved in the nick of time, but this incident reinforces the theme of the film. It would appear that Babe has stepped out of his place (by killing a sheep) and will be punished by death. But Babe is saved for the second time. Then Mrs. Hoggett leaves for the Regional Fair and Farmer Hoggett enters Babe in competition in the Sheep Dog Trials.

We have a reversal in which Babe replaces the cat by being brought into the house — the traditional home of the cat. But the cat, seeking revenge, drops a piece of hidden information that leads to another crisis. The cat tells Babe that pigs are food and that Babe is, in fact, pork. Everyone, of course, has known this all along. Everyone except Babe.

This leads to the final crisis. Babe is shattered emotionally and runs away into a raging storm and almost dies — for the third time. Rex finds Babe and an antagonist becomes an ally. Farmer Hoggett saves Babe, and thus the crisis paves the way for the climax. This sequence is the Second Turning Point, or the Second Act Climax, and also the end of the second act.

In Act 3 there are several key points — the Third Act Climax(es), the Resolution, the Obligatory Scene, and the Final Image. The Second Turning Point brings us to the climax, which is actually a series of escalating climaxes, often each is preceded by a piece of hidden information.

Act 3 of *Babe* takes place at the Sheep Dog Trials. The final piece of hidden information is retrieved by Rex. It is the password that enables Babe to get the sheep, whom he doesn't know, to co-operate: "Baa Ram Ewe." The climax is the trial itself. After first being denied entry into the trials, Babe wins.

There is very little resolution in *Babe*, but there is some. We are treated to a brief glimpse of all the central characters responding to the victory. The Resolution is followed by the Obligatory Scene in which the theme of the film is restated. It occurs in *Babe* when Farmer Hoggett says, "That'll do, Pig." The final image of *Babe* is of Babe. Perfectly appropriate. Who or what else would we rather see?

✐ 🖅 ☼

Babe is a comedy. As a genre, comedy challenges the status quo. And in *Babe*, the status quo of "some animals are meant to be eaten" is transformed into "we can be more than we are meant to be."

Marshall McLuhan famously said that current technology uses the form of previous technology. Following that premise, we understand that the past technology of the three-act feature films of today are the well-made plays of Ibsen and Chekhov, which evolved from the five-act plays of Shakespeare.

And so the question challenging filmmakers is: Does form define content, or does content define form? Some writers say that screenwriting is only form. I don't think that's entirely true. I like to think that there's hard form — which is critical in genre work like action films — and soft form, more suitable to what we might call art-house films. And whoever knows form can always subvert it.

There are many more elements of screenplay that a writer must learn: the meaning of tone, images, theme, character; the revision process; the collaborative process; and more. But the basics of screenplay described here are the foundation of any strong script. The student who masters them will have a solid footing as she takes the next steps.

He Put His *What WHERE?* Or: How to Teach Creative Writing Students to Write Plausible Sex Scenes, and at Least Prevent Them from Winning the "Bad Sex Award"

Nicole Markotić and Suzette Mayr

INTRODUCTION

Bad sex scenes have entered the literary consciousness not only as trite passages that readers must endure (or quickly pass over), but as an ongoing joke, usually (but not always) at the expense of inexperienced writers. In the United Kingdom, the *Guardian* posts shortlisted samples of its annual Bad Sex Award, given out to any bad sex scene in a published novel. The 2010 award went to novelist Rowan Somerville who, says the *Guardian*, with "one killer sentence ... demolished all comers" (his sentence: "like a lepidopterist mounting a tough-skinned insect with a too blunt pin he screwed himself into her"). Musing about why so many sex scenes slip into accidental comedy, author Ian Coutts says, "I think it's because sex is one of the very few human activities that can't be seen as standing in for something else.... A carrot can be a phallic symbol; a phallus is never a carrot symbol. We often use metaphor and euphemism to hint at sex, but once you're actually describing it, further metaphor only looks ridiculous ... Trying to get those subjective experiences down on paper in a way that resonates with others is tricky."

Given that a "good" sex scene in life has a good probability of being a "bad" sex scene on the page no matter how experienced the writer, our aim is not to analyze or critique sexual dynamics so much as to help creative writing students figure out how to further their narrative without simply dropping in extraneous sexual content. We are not comfortable with a format that would present examples of "good" sex scenes versus "bad" sex scenes, as "good" depends so much on context, and can be ambiguous. We are far more interested in encouraging students to think away from the obvious and expected than we are in presenting a prescriptive formula with ironclad, specific examples. And our idea of "good" and "bad" sex scenes would of course be informed by our own tastes (no matter how hard we might try to keep our tastes out of the discussion). To that end, we emphasize that this essay critiques the clichés of male-dominated, one-sided sex scenes; ours is a pedagogy paper in which we set out to explore these writing issues in the classroom.

As our title demonstrates, we aim specifically to take on the proliferation of masculinist sex scenes that dominate twentieth- and early twenty-first-century sex scenes in English-language novels. Such scenes — where the focus is entirely on a male character who "puts" his penis somewhere — tend to restrict the representation of female pleasure as strictly passive and heteronormative. This is a problem for feminists who wish to write feminine sexuality as empowering and female-driven, rather than present female characters as simply pliant receptacles. But it is especially troubling for those writers who have no interest in the clichéd sexuality of male-defined characters. So how might creative writing teachers go about teaching sex scenes that are purposefully inclusive of sexual and gender minorities in undergraduate creative writing classes? Perhaps one of the most tedious experiences in a creative writing workshop is when a student submits fiction that contains a poorly written and/or gratuitously pornographic and/or gratuitously violent sex scene. We both have spent many years teaching creative writing and somehow sidestepping or evading, or outright attempting to avoid, student sex writing. Suzette remembers being horrified at how many times students' stories opened with or included a graphic rape and murder, clearly in imitation of the many police procedural and forensic detective shows on television. And Nicole finds that students still hand in material — whether in imitation of TV or because they believe such topics to be "gritty" — that spirals around graphic and sexual violence. A similarly discouraging situation for a creative writing instructor might be when students deliberately choose *not* to include sex scenes in their work because of anxiety about how certain sexualities might be received, even when a particular text would be enhanced by the inclusion of more explicit sexuality. Suzette recalls asking a student why she skipped over the sex scene between two key characters in her short story — a sex scene that was essential to understanding the characters — and the student's response was that writing *any* sex scene made her "uncomfortable."

Russell Smith advises in a *Globe and Mail* article that lists his "top ten rules for fiction" as his rule number nine: "Don't be afraid of sex scenes. There is no reason to avoid them other than prudery. Sex is just as important to people's relationships as dinners are. You wouldn't skip the dinner scenes out of decorum, would you?" (R1). Interestingly, Smith is not the only writer to liken eating to sex. Foodie Jeremy Iggers has a similar, yet opposite, position on the subject: "In a culture in which consuming rather than connecting is the central motivating force, it is only natural that eating has more erotic potential than sex" (109). For many writers and readers, sex and food are fitting companions: both suggest corporeal pleasure, excessive devouring, and sensual "treats." Yet sex is also — at least in literature — aligned with death. Starting with Freud's *Beyond the Pleasure Principle* (1920), analysts have often cited "Sex and Death" as the two driving forces of literature. As one example of a writer who further aligns the two, Georges Bataille observes in *Death and Sensuality*, "The orgasm is popularly termed 'the little death' — la petite mort" (239).

Many a creative writing teacher has lamented that the majority of students in a creative writing class will choose to write about death (of which, presumably, they have no first-hand experience), yet will shy away from writing about sex (of which, usually, they have *some* first-hand experience). Such reluctance to explore the more carnal nature of love may come from student cynicism with the notion of love itself. As Catherine Belsey muses, "The postmodern condition brings with it an incredulity toward love. Where, we might ask, in the light of our experience, the statistics, our philosophy, or any documentary evidence outside popular romance, are its guarantees, its continuities, proof of its ability to fulfill its undertakings?" (683). It could be, too, that students are merely channelling North American culture's contradictory and ambivalent attitudes toward the portrayal and purpose of sex. Sex is regularly used to sell consumer goods, but the sex advertised to consumers is incomplete and partisan, often relying on misogynist or homophobic versions of sexuality. To be a responsible writerly citizen, some students might feel it's best not to write about sex at all. Or perhaps students don't appreciate that sex scenes need not rely on shame, violence, or exploitation. But as director John Cameron Mitchell so pithily laments, "Some people ask me, 'Couldn't you have told the same story without the explicitness?' They don't ask whether I could've done *Hedwig* without the songs. Why not be allowed to use every paint in the paintbox?" (qtd. in Schimpf).

PEDAGOGY

When Nicole taught from the anthology *Sexing the Maple* for a survey CanLit course, her students came to the (not far-off-the-mark) conclusion that all Canadian literary sex scenes are dysfunctional at best and rotten at worst. In a good way. In Leonard Cohen's *Beautiful Losers* not only does the narrator spend the entire novel in bed with his best (male) friend, F, screwing their asses off all while proclaiming their heterosexuality, but F and Edith (the narrator's wife) also have brutal sex with an insatiable Danish vibrator. Canada is well known for producing writers who embrace cutting-edge sexual explorations (for example, Barbara Gowdy's title story in *We So Seldom Look On Love*), disturbing sex (the Impregnation Ceremony scene in Margaret Atwood's *Handmaid's Tale*), and sexual descriptions excessive to the point of parody (not only does Robert Kroetsch's protagonist "stud" himself and his horse out in *The Studhorse Man*, but Hazard must also work at one point butchering pigs, slicing from their "dainty male nipples," past their anus, and through the penis shaft). Equally prominent are sex scenes that perpetuate heterosexual stereotypes (for example, in Morley Callaghan's *They Shall Inherit the Earth*, Bishop Foley imagines the scandal that would harm his charity campaign, should it get out that a priest has been meeting with two [female] prostitutes [198]).

We recently arrived at the conclusion that the best possible strategy for dealing with bad writing about sex is to opt for the preventive route — that is, build into our classes a structured unit and/or an exercise on writing about sex. To that end, Nicole created a "sexercise" and Suzette designed a lecture on the differences between writing a standard sex scene versus writing erotica versus writing pornography.

Here is the "sexercise" assignment:

> Write a sex scene. A good sex scene! Many, many, MANY
> writers have relied on sex scenes to offer readers a more fully

rounded, or contrasting, or surprising experience of characters or language. Many writers believe (usually erroneously) that simply describing characters having sex is titillating. Only a few manage to make their sex scenes sexy. Most writers, however, do very consciously write a sex scene to somehow provoke a response in their reader. Not necessarily to scandalize, but to show an aspect in the writing that would come out in no other scene. Consider how (and *why*) your characters might explore the sexual act on the page. This assignment is not restricted to fiction writers. What happens to sex and sensuality in a poem? Who has written intriguing poetic language about sex? Read the following creative writing CanLit examples (Leonard Cohen, Robert Kroetsch, Michael Ondaatje, Phyllis Webb), though you may bring in other literary examples on your own.

Not only were the student hand-ins that week particularly revealing, but the class discussion also took an unexpected turn. To begin with (and we realize we are using examples of only one class each), out of eighteen students, not a single one wrote a scene that didn't involve a heterosexual couple. Nearly a third wrote sado-masochistic sex scenes, with all but one writing the female characters as submissive and the male characters as physically cruel. In the one scene where the female character was dominant and the male character submissive, the student ended the scene with a jokey corrective that allowed the dominated male to stand up for himself and end the "imbalance" in their relationship. Another third of the class wrote stories and poems in which the female character was sexually unfulfilled, either because her male lover was inept, or because the couple had been married for over ten years. Sadly, the class discussion about these pieces turned on the weariness of why "we" have to read about frustrated, cold women. Only *two* students wrote sex scenes where the female characters experienced sensual pleasure. One was so metaphoric that Nicole first read it as a sci-fi scene, as there was a great deal about planets and beaches and animal avatars. The other, about a female character who attends sex-addiction meetings in order to hook up with men, was written by a male student. Ironically, the one student whose hand-ins until that assignment centred on teenage boys in love, wrote a sex scene in which his female protagonist beats up another girl, and then gets very turned on by how much her boyfriend delights in the *Carrie*-like gore.

During the workshop, Nicole turned continually to the literary examples she had given her students, asking pointed questions about the minimalist language of Webb's poetry, the overt sensuality of the Ondaatje, the raucous humour of the Kroetsch, the unacknowledged homoeroticism pervading the Cohen. The students were surprised that Nicole read the Cohen characters (who declared themselves heterosexual) and the Webb lines (which, being poetry, they read as entirely metaphorical) as queer. As our discussion widened to include the question "Why write a sex scene in the first place?" students came to the conclusion that in fiction, showing a character vulnerable (or at least partially stripped of their character coverings) allows writers to reveal character inconsistencies without merely throwing gratuitous contradictions onto the page. And in poetry, a sexual or fleshly reference may disturb the lyric line, or normative image, in ways that allow various modes of difference to emerge. As an interesting footnote, Nicole's students were so enamoured of the exercise (not always their response to these weekly assignments) that they titled the class chapbook accordingly: *UNcensored*.

Suzette found herself in an unusual but serendipitous situation: she was approached by a female student (whom we'll call Tammy) enrolled in an otherwise sex-scene-less, mid-level fiction writing class, who wanted to write erotica and had already distributed her erotic story to the class for the following week's workshop. Tammy was worried because her last creative writing instructor had said that any pornographic submissions would be given an automatic F. Suzette commented that there was a difference between erotica and pornography. Suzette had to be strategic in figuring out how to help this student write the best possible scenes for her fiction. She also knew to prepare the rest of the class to respond to Tammy's work in a constructive way that would generate fruitful discussion and provide a useful lesson to everyone in the class.

Suzette consulted and reproduced for the students in the class two texts: Ian Coutts's short article "Good Sex, Bad Writing" and an excerpt from the preface to Anaïs Nin's book of erotic short stories, *Delta of Venus*. Coutts's article makes fun of bad writing about sex, but is explicit about what constitutes bad writing, and advocates that sex scenes should stay away from metaphor. Coutts praises a sex scene in David Lodge's novel *How Far Can You Go?* because "the language is straightforward, neither crude nor euphemistic." Coutts concludes that a writer should "keep the prose simple. Stay out of people's heads." Suzette worried that Coutts's theory — that the simpler and more unadorned the language the better — would appeal too much to students who wanted to merely describe sexual actions, without considering resounding contexts. As an alternative point of view, Suzette looked at the preface to Nin's *Delta of Venus* in which she describes what makes effective erotic writing. To give a bit of context: in the early 1940s, Nin and other impoverished, writerly friends such as Henry Miller, George Barker, and Robert Duncan made money by writing erotica for one dollar a page for a wealthy, anonymous patron, a collector. At first Nin wrote the erotica fairly easily, but she eventually became more and more discouraged as the repeated response from the mysterious patron was, "[Your writing] is fine. But leave out the … descriptions of anything but sex. Concentrate on sex" (ix). In spite of the excellent wages, in her diary Nin composes a rebuttal (which she never sends):

> [Does] anyone ever experience pleasure from reading a clinical description? Didn't the old man [the collector] know how words carry colors and sounds into the flesh? … Dear Collector: we hate you. Sex loses all its power and magic when it becomes explicit, mechanical, overdone, when it becomes a mechanistic obsession. You have taught us more than anyone I know how wrong it is not to mix it with emotion, hunger, desire, lust, whims, caprices.… No two hairs are alike, but you will not let us waste words on a description of hair; no two odors, but if we expand on this you cry "Cut the poetry." (xiv–ix)

Of course, what Nin touches on in this rebuttal most explicitly is the difference between erotica and pornography. For many writers, pornography is the "clinical description," the "mechanistic obsession" — sex is the story. Whereas in erotica, sex is informed by context, conveyed with "poetry" — the story is in service of the sex (unlike the admittedly loose and contestable category of "literary" sex in which the aim of the sex scene is to be in service of the story). And because Nin's sex scenes are meant to titillate the mysterious collector there *is* a "lot of" sex in *Delta of Venus*. But there is also a surprising amount of context and enticing story. Unlike what Coutts suggests, the narrator in *Delta of Venus* often goes "into people's heads," and in many of the sex scenes it is important that the narrator enter characters' heads because so many of the stories describe female desire and lust rather than just "objective" sex. So much of the desire performed in these stories relies on context, character connection, and dynamic, and does not follow Coutts's advice to leave out the "subjective component — how it felt, what it meant." Frankly, it would be a shame if Nin's stories did not have these moments of reflection — many vividly portray a side of mid-war Europe that contemporary readers would not otherwise have a chance to witness. Nin herself comments in her diary, "I had a feeling that Pandora's box contained the mysteries of women's sensuality, so different from a man's and for which man's language was inadequate. The language of sex had yet to be invented" (xv–xvi). We suggest that a creative writing student wanting to include a sex scene in her work might find a happy medium between what both Ian Coutts and Anaïs Nin propose, and that, yes, sex scenes should likely stay away from excessive metaphor (a "phallus is never a carrot symbol"). But without the context, without the "poetry" of knowing that — as Nin suggests — "no two hairs are alike," the sex scene doesn't really entice the reader with sensuality, or seduce a reader into inexplicable pleasure in literature that the same reader would most likely avoid in life (think, for example, of Leonard Cohen's *Beautiful Losers*, where the Anglo narrator has sex with a pro-separatist Quebec crowd). Sex scenes, we're trying to teach our students, don't just titillate, they *enthrall.*

Discussing Anaïs Nin's reflections on what makes good writing about sex likely benefited the student, Tammy, and *all* the students in the class. It also allowed Suzette to establish some criteria for what could constitute a so-called "literary" sex scene versus erotica versus pornography. The Coutts and Nin texts together gave the class an opportunity to discuss sex scenes as another tool in the writer's toolbox. As an aside, we have both taught students who wished to write scenes that challenge other students' ideas about sexuality. For example, Suzette had one student (we'll call her Judy), who wanted to write a lesbian sex scene but was nervous about presenting such a scene to the class — nervous, in particular, about how other students in the class would respond, and eager for recommendations of lesbian scenes she could read that convey characters' sexuality without tipping over into a cliché of titillation.

And Nicole had a student (we'll call him Charles) who veered away from emotionally demonstrative queer scenes for similar reasons.

Neither Coutts nor Nin completely agrees about what makes a "good" or "bad" sex scene. Coutts's and Nin's lack of agreement presents an ambiguity that we aim for as a useful, general guide for creative writing students and teachers. We both took a more proactive approach with these students' literary challenges, bringing in various fiction scenes, poetry, and articles about writing beyond readers' comfort zones. Beginning writers may often think a text (especially in fiction) needs to resonate with a "universal" audience. We found that class discussions around audience, in particular, and place give a wider context for allowing students — to cite a long-standing creative instruction adage — to write what they know.

CONCLUSION

Given that students continue to write problematic sex scenes or avoid writing them altogether, and that the Bad Sex Award never fails to find many contenders and clear winners, it is obvious that writing sex scenes is fraught territory for both emerging *and* established writers. In the spirit of Russell Smith's "Ten Rules of Fiction," we would like to offer "Six Rules of How to Teach Sex Scenes." To sum up:

1. As a creative writing instructor, don't shy away from talking about effective sex scenes and how useful they can be for a writer, even though discussing sex scenes in class might inadvertently let your students know that you are a sexual being with a life outside the classroom. Be smart: stick to literary examples.
2. Definitely include literary examples that show a range of writing styles and content you want to bring up in class discussions, and make sure you discuss *why* these scenes are effective for the piece as a whole. You may even wish to hand out "bad sex" examples, as a way of showing students that many of their "original" and "scandalous" sex scenes have already been (ineffectually) written (and many times).
3. Time allowing, do give students a "sexercise" that will allow you to focus the writing and/or shape the class workshop within particular parameters.

4. Don't be shocked or surprised when students write aggressively heterosexual sex scenes. And don't be overly shaken, when a female character experiences unfulfilling sex, that both male and female students may comment on the female character's lack of agency, or even "frigidity"!

5. For a junior writing class, set out instructions in your course outline that overly graphic or violent sex scenes are not welcome. We also suggest that you might invite students to show you their work ahead of time if they have any concerns about how their sex scenes might be received in class.

6. And finally: have fun, and always use protection!

WORKS CITED

Atwood, Margaret. *The Handmaid's Tale*. Toronto: McClelland and Stewart, 1985. Print.

Bataille, Georges. *Death and Sensuality: A Study of Eroticism and the Taboo.* Trans. Mary Dalwood. Salem, NH: Ayer, 1962. Print.

Belsey, Catherine. "Postmodern Love: Questioning the Metaphysics of Desire." *New Literary History* 25 (1994): 683–705. Print.

Callaghan, Morley. *They Shall Inherit the Earth*. New York: Random House, 1935. Print.

Cavell, Richard, and Peter Dickinson. *Sexing the Maple: A Canadian Sourcebook*. Calgary: Broadview Press, 2006. Print.

Cohen, Leonard. *Beautiful Losers*. Toronto: McClelland and Stewart, 1966. Print.

Coutts, Ian. "Watch Your Language: Good Sex, Bad Writing." *Quill and Quire*, Nov. 2008: 10. Print.

Freud, Sigmund. *Beyond the Pleasure Principle*. New York: W.W. Norton, 1990. Print.

Gowdy, Barbara. *We So Seldom Look On Love*. Scranton: HarperCollins, 1993. Print.

Iggers, Jeremy. *The Garden of Eating*. New York: BasicBooks, 1996. Print.

Kennedy, Maev. "Bad Sex Award Goes to Rowan Somervillle." *Guardian*, 30 Nov. 2010. Web. 29 Jul. 2012.

Kroetsch, Robert. *The Studhorse Man*. Toronto: Macdonald, 1969. Print.

Nin, Anais. *Delta of Venus*. 1969. New York: Simon and Schuster, 1990. Print.

Schimpf, Rich. "This Week's Movies: Review of John Cameron Mitchell's *Shortbus*." *Scriptwrangler*. Web. 3 May 2008.

Smith, Russell. "Want to Write That Book? Read On." *Globe and Mail*, 29 Dec. 2001. Print.

B. By Approach

Creative Reading as Hybrid Pedagogy

Rishma Dunlop

Tu le connais, lecteur, ce monstre délicat,
— Hypocrite lecteur, — mon semblable, — mon frère!
                                              — Charles Baudelaire

The *Oxford English Dictionary definition of hybrid:* 1 *Biology* the off-spring of two plants or animals of different species or varieties, such as a mule; 2 a thing made by combining two different elements; 3 a word formed from elements taken from different languages, for example *television (tele-* from Greek, *vision* from Latin); 4 a hybrid car, a car with a petrol engine and an electric motor, each of which can propel it. Origin: early 17th century (as a noun): from Latin *hybrida* offspring of a tame sow and wild boar, child of a freeman and slave, etc.

THE READER

"All she did was read. This left a commotion in her wake. Reading as faith" (Dunlop 92). My love affair with books began as a young child. I haunted the library and spent hours sitting outside, on its concrete steps, reading. As a voracious reader, I discovered books as windows onto the world, as *objets d'art,* as talismans, and as the collectible mementos described in Walter Benjamin's "Unpacking My Library." Above all I came to recognize books as the ground of reading and as the means to learn how to write. In effect, I understood eventually that reading comes before writing, and that reading locates within the reader an original poetics that can make conscious the immense possibilities and salvific forces in the realms of literature, human imagination, and creativity.

In my view, the act of creative reading is the first axiom that identifies creative writing as a field of research. Forms of art and scholarship never remain static; they change constantly, shifting into new patterns of significance. To address some of these changing patterns, I developed Research and Artistic Creation, a graduate seminar at York University in Toronto, designed for students who wish to include artistic components in their scholarly work. It is a hybrid course that draws on multiple literary disciplines.

A hybrid approach forms an essential part of the creative process in any discipline, but in writing, it is a process of gathering and combining disparate bits of knowledge and unifying them into a whole that is a mongrel or mixed-breed genre. To teach the fundamentals of creative writing, I find it best to begin by enabling students to research and annotate their own life experiences. Only after they learn how to read their selves in the world, and only after they learn to combine their experiences with their critical readings, do they begin to write their own authentic, affective, creative works.

READINGS

> The object we call a book is not the real book, but its potential, like a musical score or seed. It exists fully only in the act of being read; and its real home is inside the head of the reader, where the symphony resounds, the seed germinates. A book is a heart that only beats in the chest of another.
>
> — Rebecca Solnit

To stimulate the creative reading process in a workshop setting, I assign a selection of hybrid and autobiographical readings designed to provoke thoughts about a joyful or traumatic incident, its memory, and attendant emotions. The overall aim is to have students produce a significant piece of autobiographical writing. Over the years, the course and readings have evolved and changed. I'll discuss here the most recent resources that I have found useful for teaching. I begin with two general introductory texts, Carolyn Forché and Philip Lopate's *Writing Creative Nonfiction* and John D'Agata's *The Next American Essay*. For the purposes of this memoir assignment, some of the readings I recommend are Anne Carson's "The Glass Essay" (from *Glass, Irony and God*) and "Kinds of Water," and Sherman Alexie's "Captivity," collected in the D'Agata anthology. The important thing is to expose students to an eclectic, hybrid range of readings, texts of mixed origin or composition.

We consider excerpts from the memoirs *Vertigo* by Louise DeSalvo, in particular the chapter titled "A Portrait of the *Puttana* as a Middle-Aged Woolf Scholar," which is constructed of non-chronological dated entries. We read memoir excerpts from Patti Smith's *Just Kids*, Mark Doty's *Still Life with Oysters and Lemon*, and Salman Rushdie's *Joseph Anton*, an interesting example of a memoir told in the third person, drawing from elements of fiction.

Then, to raise the discourse on the differences between fiction and non-fiction, we read the fragmented text of "Unguided Tour," by Susan Sontag and the story/poem "Girl" by Jamaica Kincaid. We read C.D. Wright's *Deepstep Come Shining* as an example of documentary poetry. These hybrid works reconstruct history and memory in genre-blurring styles. In *American Hybrid: A Norton Anthology of New Poetry*, edited by David St. John and Cole Swenson, the hybrid poem is identified as a synthesis between traditional and experimental styles. In the introduction, Cole Swenson argues that the long-acknowledged "fundamental division" between experimental and traditional is disappearing in American poetry in favour of hybrid approaches that blend trends from accessible lyricism to linguistic exploration. The majority of graduate students have had classes that teach them traditional and metrical forms, as well as the conventional borders between genres. Understanding that the borders are permeable and can be crossed, students can step outside their comfort zones, taking risks to find their own styles. Aleksandar Hemon's *The Book of My Lives* provides an example of a hybrid memoir that uses loosely linked essays. Lisa Robertson's prose experiments in *Occasional Works* and *Seven Walks from the Office for Soft Architecture* spark heated discussions on artistic form and research. Reading in this radical way, students begin to understand, as Robertson states, that "reading is a willed reception" (26).

After several weeks of reading and writing exercises, I ask students to write critical responses to their readings of experimental works like Lyn

Hejinian's autobiography, *My Life,* and Jenny Boully's "The Body" — an unconventional essay composed entirely of footnotes. Other valuable resources include *Creative Nonfiction,* which frequently publishes calls for themed issues, essays from *Harper's,* the *New Yorker, Agni,* the *Paris Review,* and *Granta,* to name just a few of the myriad resources for inventive non-fiction and hybrid prose. Pulled together, these readings help students internalize texts first and develop their own aesthetics.

I use similar techniques in creative non-fiction classes and mixed genres courses for undergraduates. The practice of doing creative reading first, followed by the generation of writing, establishes the classroom as a space of acute listening where students first hear each other's voices through reading out loud excerpts of what they have written. An atmosphere of trust, respect, and open communication is fostered as a community of writers gets to know each other's voices and creative styles. Hearing the writing through participants' readings of excerpts week after week builds, in incremental steps, a sense of confidence, and allows new writings to be shared without fear.

In a digitally mediated world, students are able to engage their narrative skills in various technologies and new media. This environmental shift leads the pedagogy of creative writing into a field in which hybridity (the combining of elements, like fiction and non-fiction, text and images) becomes an essential part of the creative process. In effect, hybridity becomes a new, cohesive force, a way of focusing various media or theoretical influences on a single subject. Hybridity is also a method of expanding the boundaries of fragmentation, compartmentalization, and specialization, as well as a way of releasing new energy.

After the students have discussed their creative and critical readings, I ask them to produce a piece of memoir-like writing made up of five dated entries, each entry no longer than a paragraph, recording significant events from five stages of their lives (infancy and early childhood, adolescence, adulthood, and the present day). Then they use their five dated entries to develop their factual or fictional autobiographical narratives. Students are asked to become bio-cartographers, to map life events with sensory detail, and become unflinching observers of the difficult stories they might wish to write. They are invited to think about writing the unthinkable, the unimaginable, to think about the implications of being the central character in a story, and to write about what scares them most, since the great dramas reside in dark places that are difficult to expose.

Once students select an event to expand on, I ask them to write a narrative of approximately 1,500 to 2,000 words. The next step is research: interview someone who was at the event or conduct research in print or graphic archives and write a 1,000-word narrative about the experience. Then I ask them to use both steps to develop a final essay. By the end of the course, students should have 3,500 to 4,000 words — a draft that can be refined and revised, and that demonstrates borrowings across genres or traditions and forms.

Reading a memoir is a creative act that defies the self-centred exhibitionism of the genre. Writing in a memoir form is a process of researching one's life and perhaps rethinking, reimagining, or revising one's past. Seeing things anew, through systematic research into the subject, may lead to unexpected discoveries or new facts and opinions. Readers experience these kinds of autobiographical writings through the lenses of their own lives. Creative readers, however, conduct a form of literary scavenging, searching for what serves them best and reusing what is useful for new purposes.

PRAXIS AND HEALING

Invariably, year after year, the majority of seminar participants choose to write about personal events that scared, or wounded, or silenced them in some way. Research and Artistic Creation is set up to encourage students to write about a deeply felt experience, a joy or wound they do not usually express in words. If trust has been established in the classroom, students will pursue such topics in an environment that is safe, yet challenging. They work from a sense of excitement, rather than fearing failure or humiliation. Over the first weeks, students share excerpts from their work without judgment, with a sense of connection to others. Critique begins when solid first drafts are generated. Student evaluations consistently indicate that the range of hybrid readings and in-class processes were highly valued and enabled them to approach their work in new ways.

While students will complete a finished piece for the course, many go on to expand the essay or progress to a thesis or dissertation project. Writing about trauma and other radical experiences can lead to a cathartic, potentially healing experience that could be represented or rendered in the student's essay or story. In *Writing as a Way of Healing: How Telling Our Stories Transforms Our Lives*, Louise DeSalvo considers personal writing as a restorative tool. She illuminates how the writing process transformed writers such as Virginia Woolf, Henry Miller, Audre Lorde, and Isabel Allende.

The importance of considering creative writing as healing praxis is reflected currently in the burgeoning of programs in Narrative Medicine and Medical Humanities found in medical schools across Canada and the United States, a clear indication of the growing emphasis on creative writing as a pedagogical-healing tool for physicians and patients. The *Bellevue Literary Review*, for example, is a long-standing publication of the Department of Medicine at New York University. In Canada, the University of Toronto publishes a literary medical humanities journal called *Ars Medica,* and has established an artist-in-residence program to work with physicians in training, faculty, and scholars on their narrative skills.

In each of my classes, I have encountered students who came to terms with long-lost or more recent traumatic memories by sublimating them in their creative writing. To illustrate, I'll describe two case studies of students who found the courage to give voice to a difficult experience that they wanted to write about but did not know how to articulate. The first student went on to complete an MFA at another Canadian university and win a prestigious national award for best emerging writer, and has recently published her work in book form. Her participation in my courses enabled her to break through her resistance to writing and develop a moving, complex fictional story about mental illness and depression. Her work included forays into forensic science and biblical research. The story she originally envisioned as a lyric essay became a work of experimental fiction and later an extremely affective, insightful piece of non-fiction, which expanded on the origins of her fictional narrative and revealed her understanding of the psychological and philosophical reasons behind mental breakdown.

The subject of the second case study is a writer who found his voice by exploring and writing in hybrid forms. He has won several creative writing awards and has also recently published a book of poetry. The lyric essay laid the foundation to his experiments in combining non-traditional elements with aspects of formal poetry. These experiments enabled him to write a series of poems about his mother's bipolar disorder.

These two examples indicate how students engage in critical reading exercises that help them reach inwards and find their own ways of writing about their traumas and significant events. The course becomes generative of new knowledge and a location of generous scholarship. This process has been effective, in part, because teaching creative writing to digitally literate students means first and foremost encouraging them to slow down and read, research, and analyze every word or bit in its context. In fact, creative readings become a way of training, and the writing becomes a way of fighting for the healing process by confronting the wound in an articulate way.

Reading Freud's *Interpretation of Dreams* initially provoked in me the principal idea behind creative reading as pedagogy. It made me aware of how the complexity of our lives is often only articulated in dreams and works of literature, as well as how dreams and literature are related to the subtlest ways we express our deepest and often repressed concerns. Consequently, provocative literary narratives that deal with oppression or repression are my most valued teaching tools. I use them to inspire connections between my students' lived experiences and the art of writing creatively.

Reading, to me, is above all a creative activity, an imaginative way of making our human experience intellectually or emotionally visible. In this context, I have shaped my pedagogical project as a university professor in the field of creative writing, which begins in the field of creative reading and becomes a hybrid that incorporates the fields of cultural literacy, literary studies, and arts education in general. I view these fields as intertwined aspects of the need to read, write, and engage intellectually with the world in which we live.

Encouraging students to appreciate narrative alterity, as a formal cause of literature and as a passion for students' contemplation, provides a counter-environment to the numbing materialistic forces of an entertainment-based society that frequently hides or obfuscates the creative, interpretive readings that artistic creation requires. In that sense, creative writing as a field of research is a pedagogical extension of the act of creative reading, as distinct from semiotics, or general semantics, or aesthetics.

THE HYBRID ARTIST-SCHOLAR

Like all writers, student-writers are influenced by multiple sites or locations. Their identities have not only been shaped by reading but also by experiences with multilingualism, post-colonialism, diasporic cultures, as well as politics and globalization. As a hybrid artist-scholar, my creative writing and my pedagogy aim to reflect how new works, and new knowledge, originally appear as the consequence of some unconventional formulization that produces a new impression, as a response to questions of identity. Hybridity permits students to engage with the kind of complexity that has already shaped them as persons in the digital age. Whether in scholarly writing or in poetry, or in any another medium, I consider the combining of two or more disciplines an intellectually liberating process. I encourage students to consider forms of "radical juxtaposition," as Umberto Eco called it, because I deeply value what Francis Bacon, in his essay "The Advancement of Learning," called "broken knowledge." Hybridity, juxtaposition, and "broken knowledge" are approaches I implement to help students externalize the stories that are buried within them. Hybridity is also an approach taken up by Marshall McLuhan, as a way of spontaneously accessing new thoughts and engaging with culture and media as an integrated ecology. As he states in *Understanding Media*, "The hybrid ... is a moment of truth and revelation from which new form is born" (63).

Teaching creative writing is, for me, above all a question of creating an open space for creative and critical thought to take shape. Roland Barthes referred to "the pleasure of the text" as a space in which both reader and writer are integral to a process in which independent-minded readers are able to challenge arbitrary authority and hierarchical attitudes. The digital age is amplifying this challenge and bringing higher education to a critical crossroads, locally and in a global context. Consequently, the teaching of creative writing as a field of research needs to explore new questions that arise from new media and from viewing creative reading as a form of pedagogy in all media.

Regardless of media used, creative reading can lead to creative writing, and creative writing can lead to historiographic *poiesis*, that is, art-making in response to history. In today's new media environment, particularly with the digital possibilities of hybridity and the Internet, new questions about a student's learning experience are being raised constantly, questions about the long-term effect of electronic devices on language, on reading, and on writing. These questions must intensify our research into the impact of new media on the pedagogies we employ to provide an enduring worth.

In her book *Proust and the Squid: The Story and Science of the Reading Brain,* neuroscientist Maryanne Wolf claims that we are not naturally wired to read. Reading must be learned through the brain's plasticity; when we read we are changed physiologically and intellectually. Creative writing courses produce opportunities for learners to figuratively reintegrate their so-called non-linear, artistic, right brain hemisphere with their linear, conventionally literate, left brain hemisphere. In that sense, my pedagogical goal is to bring together the two hemispheres, the empirically academic and the intuitively creative, just as the *corpus callosum* does in the neurobiology of the brain.

READING HYBRIDITY

> We spend our lives attempting to interpret through the word, the readings we take in the societies, the world of which we are part.
> — Nadine Gordimer, Nobel Lecture, December 7, 1991

Hybridity in education is emerging through the ever-growing presence of digital online learning. We are entering an era in which the relationship of our students to digital technology is making new teaching modalities possible and necessary. Hybrid forms have transformative power, the power to alter and dismantle forms, and the power to create new forms. We need to foster writers who understand modernism within the tradition, and who are committed to the development of language and new forms of writing. But as Wallace Stegner said in *On Teaching and Writing Fiction,* "We learn any art not from nature, but from the tradition, from those who have practiced it before. Writers teach other writers how to see and hear" (41). Books are made from other books, and we turn to writers, past and present, to understand the significance of our lives. In that sense, I propose that we consider the critical art of creative reading as a form of pedagogy that aims to legitimize creative writing as a field of research.

WORKS CITED

Baudelaire, Charles. "Au Lecteur." *Les Fleurs du Mal.* Paris: Gallimard, 1972. Print.

Dunlop, Rishma. "Claim." *Reading Like a Girl.* Toronto: Mansfield Press, 2011. Print.

Gordimer, Nadine. "Writing and Being." *Nobelprize.org.* Nobel Lecture, 1991. Web.

McLuhan, Marshall. *Understanding Media: The Extensions of Man.* New York: McGraw-Hill, 1964. Print.

Robertson, Lisa. *Nilling.* Toronto: BookThug, 2012. Print.

Solnit, Rebecca. *The Faraway Nearby.* New York: Penguin, 2013. Print.

Stegner, Wallace. *On Teaching and Writing Fiction.* New York: Penguin, 2002. Print.

"I'm Stone in Love With You": Stylistics in the Creative Writing Classroom

Louis Cabri

Linguistics has become increasingly important to me in teaching literature courses. What I've learned is that some of my creative writing students who also enrolled in linguistics-leaning literature courses of mine have found transferable from those courses not literary history or interpretation, ironically, but some of the linguistics. One creative writing student began to experiment with sentence construction after becoming aware that the transitivity model could describe the way language represents experiential processes: they fell into six basic categories. So my student asked, "Why are there six kinds and not seven? Can there be a seventh? What would an experiential process look like that defies the six basic types, and what would such a process require of language?" These would seem to be speculative questions far removed from the creative writing page, but they speak to how linguistics can feed the imagination concerning not just what is language but what is literature.

Some of my creative writing students appear to be interested in what linguistics in the broadest sense has to offer them because linguistics gives them a way of speaking, of perceiving, and of thinking about the language that is all around them — both inside and outside them. Linguistics offers a way to objectify language, including literary language in written form. I agree that linguistics potentially gives a creative writing student a conceptual toolbox for understanding and for articulating in minute detail why it is they respond the way they do to what it is they read and what it is they write.

It's not that I plan to have my students exclusively reading linguistics texts in a creative writing class; nor do I wish upon them listening to me lecture about grammatical structures, semantic features, or allophones. Linguistics informs, nonetheless, the way I talk about student writing and the coursepack readings I choose. And when I am successful in my approach, then the disciplinary trappings of linguistics, its jargon, methods, theory, and history, remain hidden in plain sight. I would want it so, at the undergraduate level: what's most important is the student writing.

Concepts of linguistics also appear to be of interest to some students because they give students a way to play around with making the significant *distinction* between the language in general everyday use and the language that is presented as having a specific literary or aesthetic dimension. Linguistics helps them differentiate and identify stylistic — in other words, aesthetic — effects in language.

What is great about a language focus in a creative writing classroom is that language is something students already have a sophisticated knowledge about, even though that knowledge is largely unconscious (as it is inside us all) — intuitable, yes, but always presupposed by everything they say and hear. Turning to linguistics in the creative writing classroom is also due in my case to some basic questions that confront me at the start of the teaching year: How do I introduce and present formally challenging poetry within an undergraduate creative writing class? How do I present formally innovative poetry to students who have not yet accumulated enough experiences as readers of literary and cultural norms and conventions, and of literary history and aesthetics, to grasp what might otherwise strike them — and with mixed emotions perhaps of insecurity and indifference — as difficult?

From my perspective, to answer these questions about difficulty that teachers experience regarding almost any subject, to answer with a *lecture*, in a creative writing class, pointing out literary and cultural norms and conventions operating in a given poem, and the literary history and aesthetics — "placing the work in context" — now has little appeal to me. (Admittedly, I've subjected my students to monologues of this sort in the past.) Instead of reaching down through literature with a capital *L* for the sources that will help to deliver this kind of lecture, what about reaching across to another discipline entirely? This reaching across could be toward the visual arts, or music, or even toward a scientific discipline; the step I've chosen is toward linguistics.

There is an interdisciplinary study located at the intersection of linguistics and literature, called stylistics, which has been around for more than half a century. Stylistics is, to cite one textbook, a "method of textual interpretation in which primacy of place is assigned to language" (Simpson 2). And what I find compelling about some of its theory and application is how stylistics argues that one can present formally challenging poetry by drawing from the students' own *already-developed* sense of norms — not their weak sense of *literary* norms, but their strong — even rigid — sense of the norms of everyday language use. As when a student exclaims, on first reading Gertrude Stein's *Tender Buttons*: "You can't write 'Roast potatoes for,' because that's just stupid — it's an incomplete sentence." My fantasy rejoinder will be, "Student A, you are remarkable! You have a strong and highly developed — even rigid, as in righteous — sense of the norms of everyday language use! Bravo for recognizing them! Now let me ask you something. What if poets are meant to draw a reader's attention precisely *to* the presence of those norms, even if in order to do so they must contravene them, as Gertrude Stein has so deliciously done herself?"

The idea here is to help students consciously articulate what strikes them as stupefyingly obvious, articulate what it is that students, teachers, and writers, as language-users, already intuit about so-called acceptable language use. The idea of encouraging students to consciously recognize their implicitly agreed-on conventions of acceptable language use turns out to be a key to unlocking — to perceiving — the nature of literary language.

That is, stylistics often works from the premise that literary language is literary because of how it deviates (or detours away) from acceptable language use. Thus a stylistics analysis will contrast a present *literary deviation* to a pre-existing *language norm*. For example, in a literature course, I've asked students to read the opening two stanzas of "Berkeley St Bridge" by John Wieners:

> Petrified the world
> wherein we walk.
>
> Frozen the fields.

I then asked students to rewrite these two sentence-*like* word sequences using the most normative syntax and grammar they could conceive of. Many students came up with something like

The world is petrified where we walk. The fields are frozen.

Then, finally, I ask them to demonstrate the literary effects caused by the poet's words deviating the way they do from these grammatical norms. The work of a creative writing classroom, then, might also lie in such a pedagogical direction, in collectively making manifest these language norms at play in literary texts (norms that underlie hasty judgments upon these literary texts). Even *literary* norms were once perceived as deviations from *language* norms. But because they're no longer perceived as deviations but as standard literary customs, they've become clichés. After all, "Petrified the world / wherein we walk" is arch, haute-poetic — with a capital *P*!

I repeat: A key to unlocking — to perceiving — the nature of literary language is recognizing the implicitly agreed-on conventions of acceptable language use that the literary language deliberately contravenes. And I mean perceiving "the nature of literary language" in the broadest sense. So I'll switch up the register through which to perceive a play of norm and deviation, from the proto-camp lyrical register of Wieners's gay angst to the manufactured consent of the advertisement slogan: "So good it's riDQulous."

Dairy Queen's 2011 slogan is a good example, at the micro level where sound and spelling interact, of how deviation can make norm perceptible, and how norm, likewise, can make deviation perceptible. For how *does* one spell "ridiculous," anyway? How *does* one usually pronounce it? What's ingenious about this particular slogan is that it does more than slow down perception enough to allow one to recall and then relish identity and difference between orthographic deviation and norm. In addition, the corporate slogan demands that viewers *change* the way they utter the word, because the consonant-vowel-consonant-vowel sequence -*dicu*- in the word *ridiculous* is not pronounced the same way as the letter-sequence -*dq*- in *riDQulous*: it's something like /dəkI/ versus /dikju/. (That is, the slogan impels us to pronounce the names of the two letters that constitute the brand name: *d* and *q*.) Substituting the deviation in pronunciation *dq* for the norm -*dicu*- constitutes one of the slogan's literary effects. To pronounce *ridiculous* as "*ridqulous*" is not phonotactically unacceptable. Moreover, the altered pronunciation creates the allure of a "foreign accent" at play, even retroactively leading one to consider rolling the initial *r* (as in, say, Russian), because the word-form itself (in its totality) is affected by pronouncing /dəkI/ as /dikju/.

Dairy Queen advertisers evidently know their concrete poetry! At this point in a classroom discussion I might say something like: Formally innovative poetry always anticipates larger mass-cultural trends. The problem I have with making such statements these days, as truthful as they may be (and I am about to give one further proof of this), is that such authoritative statements alone don't give the students the tools to analyze language and incorporate its play into their own writing. So, in my creative writing classes, I sidestep the literary history lesson about Mallarmé, futurism, advertising, and fashion, and go straight to a comparison of norms and deviations between the DQ slogan and what bpNichol was doing decades ago — for instance, in this complete poem:

em ty

Nichol's poem indicates how the sound of the letter *p* is emptied out, or is absented from the norm of pronunciation that readers intuit and use when uttering the word *empty*. The absence of the *p*-sound in the sound-sequence "*emty*" is cleverly disguised from ordinary perception because readers need to bring lips together to articulate the next sound in the word's sequence — the *t*-sound. Nichol is not demanding that his readers change the way they pronounce *empty*. He's in fact *pointing out* how we pronounce it normally. That's the literary effect: contravening one norm (spelling) while confirming another (pronunciation). Incidentally, if Dairy Queen had asked Nichol to come up with a name for a line of plastic refillable water bottles (for cyclists, say), perhaps Nichol would have called it "MT" — which of course would be TM.

Another variation at this micro-level of sound-and-letter play is the concrete poetry classic by Aram Saroyan

Lighght

which poses the opposite end of the spectrum of Nichol's point, in that Saroyan's poem highlights exactly those letters whose visual presence is overt, and yet do not exist orally.

What the DQ slogan and Nichol's and Saroyan's poems have in common is that each *gently* tests the limits of word-form structure and of word formation rules in English. From a linguistics viewpoint, underlying such verbal inventions as these is a fundamental, yet vexing, and terrifyingly simple question: What is a word? Our intuition-based norms about language tell us that of course we know the answer — at least we could be reactive and say we'd recognize a word when we see one. But in fact a word is difficult to describe, let alone define or even formulate as principle. Most poets *don't* test word-form norms. And for Robert Grenier, John Keats is an exemplary poet in this regard. Notice that, in order to describe what Keats *does* do so well within the universe of the well-made word, Grenier resorts to the vocabulary of linguistics, defining syllable and word as a linguist would:

> think of *Keats* as really 'milking' words of all possible letter/phonemic qualities without really challenging notion of English word/morpheme as basic unit of 'meaning' — hence 'best effects' all-stress monosyllabic —"No, no, go not to Leth(e)" — "Where are the songs of Spring? Ay, where are they?" — because mind in work really does *want* to think phonemically, one sounds so 'dense & rich,' tongued — slows down articulation so teeth, lips, whole vocal apparatus drawn in to pronouncing letters, reading it aloud — counting 'syllables' (convenient grouping of phonemes/smallest unit one normally hears) thus more than old poetic habit, focuses attention toward primary semantic unit ... 'meaning' identical to physical fact of *a* sound ... in series of discrete particles strung together (by Keats, etc.) with gaps.... (19–20)

The last statement in this quotation contains Grenier's linguistic definition of a word: "a series of discrete particles strung together ... with gaps." And, as well, it contains a definition of language's minimal meaningful unit, the morpheme: "'meaning' identical to physical fact of *a* sound." While these abstract definitions derived from linguistics are at odds with the sensuous language Grenier uses for Keats ("'dense & rich,' tongued," "milking" of words), they are entirely appropriate for Clark Coolidge's non-narrative text *Suite V.* Coolidge's *Suite V* is a paradigmatic example of the minimal pairs of sound difference — such as the meaning-making difference between the *s* and *z* in *sip* and *zip* — that constitutes the system of a language. *Suite V* features one word centred and typed at the top and one word centred and typed at the bottom of alternating pages for a total of seventeen pages. Here are three sequential pages, with the two slashes indicating the empty page space.

hats
//
gars

pins
//
wens

webs
//
cups

Each word is one syllable long and ends with the same bound morpheme, the suffix -s. The sequence of pages I've shown here stands out from the rest of *Suite V* in that it presents two words from specialized vocabularies: ichthyologists and some fishers know "gars" as plural for "a fish of the Pike or Esox family," and medical doctors and some patients know "wens" as plural for "sebaceous cystic tumour under the skin, occurring chiefly on the head"* (*Oxford English Dictionary*). These slight irregularities function to heighten readers' awareness of the structural integrity of the text, focusing their attention on the lexical level of language and on the relational movement of phonemic differentiation between words. Each word-pairing demonstrates the structure of language itself in the abstract, a synchronic system of differential phonemes, what the Swiss linguist Ferdinand de Saussure called *langue*.

And each demonstrates what the poet Bruce Andrews calls, in a moment of pique, "chaise *langue*." Andrews has recently invited readers to "bring the internal word investigations." The English language reputedly has a comparatively high number of unused morphemic slots in many of its words (we say "pluralistic" not "pluralitic"), slots that could be filled to form

---

* I would like to thank Cy Strom for help with the words *wens* and *gars*.

productive new words. Andrews's three long poems in his book *You Can't Have Everything ... Where Would You Put It!* search out those morphemic vacancies to create new words conforming to morphological rules. One is the word *lacerability* in the line

lacerability per lahlahlah syllables in touch

that converts the verb *lacerate* by way of two suffixes — *-able* and *-ability* — into this overstuffed noun. In other lines, Andrews tests the limits of word-form by drawing attention to discrepancies that a letter or two can make in identifying whether a sound- and letter-sequence is a syllable, a morpheme, or just a letter in the phonetic alphabet, and how exactly it is to be pronounced:

oring^hon
....
aterial^m
....
dling^mid

In contrast, Dorothy Trujillo Lusk, in "Sclebiscite," tries to expunge all morphological proprieties from the insides of words.

p a n a x
Retreaxelle

w o m
p o u t

neutricidic   frustrum

The word with the capital first letter, "Retreaxelle," suggests a product-name composed of the oxymoronic sound-blend of "retreat" and "excel." Word-form play also occurs within an existing product-name, "panax," which is a type of ginseng: the extra spacings on either side of each interior letter — the "gaps," to use Robert Grenier's term — test our sense of the identifying boundaries of a written word. The astonishing "neutricidic" leans on both sound play and faux morphemes. One route through its construction is as follows:

> "neutricidic" *nutrition* → *nutricide* (as in *suicide, genocide, insecticide,* etc.) → *nutricidic* (with sound of word *acidic* added) → *neutricidic,* which therefore cumulatively suggests the quality of a subatomic suicide (perhaps a nuclear plant meltdown? or self-destructive personality?)

I mentioned that *most* poets don't alter word-form norms — for me, though, this means that in the classroom I can simultaneously invoke general linguistics principles of the norms of the English language and at the same time describe rare or singular poems. For example, I can specifically describe poems that test the norms of word-form boundaries. Deviation is only perceptible against a fully conscious recognition of language norms constituting everyday language use.

There is a role for the formally innovative text and its student reader/writer in the creative writing classroom: to perceive how perception itself is constituted by deviation from a language norm. And there is a lesson about language norms. After all, such norms may *appear* to be based on intuition. But they are in fact historically informed, socially contingent constructions that change over cultural time as language changes due to the ways it is spoken by different groups of people. A lesson, or hope, is that coming to perceive how perception itself is constituted by deviation will open students to language beyond the classroom — by using what linguist Hermese E. Roberts calls their "third ear." "Could it be," she wonders, "that we have used our two ears to listen to the communication-network variety of English for so long, we unconsciously have shut ourselves off from hearing, understanding, appreciating, and enjoying the colorful language varieties minted and used by specific groups of people?" Thus the distinctive use of the word "stone" in my title, which comes from a song by the seventies soul group the Stylistics. In *The Third Ear: A Black Glossary*, Roberts defines "stone" as "adj., adv. used to intensify the quality of another word; i.e. a *stone* fox is a very beautiful girl; I *stone* took care of that means I really took care of that." A lesson, then, in which language refuses standards — "the norm" itself changes: in new slang words, in new grammatical phrases, in poetry.

Acknowledgements

A modified excerpt from this essay appears under the title "Crashing the Craft Zone" in *Toward. Some. Air.: Remarks on Poetics*, edited by Fred Wah and Amy De'Ath (Banff, AB: Banff Centre Press, 2015), 224–28.

WORKS CITED

Andrews, Bruce. *You Can't Have Everything … Where Would You Put It!* London: Veer, 2011. Print.

Coolidge, Clark. *Suite V.* New York: Adventures in Poetry, 1973. *Eclipse Online Archive.* Ed. Craig Dworkin. Web. 31 July 2012.

Grenier, Robert. "Hedge-Crickets Sing." *The L=A=N=G=U=A=G=E Book.* Eds. Bruce Andrews and Charles Bernstein. Carbondale: Southern Illinois UP, 1984. Print.

Nichol, bp. *The Alphabet Game: A bpNichol Reader.* Eds. Lori Emerson and Darren Wershler-Henry. Toronto: Coach House, 2007. Print.

Lusk, Dorothy Trujillo. "Sclebiscite." *W6.* Kootenay School of Writing. Web. 10 Aug. 2011.

Roberts, Hermese E. *The Third Ear: A Black Glossary.* Chicago: English Institute of America, 1971. Print.

Saroyan, Aram. *Complete Minimal Poems.* Brooklyn: Ugly Duckling, 2007. Print.

Simpson, Paul. *Stylistics.* New York: Routledge, 2010. Print.

"So Good, It's RiDQulous!" Dairy Queen TV Commercial. *YouTube.* Web. 27 July 2012.

Stein, Gertrude. *Tender Buttons.* 1914. Toronto: BookThug, 2008. Print.

The Stylistics. "I'm Stone in Love with You." By T. Bell, Linda Creed, and Anthony Bell. *Round 2.* Avco Records, 1972. LP.

Wieners, John. *Selected Poems.* New York: Grossman, 1972. Print.

Textual Culture: A Postmodern Approach to Creative Writing Pedagogy

Jennifer Duncan

A textual culture approach to creative writing pedagogy is an idea, based on the visual culture approach to art education, for how to reinvigorate not only the study of creative writing but also the field of English. It aims at giving post-secondary education the tools to better address challenges brought by the conditions of postmodernity while benefiting from postmodern values on heterogeneity, plurality, and inclusivity to give both students and faculty more critically rigorous authority and playfully creative engagement with textual practices.

The story of this idea begins not in the academy but in the Yukon, where, while writing my second book, I collaborated with artist David Curtis in developing a visual art foundation year program in Dawson City, now known as the Yukon School of Visual Arts.* As I had studied Aboriginal Pedagogy at OISE/University of Toronto and had already designed a community-based writing program for Dawson, I knew that the art school would need to be inclusive of the local culture and peoples, build on local skills and traditional knowledge, and be developed in consultation with the local First Nations government and the larger community. It was immediately apparent that a traditional discipline-based model that hierarchizes fine art over design and craft and that focuses on the main subjects of drawing, painting, sculpture,

---

* The school was previously called the Klondike Institute of Art and Culture School of Visual Art (KIAC/SOVA).

art history, and design principles would be completely inappropriate. Also obvious was the fact that, without any entrenched institution in place, we had a free hand — a rare and exhilarating opportunity to create something entirely new, something as wild and rigorous and intense as the Yukon itself.

I was aware of the recent paradigmatic shift in art theory from looking at art as the products of the art world to seeing art as the practices and products of a visual culture. I began to delve more deeply into what this could mean for art education. Paul Duncum's "Visual Culture: Developments, Definitions and Directions for Art Education" provides a definition of visual culture useful for educators, in which visual artifacts "are viewed in their contextual richness, as part of an ongoing social discourse that involves their influence in social life" (107), but concludes that this will only widen the field of study without changing the practices of the art teacher. Without focusing on the term "visual culture," Arthur D. Efland, Kerry Freedman, and Patricia Stuhr's *Postmodern Art Education: An Approach to Curriculum* compares modernist to postmodernist values, theoretical premises, educational modes, and art practices, and develops a vision for the use of postmodern concepts in instruction. In this vision, pedagogy would resist meta-narratives by including mini-narratives of those excluded from the canon, explicate relations of power in the constitution of art knowledge, employ deconstruction to avoid privileging singular viewpoints, and explore artworks as "multiply coded within several symbol systems" (72). Synthesizing these and further works of theorists such as Paul Duncum, Chris Jenks, Kerry Freedman, and Theresa Marché,* I came up with the following picture, included in the program design I wrote with artist David Curtis in 2006:

> The visual culture approach sees art as a form of meaningful cultural production that is a carrier of conventions reflecting the society in which it was created. Visual culture includes all aspects of fine art, craft, and design within a diversity of cultures. An integrated approach makes connections and provides continuity between art making, art history, art theory, and art criticism; between

---

* In fact, I spent over a year researching a visual studies approach to art education, far too extensive a study to summarize here. See the Works Cited for further foundational texts in the subject.

a multiplicity of cultures and historical periods; and between a variety of materials, techniques, and modes of expression. An integrated visual culture approach thus creates authentic opportunities for students to connect theory to practice and recognize the connection between art, their lives, and their communities. (1)

The design we came up with breaks down boundaries between the school, the community, and the environment; between fine art, design, and craft; and between art history, theory, and practice. Local artists, elders, and experts are invited in to share knowledge. Studies are organized by thematic units to allow greater integration of all disciplines and subjects. Our themes were chosen to support certain foundational skills, such as drawing a still-life; include First Nations values and practices; and introduce key issues in cultural theory. These themes were Harvest, Objects, Animals, the Body, Clothing, Masks, Carnival, Ritual, Memory, Shelter/Home, and Landscape/Mapping/Boundaries. Every lesson begins with the students' own knowledge, generates critical questions, and incorporates history, aesthetics, and theory with practice so that students are always questioning the cultural contexts of art and the production of meaning as they hone their skills and produce their own art.

In our original design,* and in order to support the seasonal cycles of the local and traditional culture, the school year begins with a Harvest unit in which students go into the bush and the local dump to gather materials for making their own art supplies and assemblages. The middle of the year is marked by the students putting on a winter carnival for the town, while investigating Bahktin's theory of the carnivalesque and carnival practices in a variety of different cultures. The year ends with students exploring Landscape/Mapping/Boundaries and collaborating on group earthworks or community-intervention projects, directly involving the community and environment. The plurality and indeterminacy of this design de-centres dominant Western ideologies and allows for greater inclusion of marginalized values, peoples, histories, pedagogies, and art practices, as well as creating greater critical rigour and creative free play. Now that the school has been

---

* The curriculum has since been adapted and revised by the instructors teaching at the school.

running a few years, we can see the results of this approach. Administrators have reported that every single one of the first graduating students was accepted into a top Canadian program down south. Their first-year port-folios include work of fourth-year sophistication, and the administrators of established art schools had only one concern about accepting these students, which is that they will be bored in the traditional programs.

It made me wonder if a similar approach could be developed to benefit creative writing and English students. What if we changed our concept of our subject from English to textual culture, and from "creative writing" to "creative textual practices"? On what theoretical basis might this be done? How would we define a textual culture approach? How would this be dif-ferent from the mixed workshop already in use? How might this enliven and extend curriculum and program designs both inside and outside the academy? And how can we ensure that the teaching of *literary* practices and products, already endangered by the overwhelming proliferation of *popular* culture, is supported rather than superseded by a textual culture approach? How can we ensure that creative writing is not subsumed as only one of a variety of ways to enter the great literary and greater textual conversation that overwhelms us in the Information Age?

The work of Roman Jakobson, Paul Armstrong, Robert Scholes, and Gerald Graff can be used to propose a theory of heterogeneous textual prac-tice and develop a practical pedagogical model of textual culture studies. In "The Future of Theory in the Teaching of Literature" and *Professing Literature*, Gerald Graff argues that the English department *is* a theory, and an incoherent theory due to the field-coverage principle (which business calls silo engineer-ing) isolating individual courses to submerge conflicts between them. With reference to James Kincaid, Graff proposes that we need a new model that centres not on the texts themselves but on how we situate ourselves in rela-tion to these texts — in other words, a model that centres on textual cul-ture. Scholes's argument in *Textual Power* that English studies are organized by the three binary oppositions between literature/non-literature, production/consumption, and real world/academy, in which consumption is privileged over production (and creative writing is at the bottom of the hierarchy as the production of pseudo-literature), is a call to deconstruct these boundaries. Furthermore, Armstrong's definition of literature as "an inherently multifar-ious entity which conflicting communities define in sometimes irreconcilable ways because of their different presuppositions, interests and purposes" (124) and his identification of the central paradox of conflict and validity in literary studies "that critics can have legitimate disagreements about what a text means but they are also able to say with justification that some readings are wrong, not simply different" (2) can be the premise for a postmodern definition of literature as textual culture and a practice of multiplicity in ways of engaging with texts. Thus, an English department that was a heterogeneous, rather than incoherent, theory would focus on how we situate ourselves in relation to literature, would see literature as subject to conflicting definitions, would make conflicts explicit and subject these to tests of validity but see them ultimately as an irreconcilable plurality of beliefs, and would then be engaging in a textual culture approach.

The textual culture approach begins, then, with the premise that reading and writing text are practices that are productive of particular and diverse ways of experiencing, thinking about and constructing our lives, communities, and cultures, including both visual (literate) and oral (linguistic) cultures. Textual culture includes literature, composition, creative writing, and professional writing, as well as forms of art, performance, and technology that involve text. A textual culture approach is integrative and makes explicit the connections between cultural knowledge, critical analysis, and creative practices to produce authentic and meaningful learning experiences that allow students to situate themselves in relation to texts, contextualize texts in relation to their worlds, and critically and creatively enter the ongoing, generative textual conversation and consciousness.

In practice, this approach would begin with establishing a learning community to collaboratively design an integrated curriculum, instead of following the "field coverage principle" in which instructors operate as silos, independently covering a certain field such as Romantic poetry or post-structuralist feminist theory. Rather than mounting individual courses, the following converging streams would be offered: Textual Practices/Creative Processes, Cultural/Historical Understanding, Critical Inquiry, Aesthetic Issues, and Discourse Analysis, and these could move through a series of theme-based units.

Let's say the theme is the Journey. In Textual Practices/Creative Processes class, students would be working on a short story involving a trip. In the Cultural/Historical Understanding class, students might be reading the Oedipal myth, *The Pilgrim's Progress*, Victorian women's travel diaries, *Huckleberry Finn, On the Road*, and Anne Carson's "Kinds of Water." In Critical Inquiry class, students could be exposed to Baudelaire's and Wittgenstein's concepts of the *flaneur* and Janet Wolff's figure of the *flaneuse*, Joseph Campbell's *The Hero with a Thousand Faces* the post-colonialist theories of Edward Said and Gayatri Chakravorty Spivak, and more, to generate their own questions about translation, diaspora, urbanization, the frontier, and so on. In Aesthetic Issues, students would be exploring narrative, the characteristics and questions involved in different kinds of short story narrative structures. In Discourse Analysis, students would be comparing contemporary travel blogs and tourist guidebooks with literary travel memoirs, poems describing places, road trip films, and songs about journeys. The classes would all be in conversation with one another so that *Huckleberry Finn* can be questioned in post-colonial terms as well as explored structurally as a linear narrative. This entire methodology, then, is a real-world experience of how (many) writers write: by exploring the formal, theoretical, and literary dimensions of their subjects to inform their own creative process.

Now, many of the mixed workshops in creative writing basically achieve this same kind of integration, but this leaves much less time for students to write and critique. As well, we can no longer count on creative writing students having a strong background in the literature of the past or current cultural theories, or being able to make connections between the disparate English classes they take. A textual culture approach would directly address these problems and would produce a more enriched and generative structure and pedagogy to transform both creative writing and English studies into a postmodern form of education that allows for a more comprehensively critical and creative engagement, not just with textual culture but with the ways in which reading and writing shape consciousness.

There are still a few problems I'm working on with the idea of a textual culture approach to creative writing and English studies. The first problem centres on the difference between art in relation to visual culture versus literature in relation to textual culture. In the art world, it is no longer necessary to know how to draw to be an artist, as conceptual, performance, and installation art have freed art from paper and canvas. As well, there is much greater hybridity in the art world between art, design, and craft. This is not the situation in the world of letters. Writers still need to know grammar, and the literary world, despite the work of writers such as Rachel Zolf, Christian Bök, and Darren Wershler, is not deeply involved in a hybridity of forms that plays with academic, technological, and professional writing as a matter of course. As well, art education in the academy has always had practice (the creation of art) at the centre of study, whereas English studies have always had interpretation at the centre, with practice (creative writing, not composition) either absent or marginalized. These differences mean that a textual culture approach might not yet be appropriate unless it can be applied in a way that ensures a strong foundation in basic skills and a structure that upholds the importance of creative writing (as well as reading, composition, and professional writing skills), while stressing and problematizing the differences between literature (as art) and other textual practices and products that may not have art as an aim.

The second problem centres on the similarity between a visual culture and a textual culture approach: while rigorous, the plurality and indeterminacy of these approaches destabilizes specialization. Anyone who has spent the years of practice with technique that it takes to become accomplished at drawing a detailed sketch or writing a multi-layered poem knows that to become truly talented within a given art form means specializing to a certain extent. This is why I saw the visual culture approach as eminently suitable for foundation year or undergraduate studies, with the understanding that specialization would be the next step, when students would take courses specifically dedicated to particular practices.

The third problem is institutional. A textual culture approach is a radically different pedagogy and structure that requires instructors to work collaboratively and flexibly. While many Canadian art school administrators may deeply want to switch to a visual culture approach, it seems impossible, as this would dismantle all the current structures for job descriptions, enrolment systems, course selections, evaluation structures; the entire organism would need to change shape. In English departments, this would mean altering teaching positions and compensation to incorporate more team teaching and changing from a course selection structure to a fixed program of study to build a learning community.

However, I believe that these are ultimately resolvable problems and that the site for a shift to a textual culture approach to English studies as a whole would be in existing creative writing programs and writing centres.

And I think the success of the Yukon School of Visual Arts students shows the benefits of such an approach: students who are critically aware and questioning, conversant with both traditions and experiments, experienced in a wide variety of skills, personally engaged with their studies, and committed to becoming meaningful creative forces. The art world exploded when the boundaries between art, craft, and design, and between theory and practice were challenged by feminists, post-structuralists, and post-colonialists, creating an entirely new visual culture. Imagine what playing with the boundaries between creative, academic, and professional writing, between theory and practice, and between institution and community could do for English studies and the literary world: no less than inventing new literatures and a newly relevant and reinvigorated academy.

WORKS CITED

Armstrong, Paul B. *Conflicting Readings*. Chapel Hill: U of North Carolina P, 1990. Print.

Curtis, David, Jennifer Duncan, and KIAC Curriculum Development Advisory Group. "Foundation Year Visual Arts Program: Program Design." Dawson City, YT: Klondike Institute of Art and Culture, with Yukon College and the Tr'ondëk Hwëch'in Government, 2006. Print.

Duncum, Paul. "Visual Culture: Developments, Definitions, and Directions for Art Education." *Studies in Art Education* 42.2 (2001): 101–12. Print.

Efland, Arthur, Kerry Freedman, and Patricia Stuhr. *Postmodern Art Education: An Approach to Curriculum*. Reston, VA: National Art Education Association, 1996. Print.

Fehr, Dennis E., Kris Fehr, and Karen Keifer-Boyd, eds. *Real-World Readings in Art Education: Things Your Professors Never Told You*. New York: Falmer, 2000. Print.

Freedman, Kerry. "Social Perspectives on Art Education in the U.S.: Teaching Visual Culture in a Democracy." *Studies in Art Education* 41.4 (2000): 314–29. Print.

Graff, Gerald. "The Future of Theory in the Teaching of Literature." *The Future of Literary Theory*. Ed. Ralph Cohen. Chicago: U of Chicago P, 1989. Print.

———. *Professing Literature*. Chicago: U of Chicago P, 1987. Print.

Jakobson, Roman. "Linguistics and Poetics." *Modern Criticism and Theory*. Ed. David Lodge. New York: Longman, 1988. Print.

Jenks, Chris, ed. *Visual Culture*. New York: Routledge, 1995. Print.

Marché, Theresa. "Toward a Community Model of Art Education History." *Studies in Art Education* 42.1 (2000): 51–66.

Scholes, Robert. *Textual Power*. New Haven: Yale UP, 1985. Print.

Stankiewicz, Mary Ann. "Discipline and the Future of Art Education." *Studies in Art Education* 41.4 (2000): 301–13.

Sullivan, Graeme. "Art-Based Art Education: Learning That Is Meaningful, Authentic, Critical and Pluralist." *Studies in Art Education* 35.1 (1993): 5–21.

The Joys of Adaptation: Pedagogy and Practice

Priscila Uppal

Professors of creative writing commonly claim that our raison d'être is not only to train writers, but, and perhaps more importantly, to create readers. With the aims of teaching our students to become more sophisticated, more critical, more contextually (historical, aesthetic, cultural) informed readers, many of us supplement creative writing assignments in our courses with specific required and recommended readings, including exemplary novels, poems, short stories, essays, and theoretical works. We also frequently guide workshop discussion toward more sophisticated readings of each other's creative products, which we hope will then, in turn, facilitate more astute reading in general. When we teach a specific genre or subgenre of literature, we may deliver mini-lectures on the conventions of each form and cite examples from published works by classic writers and contemporaries. All of these pedagogical strategies effectively contribute to the training of active, engaged, and knowledgeable readers, as well as to the training of active, engaged, and knowledgeable writers.

One of the limitations of teaching literature — whether in a strict literary history framework or in a creative writing workshop context — is that we teach our subject from our own historical and cultural moment, our own academic and creative background. None of us can be expected to be experts in all genres and of all literary traditions, especially outside our own linguistic, cultural, and national frameworks. And yet, while many of us teach in an increasingly multicultural, multi-ethnic, multi-religious, global environment, many of our students, perhaps eager to learn about different literary movements and their influences on English-language writing in the West, are frequently unfamiliar, and sometimes aggressively alienated, from this body of literature. The myths and classical stories and poetic tropes many professors take for granted are the same ones that mystify, baffle, bore, or enrage some of their students.

Rather than ignoring these student reactions — many of which are never voiced in the classroom but are revealed, explicitly or implicitly, as students force themselves to conform to the literary examples they have been taught — in my experience as a writer and as a teacher, they can become the basis for innovative creative works. One of the most successful — as well as the most critically playful — strategies for expressing and shaping this material is to engage in creative works that are centred on some form of adaptation.

For the purposes of this essay, and to encourage the adaptation process to be thought of as a multi-faceted, multi-generic, even multifarious, activity, I am using "adaptation" as an umbrella term that includes revisionism, parody, pastiche, approximation, translation, and any other uses of source texts to produce unique creative works. Therefore, adaptation can be understood as shaping the same source material from one genre into another — such as the novel *Don Quixote* into the musical *Man of La Mancha* — or using the source text as a launch pad for exploring certain themes in a new context — such as James Joyce's use of Homer's epic poem *The Odyssey* as the underlying myth behind his sprawling novel *Ulysses*, or Christa Wolf's use of the myth of Medea to examine the tensions experienced in post-reunification Germany in her novel of the same name. Adaptability is one of the most sophisticated and most useful forms of creativity because it involves the brain working through issues of genre, content, context, structure, transformation, and transmission all at once.

Most literary writers are attracted to stories from the past (mythologies, religious texts, fairy tales, classical works, foundational narratives). At times we are attracted to particular stories because they validate a certain aspect of one's identity or understanding about the world, at other times because the stories presented are foreign to our own experience and might express or advocate moralities that attract or baffle or offend.

For me, Charles Dickens's *Great Expectations* (required reading in my Grade 7 class), while written and set in the nineteenth century in a country I had yet to visit, spoke undeniably to an aspect of my own childhood experience. It was only fairly recently, when CBC asked me to write a script touching upon an unforgettable character from literature, that I was able to articulate the connection I felt to that novel — enough of a connection that I read it once every year until I graduated high school. I chose to honour the character of Miss Havisham, the jilted bride for whom all clocks stopped the moment her bridegroom disappeared, leaving her to live out the rest of her long life in a yellowing wedding gown among decayed pastries and cake. How did this story of a bitter, jilted lover have anything to do with me, a child of immigrants from India and Brazil, living in 1980s Ottawa? But it did. When I was two years old, my father, who worked for the Canadian International Development Agency (CIDA), was involved in a freak accident while on assignment in Antigua: a sailboat tipped and he swallowed contaminated water that attacked his immune system in the form of transverse myelitis, rendering him a permanent quadriplegic. Life in our home was never the same. Although we did not literally stop the clocks, time would always refer to pre- or post-accident. In addition, my mother, whose emotional suffering at facing the future with a quadriplegic had effects as devastating as my father's physical suffering, abandoned her husband and two children and fled without a trace. Miss Havisham's emotional trauma — and the tragic and disturbing home environment she subsequently created for herself — eerily parallelled truths from my own home life. Instead of writing an essay on the book, I asked my Grade 7 English teacher permission to write a creative work in response. I wrote a one-woman play, a monologue of Miss Havisham's inner life exploring the psychological effects of abandonment. I learned I could give Miss Havisham another voice, my voice, with which to express my own experiences of trauma. This is my first memory of the joys of adaptation.

For another example, I have always been fascinated by the Old Testament story of Abraham and Isaac, whereby God asks Abraham to prove his unshakable loyalty by offering up his only son as a sacrifice. Numerous painters have found inspiration in depicting the crucial moment when God, satisfied that Abraham has passed the test, sends an angel to halt Abraham's knife-wielding hand from slaughtering his own child. It's a story full of horror and suspense, and I was utterly mesmerized by it in my children's Bible, reading and rereading the story with awe, mostly because I was terrified of the implied moral. Over time, as I reread the story and marvelled at the paintings, I found myself wondering about what happened after the halting — the event's epilogue. Even though Isaac's life was spared, I imagined a long, long father-son walk down the mountain. How could Isaac ever feel safe in his home again? Obviously, I approached the myth from a contemporary and literal standpoint, but that became my creative impulse, to contemporize the myth and to explore whether or not the morality could transfer to our own historical and cultural moment. I wrote this poem when news coverage in Toronto regarding child abuse and child murderers was quite prominent. The last stanza turns to these pressing social and political concerns. The poem won a competition and was published in my third book, *Pretending to Die*.

If Abraham

If Abraham hadn't responded to God's command
how much better the relationship with his son
might have been. No nights of discomfort
in the dark, calling out in his sleep
for good Samaritans, no more fights
at breakfast about the day
it almost happened, no more hiding
the largest and sharpest kitchen knives.

If Abraham hadn't heard another word
and done the deed, how many days before some troupe
of angered parents hunted him down, stood
on his lawn with signs and government officials
broke every unbarred window
in his home, how many years before
the smell came off his hands,
before he could eat meat again.

> If Abraham was smart as the men in my neighbourhood
> he would have destroyed evidence of his plans,
> taken the boy no further than the basement,
> and kept the fires burning until
> not a soul could have recognized that body. (24)

Writers and readers are haunted by stories. In both my creative writing workshops and my more conventional academic arts courses, I ask my students: What myths, fairy tales, novels, poems, dramas, movies, haunt you? Can you try to think of why (something personal or relevant to today or a pressing fear or obsession …)? This is usually one of the most animated, and emotionally and intellectually invested conversations we have — and it frequently continues throughout the course. As students think more deeply about these questions, they engage in critical re adings of their own and other's works and identify the types of plots, characters, themes, images, and uses of language that fascinate or obsess or impact them most. They begin to identify an inherited imaginative space that produces emotional and intellectual reactions, and in doing so, they also begin to identify artistic techniques they might wish to explore. It is also an opportunity to discuss important issues of cultural appropriation and under what circumstances adaptation is an act of beneficial creation and response, and when it might be an act of silencing or inappropriate theft or exploitation. (While this essay concentrates on the former, it is important to acknowledge that the latter exists in adaption theory and practice as well.)

Inherited imaginative space assumes shared cultural knowledge. While this is useful for writers to exploit in terms of implied audiences as well as recognizable plots or archetypal characters, it's important to be able to identify the range of responses, particularly in a multicultural context, that writers and readers may experience as they interact with these inherited myths and stories. I have divided these responses into five basic categories and corresponding reactions:

1. Complete identification with Inherited Cultural Knowledge: Homage
2. Absence of Inherited Cultural Knowledge: Alienation

3. Inherited Cultural Knowledge that contradicts other Inherited Cultured Knowledge: Tension
4. Inherited Cultural Knowledge one admires but is outside of: Longing
5. Inherited Cultural Knowledge that is out-of-date or irrelevant: Ambivalence

Each of these categories can result in creative adaptations, as can be evidenced by the multitude of adaptations of Shakespeare plays alone. In fact, in a lecture I delivered called "Canadian Shakespeare" at the University of Bologna in Italy, offering context for my novel *To Whom It May Concern* (a loose adaptation of Shakespeare's *King Lear* set in contemporary Ottawa and featuring a quadriplegic patriarch about to have his family home repossessed by the bank), I argued that if you want to know how various immigrant communities feel about their adopted homelands, examine how their artists adapt texts of inherited cultural knowledge, particularly those taught in schools. Adaptations represent an active dialogue about one's place in the culture, whether or not new imaginative spaces are required to accommodate diverse experience, and whether or not inherited stories require a contemporary update to maintain continued relevance to new audiences.

In my graduate course, 20th Century Revisionist Mythmaking, referring to the very popular Canongate Myth series, which has included international writers such as Margaret Atwood, Milton Hatoum, Philip Pullman, Ali Smith, Su Tong, and Jeannette Winterson, I propose the following: If you could adapt a myth to represent contemporary times, what myth would it be? Why do you think it's a relevant myth for our times? What correspondences can you make between the elements of the original myth and this particular time in history or this geographical region?

Usually students have a hard time choosing just one. And their reasons for choosing particular myths run the gamut of the five categories listed above. Some identify themselves entirely with the myth; some experience deep alienation from the world of the myth and have felt helpless to counter its weight; some are fascinated by how one myth contradicts the moral universe of another; some want to adapt a foreign myth to their own cultural context; and some are attracted to the challenge of how to take a seemingly out-of-date and irrelevant myth and rejuvenate it for contemporary times.

Out of this exercise, many students begin their own creative works, and many others use the exercise to ask important questions of their readings, which results in the development of interesting essay topics.

Adaptation assignments are extremely useful tools. As students even begin to think about adaptation, the issue of fidelity is often hotly debated. I turn this into a discussion on critical reading as well as writing:

1. What elements of the original do you consider to be essential?
2. What elements can be changed or ignored? How do you decide?
3. In what context are your choices predictable, logical, or justified?
4. Will some changes be purposefully antagonistic or controversial (and for what purpose)?
5. What genre will this adaptation take? And how does genre influence the process of the adaptation, especially if you are adapting from one genre into another (such as a poem into a film, or a short story into a play)?

Some students are adamant that certain elements of the original story are untouchable. Others are more open to wild flights of fancy retaining only the loosest connections to the original. I like to point out, as Julie Sanders does in her book *Adaptation and Appropriation*, "adaptation always involves 'relocation' of some sort: cultural or temporal setting, or generic. The re-location is key. To relocate, one must make that connection of movement between one place and another" (19). Many students who have lived inside diverse cultures, religions, nations, or other communities have intimate knowledge of relocation, and of how to navigate between cultural spaces. This knowledge, if tapped into, can produce exciting strategies for creative writing, dealing with everything from content to structure, to genre, and to creative process. In my experience with highly multicultural classrooms — Toronto's York University is considered one of the most multicultural universities in North America, if not the most — adaptation assignments offer many students an opportunity to investigate various cultural and ancestral inheritances, many of which they are consciously or subconsciously hiding from their classmates in order to participate in the dominant cultural inheritances generally upheld in the course.

Adaptation is also a great way to discuss the topic of genre, something that many students frequently take for granted. Why is a particular work of literature a poem and not a short story? Why is this artistic product a film and not a play? What conventions of the original form are transferable to other artistic forms? Which are not? How can you exploit these differences for artistic effects? If we think of genre as a particular creative location, each location has its own structural and contextual characteristics that allow for certain types of interactions. Relocating from one genre to another means creating a different imaginative space that runs by different rules. Adaptation exercises are a great way to learn about the conventions of genre — why these conventions exist, why they are useful for the particular form — and how to exploit those conventions in interesting ways.

Adaptation assignments also give students the permission to explore how and why certain literatures survive. As Linda Hutcheon argues in her book *A Theory of Adaptation,* even though fidelity criticism has dominated the critical field of adaptation studies for decades, "there are many and varied motives behind adaptation and few involve faithfulness" (xiii). In fact, it is the impulse for movement, for change, that generally motivates writers. As Hutcheon continues: "Because adaptation is a form of repetition without replication, change is inevitable, even without any conscious updating or altering of setting. And with change comes corresponding modifications in the political valence and even the meaning of stories" (xvi). The reasons to teach adaptation have little to do with faithfulness, I believe, and more to do with relocation as "metamorphoses": transforming one living thing into another living thing, whose origins may or may not be easily identifiable. Adaptation sheds light on the continuity of art at the same time it emphasizes that art is continually in process. And if art is continually in process, it means that anyone can participate and inherit artistic products regardless of cultural or ancestral affiliations. This act of relocation is one of defamiliarization and collaboration — destabilizing the source text in order to search for ways in which competing values can be combined for various effects.

I also encourage students to think of their own lives and the lives around them as potential echoes of known myths, fairy tales, and other stories. One assignment that I've used successfully in the past, particularly in fiction and creative non-fiction writing workshops, is this one (originally published in *Writer's Gym: Exercises and Training Tips for Writers*): Interview a family member, eliciting as many stories as possible for as long as possible. Welcome stories that do not involve you directly, as well as those that do. Then take one of these stories and try to figure out what myth, fairy tale, or fable it most closely resembles. Think about plot, themes, archetypal characters, morals, and symbols; find correspondences between the family story and your chosen myth, fairy tale, or fable. Then write your family story within the conventions of your chosen myth, fairy tale, or fable. Keep in mind that most myths are written in the third-person omniscient point of view. This will help you look at the story in a more objective fashion, and will also help you concentrate on plot and action, rather than reflection. Because you are basing your family story on an earlier, likely better-known story, you can have a lot of fun playing with the similarities and differences between the two. (What if Eve had offered Adam a slice of pizza instead of an apple? What if Cinderella played basketball and her prince went out searching for her with one lonely size 10 sneaker?) (54–55).

This assignment has run the gamut from immigrant narratives to war stories to stories of specific family births to failed inventions to delicious secrets. As the family tale takes on a large cultural narrative, students start to see how their own lives naturally mirror many of these long-standing structures and how the microcosm of the family can frequently represent the macrocosm of a much larger community across time and space.

Other fruitful assignments include:

1. Do something ordinary with a mythical figure or historical person.
2. If I could trade bodies (pick a character from a book and imagine yourself in his/her or its body).
3. If they could trade bodies (pick a character and change his/her gender, ethnicity, age, sexuality, or other characteristic and see what happens to the story).

4. Take one of Aesop's fables or similar "moral" tales and revise the story to result in a new moral.
5. Give a mythical or religious character a contemporary occupation.

I'm also fond of this assignment, from Kevin Griffith's "Hamlet Meets Frankenstein: Exploring the Possible Worlds of Classic Literature": "[Ask] students to take two seemingly unrelated works of literature and then write a poem speculating on what would happen if those characters met" (111).

Short translation assignments can also be very enlightening and rewarding for writers and readers alike. Although the vast majority of students at first find the translation assignment daunting, intimidating, and sometimes even a boring waste of time (they'd much rather write their own material, they say), those same students are almost all converts in the end, as they begin to appreciate not just translators in general, but also the very difficult choices they are making, much of the time without realizing it, when they are writing in English. They also frequently work with family members and friends and learn about how adapting from one language to another usually opens up more worlds creatively and imaginatively — and even personally — than they knew existed. Many of my students say they have never worked on anything creative with their parents or grandparents before, and they learned a lot about their cultural and ancestral heritage in the process, as well as learning about writers from other languages they will continue to read and explore.

Adaptation exercises remind us that, as Sorouja Moll does in "On Adaptation & girlswork": "Adaptation is disobedient ... Adaptation can both destroy again and heal again ... Adaptation is blasphemous ... Adaptation asks the painful questions" (93). These assignments also remind us what it means to be a reader. As Dennis Cutchins writes in "Why Adaptations Matter to Your Literature Students": "Studying literature via adaptations offers our students a better, more effective way to study literature. In fact, I would argue that studying literature through adaptations can teach students what we mean when we say 'literature' ... [as] students must hold at least two texts in their minds at once" (87–88). He goes on to conclude: "This ability to comprehend the contextual nature of meaning is, I believe, at least part of what we mean when we suggest that a particular student is more 'literate' than another" (93). I would add that it is also part of what we mean when we say a particular writer is more literate than another, and that the ability to hold many texts simultaneously in the mind can stimulate limitless creativity. Ultimately, I would like to propose that adaptation assignments provoke action, fight against passivity, reinvigorate the essential stories of a culture, and re-stimulate creative life if it has become too complacent. Adapting or revising someone else's works can lead to a new, active, and fluid understanding of self, history, culture, and art, which to my mind is the reason the liberal humanities exist in the first place.

WORKS CITED

Clark, Eliza, ed. *Writer's Gym: Exercises and Training Tips for Writers*. Toronto: Penguin Canada, 2007. Print.

Cutchins, Dennis. "Why Adaptations Matter to Your Literature Students." *The Pedagogy of Adaptation*. Eds. Dennis Cutchins, Laurence Raw, and James M. Welch. Lanham, MD: Scarecrow, 2010. Print.

Griffith, Kevin. "Hamlet Meets Frankenstein: Exploring the Possible Worlds of Classic Literature." *Classics in the Classroom: Using Great Literature to Teach Writing*. Eds. Christopher Edgar and Ron Padgett. New York: Teachers and Writers Collaborative, 1999. Print.

Hutcheon, Linda. *A Theory of Adaptation*. New York: Routledge, 2006. Print.

Moll, Sorouja. "On Adaptation & girlswork." *Shakespeare Made in Canada: Contemporary Canadian Adaptations in Theatre, Pop Media, and Visual Arts*. Eds. Daniel Fischlin and Judith Nasby. Guelph: Macdonald Stewart Art Centre, 2007. Print.

Sanders, Julie. *Adaptation and Appropriation*. London and New York: Routledge, 2006. Print.

Uppal, Priscila. *Pretending to Die*. Toronto: Exile, 2001. Print.

C. By Classroom

From Memorization to Improvisation: The Challenges of Teaching Creative Writing to Students in a Culture of Rote Teaching

Gülayşe Koçak

Though the prospect sounded very attractive, when I was invited to teach creative writing at Sabanci University, Istanbul, in 2003, I was very hesitant about accepting, as creative writing wasn't a well-known concept in Turkey. So I ordered various creative writing books from Amazon, found thousands of websites (all in English), added my own experience as a writer and novelist — and designed a syllabus accordingly. Everything was planned out for each week: genre, plot, character development, dialogues, metaphors, and so on ... or so I thought.

So self-confident did I feel that it came as a real shock when on the first day of teaching I realized that these (mostly imported) exercises and prompts weren't likely to work: among the many problematic issues that presented themselves, the most important was that a large number of my students didn't know how to put their creativity into motion!

By way of background information, let me offer that Turkish education is governed by a national system designed to strengthen the "moral values" of society and to produce "like-minded" citizens. Students enter university through a standardized multiple choice exam administered once a year. Most of the classes in the education system, including Turkish language classes, are based on rote teaching — the memorization of the course subjects.

Turkish "writing" lessons involve composition writing (rarely poems or short stories). Teachers have a preconceived notion of the content of the composition and deal mostly with grammar and spelling. Because most teachers themselves were students of rote teaching, the prompts in composition-writing classes are generally cliché. Therefore, writing in general is cliché, as students know exactly what ideas they are expected to present.

I believe this is a common problem for most students who have grown up in countries where courses are memorized and where authority-hierarchy-obedience play an important role in the culture. In this essay I will try to describe how to conduct creative writing workshops, based on my teaching experience in Turkey, with students coming from societies with rote teaching. I have come to strongly believe that in order for creative writing lessons to be effective for these students (both adults and young students), three teaching methods should be combined: (1) The "standard" creative writing workshop as it is conducted in Western countries — focused on genre, plot, character development, dialogue, use of language, writing skills, grammar, and so forth; (2) parallel to the workshop, creative *and* critical thinking methods should also be taught; (3) students should actively be *taught and encouraged* to *internalize* "freedom of expression" — meaning, taught the *courage* to say and write what they think. Only if these three methods can be intertwined and made homogeneous can any one of them have meaning.

ROTE TEACHING, OR MEMORIZATION-BASED EDUCATION

It might be worthwhile to see how rote teaching works, how it limits the mind's potential for using language as a tool for self-expression — and how it restrains creativity. Memorization is black and white: if I recite a poem by heart, there is nothing blurry; I either recite it correctly or I make a mistake — I am either right or wrong.

We memorize through repetition. If I am repeating a text again and again, gradually I lose the meaning of the words. It's like reciting a morning prayer: If students were asked to explain in their own words what they just recited, I wonder how many of them would be able to convey the message in the so-well-memorized set of sentences? I recall from my childhood how, during the memorization of a history or geography book, a grammatical or spelling mistake in the book could be memorized exactly as it appeared.

Students do not just memorize information in school books, but also the words and sentences, that is to say, the language *patterns* used to convey that information, the *mode of expression* in those sentences. As they never have to show any effort to communicate information using alternative words or sentences, their minds can become lazy in terms of language-use skills. If there is a certain sequence of words in a memorized sentence, when students are asked to use one of those words to create a sentence giving a new meaning to the word, very often some get clogged up. Therefore, perhaps during lessons or exams, students could be asked to respond to the questions *without* using the words or sentences in the book. In fact, maybe *all* courses' exams could be done in this way. If students were asked to try to explain even a sentence such as "water boils at 100 degrees" with different words, if they were to get into the *habit* of explaining with their *own* words and sentences, then, even if their ideas may not be very original, their language skills would definitely develop.

Moreover, in memorization-based education, in their exams students duplicate the exact ideas forwarded in the books — this is what is expected of them. They aren't writing their own mind but "the book's mind." This often causes them to think only in clichés, only in the learned patterns of thinking. This, in turn, makes it very difficult to think critically and/or creatively. Ultimately, and in line with all of this, as their language becomes cliché and deficient, students may gradually lose the ability to express their own most vital needs, to express *themselves*. Even their most personal emotional sentences resemble nothing more than memorized, cliché sentences; they cannot come up with anything more creative than "I love you madly" to express their love.

PLAYING GAMES

In English, the verb *to play* means both playing a game as well as playing a musical instrument.[*] Playing (games) is both fun and the simplest way to stimulate creativity, not to mention the most direct and enjoyable method of learning. However, for students coming from societies where courses are memorized, games play very little role in education. Even music lessons aren't much fun, because what is done is not *playing*, but rather the memorization of notes — *solfège*.[**]

---

[*] The same applies to French — (*jouer*) and German — (*spielen*). This is understandable, because playing an instrument is pleasurable, just like playing a game.

[**] In Turkish, there are two seperate verbs for "playing an instrument" and "playing a game." Interestingly, though, the verb *oynamak* means playing a game, as well as performing a (theatrical) play and dancing to a folkloric tune.

So, obviously, how can writing be playful or creative or fun?

I play the piano: I started with a piano teacher in Ankara as a child, and as a young girl was invited as a guest student to the Hochschule für Musik und Theater in Hanover, where I continued my piano lessons for four years. Whenever I wanted to just fool around on the piano, I was told that would be "harmful for my technique," for the way I hold my wrist, hands, and so on — I could get into "bad learning habits." In short, like most people who have learned to play an instrument through sheet music, I wasn't allowed to "play" with music.

Once a person has learned music through memorization (learning through written notes and playing with sheet music), unless he or she is extremely talented, even a virtuoso who can play the most difficult pieces by heart can't improvise. I love jazz, and today would love to be able to sit down and improvise and unlearn everything I have learned — but I can't! I can imagine that a very large percentage of musicians who have gone through a classical music education in the conservatory are in this state.

In creative writing lessons, the difficulty is very similar to teaching a classical player to improvise and play jazz: just like notes and musical sentences, the use of the native tongue is being presented in "casts" or "moulds." This may eliminate the need to produce new and original forms, causing the mind to become lazy, because the student has not been allowed to play with language, with words. The student's linguistic intelligence has not been given the opportunity to develop. Essentially, memorization-based education can harm the "original" use of language, because when we don't have the ability to produce new modes of expression, new forms, our language can become ordinary and dull. In addition, if we always talk in clichés, we become unable to express our ideas in a refined way and, worse, unable to *think* in an elaborate and sophisticated way.

"POINT ZERO"

Whenever I start a new creative writing class, I find it necessary to deal with creative and critical thinking first. I introduce a term, "point zero," by which I mean "unlearning" — being stripped of all the information and values we have learned so far, like a baby discovering the world from scratch. I have my students play certain "enlightening" games and give them examples regarding point zero. One of which is this: Years ago, I read a personal essay by a woman in *Reader's Digest*. Her husband had been born blind. He had learned the Braille alphabet, been sent to special schools, eventually finished university — and met the author. She was physically unattractive — bad figure, bad skin, asymmetrical features. They fell in love and got married. She was always at his side — a totally devoted wife. After many happy years, a medical breakthrough was made, and with surgery, the man could gain his eyesight. (The author described her panic: on the one hand, she naturally wished her husband to see, but on the other, "What happens when he sees me?") When the day came when he could actually see, his wife's face was the first thing he saw, and to him, it was beautiful, because he was at point zero.

I try to get my students to understand what it means to approach everything unbiased, as though it were the very first encounter with the concept. But they often find it very difficult to let go of preconceived notions. Therefore, in the first few weeks I give my students really silly and unexpected prompts that render them speechless, that later make us all laugh when the writing is read aloud. This serves to shake their beliefs about what always happens in a classroom and to give them the message that here in *this* workshop, everything is allowed. Also, I believe humour in a classroom is the most efficient binder and relaxer.

One exercise that I demand of my students on the first day of a creative writing workshop is to have them imagine they love eating (and here, one can insert anything one likes — be it coal, pencils, paper, shoes, candles, matches ...) and to write a text describing the great taste of whatever has been chosen, and the great pleasure they get out of eating it. It is an exercise in "unlearning": describing as delicious something we have grown up believing would taste disgusting.

One year, on my first teaching day, I had to combine university personnel and students in the same workshop. My prompt was: Imagine you love eating cigarette stubs. Describe the taste and the enjoyment you derive from eating stubs in such a persuasive way that, when you read out aloud what you have written, we should wish to have a taste! All the participants looked at me in disbelief; some laughed, some smiled, some said "Yuck!" and all were at first very reluctant to write. "Just five minutes!" I told them (as usual). "Just do your best and try to write this for five minutes. Disregard spelling or grammar mistakes, don't look back at what you have written, write as fast as you can, and *don't think*. Let go. The purpose is to get really silly. Show us how incredibly silly you can get." Five minutes later they were all still writing like mad, so I let them write for ten. The most unbelievable texts came out of some of the students. One described in detail chewing the filter like gum, and the pleasure of the bitter nicotine trickling down her throat. Another one had fried the stubs and described the process as if it were a recipe: "… but the paper should turn just slightly pink, otherwise the fried stubs may become bitter!" Another one ended his text as follows: "Yes, stubs with yoghurt and garlic is my favorite dish, but nobody can cook it like my mother can!" Yet another one had ended: "Nevertheless, if you ask my opinion, stub salad should be eaten *sec …*"

Interestingly, none of the university personnel had imagined eating the cigarette stubs! Most of them had written compositions and philosophized: "When I look at these stubs, I try to guess the lives of who may have smoked them." I was curious: Were the staff members unable to "eat" the stubs because they had become so rigid they were no longer able to imagine or think creatively? Or had they become shy and self-conscious and censored themselves, afraid the students may find them weird if they wrote too realistically? That is to say, Did they lack the courage to write as they would have wanted? This wouldn't be hard to understand. In an education system where there is so much talking and writing around the same clichés, how can a person find the courage to express a really original idea that has come to his or her mind, in a small classroom environment? The students are probably afraid of me as an instructor as well, as there is the constant fear of reprimand and authority. To break this fear, I always write together with them and share what I have written, doing my best to go to extremes in absurdity and goofiness.

For the problem of using the same language patterns, I use brief writing exercises aimed at expanding vocabulary: "Imagine you have a friend who lives in a landlocked village with no TV, who has never left the village, has never ever seen the sea, even in a movie. One stormy night you were walking by the seaside. Giant waves were hitting the rocks. Describe to your friend on the phone *only* the sounds that you hear. Don't forget — this friend is at point zero, so you too must be at point zero in order to communicate." At the beginning, students find the exercise very difficult. Some say "a very big noise," "an enormous sound," and can't seem to get away from these words. But as they force themselves, other ideas and words start to appear. They begin using more specific verbs (roaring, moaning, exploding) and similes ("like the sound you hear when you shake a kilim from a balcony," "like the sound you hear after you shake and shake a soda pop and suddenly open the bottle").

In creative writing workshops aimed at students who have gone through rote teaching, it is important to devise such prompts that students can't resort to cliché words or ideas, even if they want to. But there are always traps: it is well and fine to demand our students be at point zero — but we ourselves may not be there (both when we choose a prompt, as well as when we are grading what has been written). When devising a prompt, we as teachers may have conventional expectations, we may succumb to stereotypes. These limitations may make it difficult for us to assess student writing fairly. For example, a writing prompt in a Turkish high school may well be something like, "Write about what National Sovereignty Day means to you." Sentimental texts centring around the glory of the country are expected, and all students know this. I tell Turkish literature teachers at seminars, "If a student has written about a family picnic he or she attended on National Sovereignty Day — if it's a well-structured text, *how* you grade it will serve as a litmus paper as to your own expectations."

Sometimes, things can be more complicated: I had a student who wrote an essay on how she abhorred dark people with a certain kind of accent, and tried to keep a distance to those kinds of people. She was obviously referring to Kurds. Yet another student had mentioned how she shuddered when a woman in a headscarf accidentally touched her. These were shocking to hear, but our students often — even if unknowingly — test us, and I believe it is very important not to be abruptly judgmental. Problematic issues such as discriminatory texts should definitely be discussed, but not at that moment; perhaps a few weeks later, within another context, approaching the issue in a roundabout way. I later brought up the topic "conscientious objection" and got the class to discuss militarism, the Kurdish issue, what the Kurds want, and other matters, asking questions designed for my students to see from the Kurdish point of view. Another time, I asked my students to think of a person they definitely wouldn't wish to share their dorm with. I then instructed them to write a story about that person visiting a psychiatrist. What is the person confiding? What's troubling her or him, or giving pain? Creative writing can be a great way to coax feelings of empathy without making students defensive.

The biggest challenge I face in a workshop is getting my students to understand that there is no "right" or "wrong," there is no "mistake." Turkish students expect the teacher to direct them so they can please the teacher. Therefore, it is important that the teacher not offer any clue *at all* as to his or her personal preferences or expectations (if he or she has any). In improvisation, there is no "mistake," no "wrong note." Just as there can be "bad jazz," but not "wrong jazz" or "shameful jazz," there can be no "wrong" in creative writing.

Another example: I was giving a lecture on teaching creative writing to a group of Turkish literature teachers. One of them asked, "But what if the students use swear words in their writing?" "Of course they will," I answered. "But then you can ask natural questions like, 'Is there a function for that word?' 'Does it move the story forward?' 'Would that character use that word?'"

By its nature, in order for creative thought to exist, it is necessary to deviate from what everyone knows as "the right track." Students need to be consciously taught, in fact, actively encouraged, to write divergent works, to not fear "mistakes" and think freely.

Writing courage is fragile. Even as professional writers we all have an internal censorship board that is constantly in force. I always have to keep reminding my students, "Whenever we hesitate to write something or feel a reluctance, or wish to go and grab a coffee, or refrain from writing, we should know that the subject matter we are resisting is the very subject or theme where something is boiling, where there is dynamism. That is exactly what we should force ourselves to write about. If we refrain from writing whenever we feel resistance, all we can produce will be shallow texts."

I am grateful to be able to teach creative writing as something more than a skill: in my mind, it is a way of living — and I judge the success of my workshops not by how many authors I've produced, but by how many students I have enabled to think creatively and to love writing.

How to Teach (Online)

Kathryn Kuitenbrouwer

When the novelist Lee Gowan asked whether I might be interested in proposing an online course to the *New York Times* adjunct (and now defunct) education component, the *New York Times Knowledge Network*, I had been thinking for some time how I might replace certain aspects of a mostly volunteer position I held as a colleague of the poet George Murray and the novelist Peter Darbyshire at the influential website and online community Bookninja. I blogged about literary news there for about a year and hadn't much liked the public nature of it. I wasn't naturally funny in the way that George and Peter could be, and my preternatural sarcasm didn't always translate. I wanted to quit but instead became the website's magazine editor, a position I loved because it gave me access to other writers in the form of interview possibilities. I interviewed (among others) the novelist Tom McCarthy and the Australian writer Nam Le, and discovered I liked the form, liked getting into the heads of other writers.

Besides being an accomplished writer, Lee Gowan also happened to be my boss at the School of Continuing Studies at the University of Toronto, where I had taught in-class workshops for a couple of years — everything from the short story to reading courses (which I fancied). His query couldn't have come at a better time. I spent about three seconds formulating a course that would incorporate the things I had liked about Bookninja, namely the social interaction among its readers and the proximity I had to writers through interview. The course I designed was a salon-style creative writing workshop called *Writer's Talk: Writing Through Reading with The New York Times*. The student-writers who registered for the course were paying for the privilege (well, I hoped it would feel like a privilege!) of interacting with one another as serious students of writing, but also of interacting with living, working writers, the very writers whose work they would be grappling with throughout each week. I assumed (mostly) rightly that the *New York Times* brand would act as a calling card and that it would at least gain me introduction to any writer working on the planet. The brilliant thing about an online course, I reckoned, was that it was international in possibility. I could invite any writer living anywhere into the course, just as I hoped the student body would be also be far-flung. The first incarnation of the course featured Roddy Doyle, Nicholas Shakespeare, Deborah Eisenberg, Lydia Millet, Jonathan Lethem, and *New York Times* editor Frank Flaherty. My students came from all over Canada and the United States. I also had students, over the years, living in Africa, Australia, the United Arab Emirates, and Europe.

Each week my students studied a particular aspect of craft with special focus on the work of one of the writers. They would generate a short assigned piece based on each specific aspect: point of view, narrative voice, structure, momentum, the child's voice, writing biography, the researched novel, the fairy tale, plot/subplot, humour, dialogue, empathy, and, well, the basics, plus whatever I happened to be interested in teaching. And each week my students entered into a question-and-answer session with the author. There were rules, of course, that structured what the students might and might not ask visiting writers, but since the focus was on craft, and since we had spent enough time parsing the writer's work, the questions invariably followed the topic of that week. So, for instance, we asked Roddy Doyle about writing the child's perspective (*Paddy Clarke Ha Ha Ha*) and Nicholas Shakespeare about researching his novel *The Dancer Upstairs* (students had been encouraged to rent and watch the film, as well, and questions ranged between the two media).

Writer's Talk ran from the fall of 2009 to the spring of 2012, at first three times a year and finally, billed as a boutique course, twice. There were seven iterations of the project, each one eight weeks in length, with a student-body cap at fifty (the course usually ranged from twenty-five to thirty students). The roster of visiting writers was impressive. Besides the first guests, Dwight Garner,

Motoko Rich, Lynda Barry, Bill Gaston, Kate Bernheimer, Francine Prose, Andrew Pyper, Miriam Toews, Alissa York, Lynn Coady, Douglas Glover, Kim Addonizio, Tom McCarthy, Daniyal Mueenuddin, and Sheila Heti all came and shared generously (outstandingly) their expertise in very particular ways. To a fault, my students asked probing and intelligent questions because they had immersed themselves in the work in the particular way I had asked of them. This allowed them a kind of authority to ask each writer *real* questions, questions that were asked to deepen their own practice. The investment they had made in the writer's work was paying off in an investment not only into their own practice, but also into the larger view of what writing means as a social exchange (how writing is something outside of the self as much as it may be of the self). Here are a couple of examples of these exchanges:

Roddy Doyle

Writer's Talk: When you are writing about a shared time and place — even when it is fictionalized and historical — how much thought do you give to those who might feel this is their story as well, people who might see themselves reflected in it in a highly identifiable way — though not necessarily people who you know personally. Though on that ... I also wonder about this in a case of a book like *Rory and Ita* when you are telling someone else's story, but it is your story too — not just as an author, but as a son. Have you ever felt you had to take this into consideration in your writing? Has it ever limited your ability to tell the story you want to tell?

Roddy Doyle: I don't give much thought to the conse-quences of what I'm writing, until I've finished the first draft. In the case of *Paddy Clarke Ha Ha Ha*, I was using the geography — and the house — of my childhood, which, in the case of the house, I shared with my siblings and parents (who still live there), and the school, streets, general locality of many people. If I'd let it become the over-riding consider-ation I'd never have written the book. So, I wrote it — then worried. Then I began to disguise it — changed names, ages. One of my sisters, when she read the book, said she found it both very familiar and unfamiliar. She read it a second time — and accepted it as a novel; the story had nothing to do with her, the parents in the book weren't hers, etc. As for worrying about people I don't personally know — I never do. I had a very early lesson: after my novel *The Commitments* was published, so many people claimed it was based on them — musicians who were still children when I was writing the book, bands I'd never seen play, etc. As recently as last week, at a Bob Dylan gig, a woman told me that I'd based one of the characters on her husband. None of the characters was based on anyone I knew, yet so many people saw themselves — because they wanted to. It had nothing to do with me.

Lynda Barry

Writer's Talk: Lynda, what is the bridge between text and graphic for you? I've been a big fan of your cartoons ever since I can remember. You have always been doing something interesting with adolescence. Taking a brave stance on it somehow. I wonder if it is the words or the drawings that come first, and if you have thought of why this might be.

Lynda Barry: It's funny because I've been thinking a lot about when words and pictures separate for people. A kid learning to write the alphabet is actually learning to draw the alphabet. When I remind people that writing by hand is actually drawing, they look surprised and then try to figure out how it is not drawing, how it is different, but there is no way to argue it. A person knows the physical moves required to make any letter of the alphabet or numeral. The same person can make these marks very small or very large. With a pencil, or a wet mop on a wall. It's just a specific movement with a mark maker.

When I'm making a comic strip these two things are not separated at all. I don't pencil my work in before I start. I just work very slowly with a brush, and as I draw the frame of the panel I'll often "hear" a sentence in my head. It's not mystical at all or deep or anything different than when a song gets caught in your head. You didn't consciously put it there, but it's playing, you can "hear" it — it's not the same as hearing it coming from a radio, but I would bet most people would describe it as "hearing the song" in their head rather than "thinking the song."

So I "hear" a sentence and I can tell who is saying it — which character — in the same way you can tell who is singing that song in your head. I'll write out that sentence, and if another one follows I'll write that out too. But if one doesn't follow I usually start drawing the character who said the sentence or the person she is saying it to. And in that way the comic strip begins. Each line leads to the next one.

In between there are times I have to just wait. So you'll see a lot of freckles on my characters or patterns on their clothes or little lines built up in the background. That's me waiting for the next line. It won't come if I'm not in motion. If I just sit there like "The Thinker" nothing comes at all.

My characters don't tend to be attractive at all. For drawings of girls in a comic strip, this isn't common. I always thought it might be the reason people say I can't draw well. If I could draw well, why would my characters be so homely?

I've written characters who have a lot about feeling very ugly, especially ones who have very beautiful mothers. That part is from my life. My mother was very beautiful. She let me know this all the time. And she also let me know I looked like a female Alfred E. Newman from *Mad Magazine*. She hated the way I looked. I always felt like a gargoyle around her. That relationship is certainly reflected in my work. I never had to put it in intentionally and I don't think I could intentionally keep it out.

The combination of reading, discussion, and interaction meant that by the time the student-writers approached their own assignment, they had thoroughly immersed themselves in the material at hand. They were thinking about the complexity of the task in a way most novices don't. In my experience, the work of reading and the work of writing are considered separate endeavours by many new writers, and my course sought to connect them in a way that showed how one could feed the other, and how there exists a reciprocity between the two experiences, a reciprocity from which the student-writer, just as the professional writer, stands to gain a great deal. If we are attuned to reading, we become (incrementally) better writers. This may seem obvious, but I had encountered student-writers who did not read, and who did not seem to think it was necessary to have read in order to give proper voice to their stories. Of course, in a sense they were right. One can simply write, but if one is to write well, coherently, and interestingly, one does well to read, and to read with one's heart and mind thoroughly open and attentive to the intention of the work at hand.

The differences between teaching online and in-class creative writing courses are subtle but particular. In class, I could assess students' temperaments more quickly and help students who were reticent or shy to find a way to speak. There was an easy inclusiveness to the in-class experience that was difficult to reproduce when one was in an atemporal course — that is, when the students and instructor are not necessarily in the "class" at the same time. Students living in disparate time zones interact in their time, not in real time, so spontaneity feels different. This is not to say that the online experience lacks authenticity, but it can feel less natural. Students are typically less impulsive in their comments and, in some instances, the forums can feel less conversational than an in-class interaction. This stems from the fact that the instructor will have initiated the conversation with a set of questions, and students with less time and inclination may simply respond before reading the discussion that flows from this initiation. Ideally, of course, discussion becomes a collective interaction, as it would in class. At times, though, an online forum can feel a bit disconnected in this regard, with some of the students interacting with the instructor and with one another, while some are less engaged and merely in conversation with the instructor.

My reaction to this, as an instructor, was to try to connect the students to one another in various ways. I would ask students to respond to one another's posts, and I would ask students to lead discussions. This last had the dual advantage of giving them agency (or position of mastery) over material and also of indicating my own non-mastery. It suggested to them, I think, that we are all students when it comes to reading attentively. It also encouraged less "chatty" students to publicly engage, and to feel less inhibited.

One of the distinct advantages to the online experience for some students is the fact that it is text-based and not oral. This allows students to think about and edit their comments before they hit "Send." Of course, there are still students who blurt and whose impulsivity sometimes requires retraction or intervention, but this is not so different from an in-class experience. My experience online has shown that the discourse often rises above what I might expect in an in-class scenario, especially given the typical demographic of University of Toronto registrants. Students can fact-check quickly, they can quote from writers and writing manuals, they can formulate their thoughts. This means that online I can often achieve a higher level of abstraction with my students and can in certain cases discuss more deeply how, for instance, point of view is flexible or narrative voice can shift (if done deftly and purposefully) depending on the skill of the writer. It's not that I can't do this in class, but, in a sense, there is more time online — students mull things over and then come back with insights, and since it is public to the rest of the class, the conversation can quickly become quite advanced. This was a pleasant surprise when I first began to teach online, but it has blowback, too. Some students become intimidated by the level of discourse and simply drop out of view. Since there is no way for me to engage them (I can't call them out online as I might be able to do discreetly in class), this can be a problem. I will add, though, that generally if the class size is over fifteen, discussion is lively and genuine — and students get to know one another. Sometimes they form writing groups among themselves once the course finishes.

Online is becoming as real as in-class. As technology advances, I expect this will only increase the authentic texture of online courses — also, as people adapt to cyber-relationships of this sort, they become more skilled at presented themselves in ways that generate camaraderie in the classroom.

My in-class approach has always been to meet the students where they are, and to help them achieve more in their writing practice from that starting point. In other words, I do not come to the class with any real idea of who they are and who they ought to become. Writing is a journey, but there are many journeys, and I have no interest in a programmatic approach to writing. Interesting writing is that writing in which the writer accesses his or her own singularity. This is the kind of writing that sparkles; it is this writing that is lively and energetic. I have taken very few writing workshops in my own career, and those I did take predate institutionalized writing programs.

I'm grateful for this, in a sense, because my unease with workshopping (as a system for generating good and proper writing) has led me to approach students individually, not as factory-farmed producers of literature. The emphasis in my classroom has always been on craft and how craft can help a sentence to do the work the writer needs it to do.

Seen a certain way, a sentence is nothing more than a web of words that captures some essential meaning. The magic is in the writer's confidence in choosing those words, and putting them in the best order to do that work. In other words, the magic is not really magic at all, but a long journey of reading attentively and practice. Writing has an aspect of meditation to it, and the writer who practises will naturally recognize the hum of his or her zone, the G-spot of an interior speaking rhythm that produces confident, authentic writing. Conveying this in-class or online is equally challenging. Students often come to class with a very hardened sense of what writing is. We all write, so why should writing be difficult, or why should it be pleasurable, or why should this sell and that not sell? Of course, I cannot teach anyone how to find the speaking rhythm that is his or her particular one, but I can recognize garbled thought and overwritten sentences. I can indicate a clogged idea, or dialogue that doesn't emerge from a character's trueness. So, I edit. That is my process as an instructor. I go in and I try my best to weed paradise. This weeding, I hope, shows new ways into each student's Eden. It's difficult to fully assess whether this feedback is more fully integrated by in-class or online students — or if it is the same — because I cannot know in any given class setting who I have, and what each will achieve in the short time span (typically eight weeks). In both settings, I encounter students who excel, who go from zero to sixty in a short time, but I also see stalled students, and ones who are simply better readers by the end but who haven't yet applied what they have learned to their own practice. I find it hard to stand in judgment of this, especially in light of the leaps some students take suddenly by course three, where I never anticipated this might happen. With writing, you never know when something exciting will happen, and transformation is not always sudden or spectacularly obvious. The least student will doggedly achieve what the naturally talented one won't, because writing is practice.

My online courses, like the in-class courses, are multi-faceted, trying to impart to students the importance of full engagement with each other's work. The online workshop runs slightly differently from the in-class one, in that I don't/can't oblige each student to give both positive and critical feedback — I can't really oblige online students to participate at all (except through grades, which have limited power in a continuing education setting). I integrate the idea of true criticism into discussions I have with students in the early days of the course, impressing upon them how important becoming an adept reader is to the practice of creative writing, and how listening (to their own work and to the work of others) will help them become more attentive to the world around them. I ask that they read their work aloud before they post it — as an editorial exercise, but also so that they get practice hearing their own work. (A few have made YouTube recordings of their readings for the class, but I have not insisted on anything like this; it might be something to look into in the future, when more people are adept at the technology.) Writing is not only about being heard, it is about learning to hear, and I truly want them to become stronger listeners, stronger witnesses to their worlds. This, I tell them, will help them write better, and will open them to story in new ways. It is my hope — and my experience as an instructor — that they will begin to bring to their own work the expertise they begin to acquire through workshopping with a fine ear and compassion.

The workshop is an emotional experience. I ask students to be open and not to comment on the comments of others to their work (except to thank!) because I want them to process critical feedback, not to answer it or defend their work. This is difficult for students, since it effectively effaces them from the work. My students will all be able to quote me: "You won't be sitting on the end of my bed when I read your book, so it better say and do what you want it to say and do." The writer *is* ultimately effaced from the work; that is the nature of fiction. It makes authors sensitive, and that vulnerability is the fuel that ignites the next book. It is my hope that the critical feedback students bring to their colleagues' work acts in a circular fashion, so that they open one another to the possibility of being ever more creative. There are rules around workshops I run so that the "reader" recognizes the "writer's" vulnerability and directs his or her gaze to the work, not to the maker of the work. In both in-class and online settings I've seen very powerful and useful responses to early drafts, inspiring students to revise the piece more toward what they wanted in the first place but hadn't completely been able to see. The student was helped to see where the work was bogged down or where it evaded the depth it could have reached. The idea is always that the student-writer becomes a writer-student. We are all learning.

Small Group Workshops in Large Creative Writing Classes: Because You Can't Be Everywhere at Once

Kathy Mac

You'd think that in a time of declining enrolments, classes would get smaller. Alas, fewer students means smaller budgets and, therefore, regrettably, larger classes. For creative writing courses, which hold workshopping at the heart of their pedagogy, large classes can be disastrous; more students means fewer opportunities for each to workshop their texts during the term. Furthermore, though millennial students (those born after 1982) are inherently team-oriented and well adjusted to creative writing courses, putting them in a large class and expecting them to participate fully on an individual basis can be disastrous. One solution to both problems is to break the class into small workshop groups. However, instructors face issues concerning leadership: those of us teaching classes capped at twenty-five or more, who don't have access to teaching assistants, worry about what will happen in groups when we're not with them: What can we do to ensure students focus on the workshop process?

Twenty-five students and no teaching assistance; that was my challenge when I began teaching creative writing at St. Thomas University in 2005. Fortunately, in 2003 I participated in a teaching workshop, Team Learning in Liberal Arts Courses, led by Brent MacLaine (a poet and award-winning professor at the University of Prince Edward Island), so by the time I came to teach creative writing I had a couple of years of experience using MacLaine's strategies for literature classes. MacLaine had adapted these strategies from

Larry Michaelsen's Team-Based Learning techniques, developed for huge (mandatory disclosure) business and science courses. I developed ways to adapt Michaelsen for my creative writing classes.

Box 1: Four Key Principles
for Successful Team Learning

1. Groups must be properly formed and managed.

2. Students must be made accountable for their individual and group work.

3. Group assignments must facilitate both learning and team development.

4. Students must have frequent and timely performance feedback. (Michaelsen 2–6)

Though Michaelsen delineates four key principles for successful team learning in academic courses, when it comes to teaching creative writing only the first two principles require effort (Box 1); the other two appear in the workshop process. First, "groups must be properly formed and managed" (2) for several consistent components. Barriers to group cohesiveness need to be minimized by ensuring that the groups are created in a random manner, so that pre-existing cliques don't persist (3). Furthermore, member resources need to be distributed so that "each group [has] access to whatever assets exist within the whole class and [does] not carry more than a 'fair share' of the liabilities" (3). In a creative writing class, assets might include things like experience in a workshop, at creative writing, or in journalism, while liabilities may include a tendency to speak before thinking, not speak up at all, or the inability to concentrate for an extended period. Finally, groups need to be big enough to maximize the creative resources of the members, and yet not so big that they prevent full participation by individuals in the group. Michaelsen has determined the optimal size for an academic group is five to seven people; my experience with creative writing is that seven is too large. However, five is a minimum, given that students sometimes miss class.

Box 2: Sample Group Creation Questionnaire

Name: _____

Choose one answer for each of the following questions:

If .... score yourself

1. Checking your writing habits

you write for yourself (i.e., not for courses, money, or employment) every day ... 20

you write for yourself every week 15

you may not write every week, but you had lots of stuff for the portfolio 10

you had to scramble to put together your portfolio 5

2. Checking for comfort sharing your work

you belong to a writing workshop that meets fairly regularly 20

you have workshopped your work periodically with peers 15

your mother and your dog love your work 5

3. Checking for rewriting/editing experience

you always rewrite your creative work 20

you sometimes rewrite your creative work 15

you never rewrite 5

4. Checking for grammar comfort level

you are pretty good at grammar and punctuation 20

you are insecure about your grammar and punctuation 10

"Commas? We don't need no stinkin' commas" 5

5. Checking your reading habits

you read obsessively whenever you can 20

you usually have a novel on the go, but it may take you a while to finish it ..15

you have read a work of fiction outside of class within the past year 10

you check your e-mail sometimes 5

TOTAL _____

The way to create correctly sized groups without pre-existing cliques, but with a fair distribution of assets and liabilities, is to administer a questionnaire at the beginning of the course (Box 2). It's important to explain to the students that it is more like a magazine questionnaire than an evaluation — there are no incorrect answers. Once they've finished the questionnaire, I have them line up around the perimeter of the classroom in the order of their final score, and then count themselves off. In a twenty-five-person class, I'll plan on having four groups, so each student calls out in order "one," "two," "three," or "four." The number they call designates their group for the first half of the term.

Michaelsen and MacLaine recommend keeping the same groups for the entire term, which is effective for academic courses that use the groups once every couple of weeks or so. However, in a creative writing class, the groups are used for at least half of the allotted time every week. Consequently, it's better to change the groups once or twice every term; this helps to keep cliques from forming, keeps a fresh critical perspective for each day's workshop, and ensures that no single group is burdened for the whole term with a socially inept or disturbed student.

I regularly have students in introductory creative writing classes write a short "Workshop Response" paper on the workshop process. In his response, Corry Melanson — a student in creative writing — reported that his first group, "instead of building a constructive workshop sandwich of 'compliment / criticism / compliment,' made an overly sweet sandwich of 'compliment / compliment / compliment'" (1). The second group of the course had a more "satisfying sprinkling of criticism and compliment," but "was still not perfected. Awkward silences often echoed through the group ... [which] often resulted in people being nitpicky about commas, apostrophes, and so on" (1). By the third group, "the process finally started to become what it was meant to be. Comparing a piece that I first wrote in the first group, then rewrote for the third group, the marks on the copies I made for my peers told a story about how much we've improved in the workshop process. The first group of copies was left mostly blank, save for an occasional smiley face or an underlined phrase. The later group of copies, however, was marked to satisfaction with many grammatical mistakes underlined and circled, comments filling the margins and a satisfying summary of what the person thought at the end of the piece" (2). The change was evident in the actual workshop as well, where "criticism was usually in such available bounty that the group often had to force ourselves to move to the next piece before we ran out of time" (2).

Corry saw such a positive growth in workshopping skills over the term because students were held accountable to each other for their work, which is the second crucial principle from Michaelsen that applies to creative writing courses: "Students must be made accountable" (4). Without accountability for their behaviour in the workshop groups, they have no motivation to actually do the work necessary for a healthy workshop — provide sufficient copies of the text that they've written by the deadline (usually several days before class), read the others' texts for class, and participate fully in the in-class workshop (4–5). Michaelsen developed peer evaluation as a strategy for ensuring accountability.

PEER EVALUATION

Peer evaluation motivates students marvellously. As Michaelsen notes: "Peer assessment is essential because team members are typically the only ones who have enough information to accurately assess one another's contributions" (5). Furthermore, in my experience students are more sensitive to the impression that they make on other students than they are to my opinion of them, and consequently they work hard to keep up their part of the workshopping bargain.

Peer evaluation is based on a form (Box 3) that individual students fill out either during their final class with a group or via email in the last week of working with a group. (If peer evaluation is done during class time, it's best if group members don't sit together while filling out the form.) As the form indicates, students assign each student a grade from 1 to 10, with a 9 or a 10 meaning that the person has given a 90 percent or 100 percent contribution, while a 5 means 50 percent or "passable." Less than 5 means he or she failed to participate adequately. The student decides on a mark according to very specific criteria that we discuss prior to administering the peer evaluation form: attendance, effort made to participate, willingness to listen and consider others' ideas, preparedness (bringing sufficient copies of their own work on time, reading the material in preparation for the workshop), and then the quality of the contribution. The rules for assigning a peer evaluation value are laid out in Box 3.

Box 3: Sample Peer Evaluation Form

This is your opportunity to evaluate the *participation* of your peers in the class. Give each student (excluding yourself) a rating out of 10.

Remember that a 9 or a 10 means that member has given a 90% or 100% contribution; a 5 means 50% (or "passable"); less than 5 means that person failed to participate adequately. You should decide on a mark according to the following criteria:

- attendance
- effort made to participate
- willingness to consider others' ideas
- preparedness (having the material read)
- the quality of the contribution

NOTE: You *must*

1. Give a spread of grades.
2. Justify your highest and lowest marks on the reverse of this sheet.
3. If you wish to give more than two grades that are the same, you must explain your reasons on the reverse.
4. If you wish to give half-increment grades, then you must also explain your reasons on the reverse.

Note that your comments will be sent to the people commented upon.

Student's Name/Grade/Comments:

_____ / _____ / _____
_____ / _____ / _____
_____ / _____ / _____
_____ / _____ / _____
_____ / _____ / _____
_____ / _____ / _____

General Comments (Optional):

Through the peer evaluation form, I acquire two sets of feedback: a number out of ten, and comments. The numbers assigned to each student by their group members are averaged together to give them their final peer evaluation value for that group, worth 5 percent of their final grade. Peer evaluation grades given through the term are added together, so when a class has three sets of groups, peer evaluation will be 15 percent of the final grade. If there are only two sets of groups, peer evaluation is worth only 10 percent. Making the peer evaluation count for more than 5 percent for each group might invite students to inflate the peer evaluation grades they assign.

Along with calculating a grade, I also compile comments on the peer evaluation forms, strip away any elements that might identify the person who made the comment, and email them to the student commented upon (Sweet and Michaelsen 27). Doing this provides a wake-up call for students who come to class inadequately prepared; their peers let them know, kindly but unyieldingly, that they are not pulling their weight in the group. Poor peer evaluation grades and comments in the first or second group often change student behaviour, in large part because students cannot remain anonymous in the course. The result is more participation as the course continues, and better peer evaluation grades at the end.

EVALUATION RUBRIC

Peer evaluation is just one part of my overall evaluation strategy in creative writing classes. The whole looks something like Box 4.

Fifty percent of the final grade is based on weekly writing and the final portfolio; determining the relative weight of these is the first group activity students undertake. First, they determine within their group how they would like to see the 50 percent divided between the two items, and then they choose one group member to represent them in a meta-group, which comes to an agreement on behalf of the whole class. The only rule is that neither the workshop writing nor the final portfolio can be worth less than 10 percent.

Workshop responses provide another method of ensuring student accountability. Due on the class after the workshop groups have changed, page-long workshop responses detail what each student has learned from the most recent group. Here's how these assignments are explained in the course syllabus:

The subject of these short assignments is your experience of the critiquing process; what you learned and from whom. Be specific; mention the titles and authors from your group that you choose to discuss in these papers, either positively (i.e., from X's comments, I learned to ...) or negatively (from Y's story, I learned never to ...). These papers should demonstrate the development of your critical "eye."

Box 4: Evaluation Rubric

Writing	50%
Weekly Writing	X%
Final Portfolio	X%
Event Review/Workshop Responses	10%
1st Workshop Response	2.5%
2nd Workshop Response	2.5%
Event Review	2.5%
Optional 4th Assignment	2.5%
Blog Entries	20%
Peer Evaluation	15%
Participation	5%

Each of these is worth only 2.5 percent; I require two, after the first and second workshop groups, and one event review. Students then have the option of responding to their third group, reviewing another literary event, or doing an introduction for their final portfolio, so that they will have earned 10 percent of their final grades. This 10 percent, plus the 15 percent for peer evaluation and 5 percent for participation (assigned by me and based in large part on attendance and getting workshop material in on a timely manner), means that 30 percent of the course's grade comes from their preparation for, and active participation in, the workshop.

The final objective in the first few classes is to encourage positive group norms. In the case of a workshop group for a creative writing class, this means setting up a useful, positive paradigm for critiquing texts. In a playwriting workshop in 2007, Kent Stetson laid out clear rules:

1. Compliment the playwright.
2. Pick out the central image.
3. Question (for criticism).
4. Urge (for next draft).
5. Pick out the theme (this is a text about ...).

In my experience the first, third, and fourth of Stetson's precepts are the most useful, though I introduce students to them all. I also request that the author not participate in the discussion initially; she or he may speak up later in the critique if requested by another member of the group — a stricture honoured more in the breach, particularly by less experienced workshoppers. By the end of a one-term course, though, even the most voluble have learned the value of listening rather than defending.

The way the creative writing program works at St. Thomas, there are always a few people in each class who have taken a creative writing course in the past, which provides another contributing factor to the success of the groups; I try to ensure that each group includes at least one experienced workshopper. Finally, along with introducing Stetson's rules for workshopping, I emphasize to the students that a critique of a text is not a criticism of the author; on the contrary, when a reader gives deep critical attention to a text the reader is in fact complimenting to the author in a most compassionate, disinterested, meaningful way.

CONCLUSION

In a perfect world, all creative writing courses would be capped at twelve students. But this world is not perfect, and nor is group learning in a large creative writing class; I am constantly adjusting my instructional practices. For example, changing the groups only once per term (instead of twice) increases the sense of community and the support for at-risk students, a disproportionate number of whom seem to end up in creative writing. However, leaving students in the same groups for too long can lead to cliquishness and off-topic gossip rather than actual focus on the texts during the workshopping that takes place when I'm out of the room. Similarly, the critical ability of students new to workshopping is fairly shallow; they are often so enamoured with the process of workshopping — with reading stuff that one of their peers actually created — that they miss some of the most egregious problems with passive verbs, pedestrian premises, ambiguous symbols, and the like. I mitigate this as much as possible by modelling and refining the workshopping process for them every couple of weeks, pointing out things they can be looking for in their own and others' work. However, there are limits to the efficacy of my front-of-class pronouncements, no matter how I ground them in their own work. Finally, even with a mandated out-of-class meeting around the mid-term, students do not get enough "face-time" with the professor.

The use of small group workshops in large creative writing courses is not a panacea. But it *can* be absolutely brilliant, and it *is* the best solution I've found to the problem of a high student-to-teacher ratio. Though not terribly significant in terms of final grade, peer evaluation has a disproportionately positive effect on students' writing, reading, and workshopping skills.

Acknowledgements
Thanks are due to Kathleen Wall for her thoughtful edit of an earlier version of this paper. A previous version of the paper was included in the *Wascana Review* 43.1 (2011).

WORKS CITED

Melanson, Corry. "Final Workshop Critique." ENGL 2013: Creative Writing I, St. Thomas University. Unpublished assignment, quoted with permission.

Michaelsen, Larry K. "Getting Started with Team-Based Learning." U of British Columbia. Web. 22 Aug. 2013.

Sweet, Michael, and Larry K. Michaelsen. "Critical Thinking and Engagement: Creating Cognitive Apprenticeships with Team-based Learning." *Team-Based Learning in the Social Sciences and Humanities.* Ed. Sweet and Michaelsen. Sterling, VA: Stylus, 2012. 5–32. Print.

PART II

RE-WRITING THE CREATIVE WRITING TRADITION

Poetic Form as Experimental Procedure: The View from Renaissance England

David B. Goldstein

O ne of our most complex challenges as teachers and critics of poetry is to explain both how writing changes and how it stays the same. Teachers of avant-garde or experimental poetry are especially called upon to elucidate these matters. Just what is "avant" or experimental about such work? How does new writing establish continuities with earlier traditions, and when is it effacing or rejecting them? One of the most pressing and least studied of these issues, especially in English-language (as opposed to French) criticism, is the distinction between form and procedure. This distinction goes by many names — what some critics call form, others call "rule," "generic convention," or "regularity," while "procedure" is also called "constraint."* The multiplicity of terms underlines the fact that there is no agreed-upon definition of the two categories. But we know it when we see it. In general, form is associated with traditional poetic structures with histories dating back before the twentieth century, often involving metre and/or rhyme. Procedure is linked to innovative, experimental, and organic poetic structures employing particular constraints, sometimes generated for use in a single piece of writing. In creative writing and critical classes, we tend (I would venture) to teach the difference between these two modes of poetic structuring as a difference not just between contrasting approaches to poetic making, but as a historical divide, between "new" poetry and "old" poetry.

---

* See the various critics cited in this discussion.

I will suggest here, instead, that procedurality has always been with us, and that while it may be useful to draw distinctions in these techniques among current poetic approaches, to view "form" historically is to discover that it is nearly indistinguishable from procedure. My argument here will focus upon Renaissance prosody, especially in the sixteenth century — the formal concepts that influenced Shakespeare and his contemporaries. In comparing Renaissance poetic practice and theory to contemporary, and especially Oulipian notions of procedure, I will suggest that the two are virtually the same in most important respects. Renaissance poets would have found themselves in significant, if perhaps not total agreement, with the Oulipo movement as well as with much of what goes by the term *procedural poetics*. What can we learn from this about our own practice as writers and teachers? Who cares if Sir Thomas Wyatt or John Donne thought of poetry as procedural? The answer, I will suggest, is that we must undertake a fundamental shift in the ways we teach "form," as well as metre and rhyme, to our students.

The concept of procedure — or its close cousin, constraint — arose in experimental circles, such as those of Language Poetry, the conceptualists, and above all Oulipo, as a challenge to the notion of form as a culturally fixed and outworn vessel into which a poem's content is poured. The goal of a procedure is to reinvigorate poetic language through restriction. Following Jacques Roubaud, one of Oulipo's primary theorists, Marjorie Perloff makes a distinction between metrical form and procedurality, arguing that form denotes a "rule" or "fixed property of the text," while a procedure is "generative," denoting "how the writer will proceed with his composition" (*Radical* 139). Elsewhere, Perloff elaborates, "Whereas a Petrarchan sonnet may be understood as a kind of envelope (octave plus sestet), whose parameters govern the poem's composition, the Oulipo constraint is a *generative* device: it creates a formal structure whose rules of composition are internalized so that the constraint in question is not only a rule but a thematic property of the poem" (*Differentials* 208). She lays special emphasis on two of Roubaud's chief Oulipian tenets: first, that "a text written according to a constraint describes the constraint," and second, that procedures are often constructed in relation to numerical and mathematical schemes.[*] As Alison James writes, procedure describes "a process of undoing an established form in order to construct a new one" (n. pag.).

---

[*] These schemes are, of course, occasionally metrical: the sonnet is listed as one of the procedures in the *Oulipo Compendium*.

Perloff draws her distinction between form and procedure not in order to separate traditional from contemporary poetry, but rather to mount a critique of traditional form as currently conceived (especially by the New Formalist movement) as a timeless and ahistorical set of rules. Conversely, Perloff argues, paraphrasing the critic Henri Meschonnic, "There is no prosodic form that isn't, at least to some degree, historically bound and culture specific" (*Radical* 136). Indeed, some proceduralists go out of their way to demonstrate continuities between ancient forms and modern procedures. Roubaud, in *La vieillesse d'Alexandre [The Old Age of Alexander]*, argues for a continuous reinvention of the French alexandrine whose latest avatar is the Oulipian experiments of Michel Bénabou and others (Perloff, *Differentials* 208). Harry Mathews and Alastair Brotchie, ruminating on the vexed question of the sonnet, conclude (invoking Roubaud's research) "that by Oulipian standards no precise definition of the form can be said to exist. All the same, Oulipians have always loved experimenting with it" (229).* Confusion, or perhaps a refreshing ecumenicalism, also surfaces on the formalist side. For example, the editors of *In Fine Form: The Canadian Book of Form Poetry*, offer a rather New Formalist definition of form: "A form poem is one in which key details of composition, including rhyme, repetition, meter, and rhythm, are accepted as givens" (Braid and Shreve 13). "Accepted as givens" seems to suggest a notion of form as fixed or received. Yet the anthology includes a selection from Christian Bök's *Eunoia*, as well as concrete and anagrammatic poems by bpNichol, all of which treat procedure as generative in the Oulipo sense. Thus, in spite of the concern over categorical distinctions between form and procedure — and, beneath it, between the *bona fides* of traditionalism and the avant-garde — distinguishing firmly between the two is a challenging, if not impossible, endeavour. I plan to muddy the waters further by expanding upon Roubaud and Perloff's arguments in order to suggest, not only that Renaissance prosodic forms were historically produced and contextualized (as others have pointed out), but that in fact Renaissance poets viewed what we now call forms as something much closer to what we now call procedures. On the continuum of form and procedure, Shakespeare's contemporaries considered not only the anagram, but also

---

* Examples of Oulipian sonnet experiments include Raymond Queneau's *A Hundred Thousand Billion Poems* and Roubaud's own debut collection of poetry, *ε*. See the discussion in Mathews and Brotchie.

the sonnet, and indeed metre and rhyme themselves to be generative and unpredictable constraints — fields of play upon which language scatters and finds itself through rigours both mathematical and mystical.

Our understanding of Renaissance prosody is conditioned above all by two pressures: selection (with respect to modern canon-formation) and fixity (with respect to modern printing). The pressures of canon have left us with the sense that Renaissance writers chose from among a narrow range of forms — above all the sonnet — and that writer and reader, as Timothy Steele puts it, "would have recognized the verse forms and could have traced ... their continuity all the way back to the misty beginnings of Greek lyric" (426). The fixity of modern print has left us with the impression that Renaissance form was static and iterative — that all sonnets looked more or less alike, with small variations (such as the replacement of Petrarchan by Shakespearean rhyme schemes) having only slight effects on the rules of the form. Open just about any modern printed anthology, and you will see the familiar result of these two biases: a sonnet equals fourteen lines of left-justified iambic pentameter, the last two lines (if the rhyme scheme is Shakespearean) always indented.[*]

To define the Renaissance sonnet as a fixed form, even in the most usual and general sense of having fourteen lines of rhymed iambic pentameter, is already to forget the well-known fact that Renaissance sonnets actually come in several line-lengths, from the alexandrines of Philip Sidney's "Loving in truth" to the tetrameter of Shakespeare's Sonnet 145, as well as varying numbers of lines (from twelve to sixteen), and experiment widely with rhythm (as in Thomas Wyatt's syllabic experiments), rhyme (as in Spenser's *Amoretti*), and subject (such as Michael Drayton's parody of sonnet commonplaces in his sequence *Idea*). All of these examples indicate that "sonnet" was less a fixed rule than a cloud of possibilities that interacted with various factors to produce something that contemporaries recognized as a poem. The freezing of the sonnet form, which played out from the 1590s through the early seventeenth century with the seemingly endless parade of sonnet sequences inspired by Sidney's *Astrophil and Stella*, heralded the form's *demise*, not its development. Put another way, from Wyatt and Surrey's resurrection of the form in the 1530s through the sonnet sequence vogue culminating in the 1611 publication of Shakespeare's attempt at the genre, the English sonnet was transformed

---

[*] For key standard accounts of the relationship between printing and fixity, see the writings of Elizabeth L. Eisenstein and Adrian Johns.

from a procedure into a rule. With the exception of Donne's spectacularly strange *Holy Sonnets*, it took several decades before the sonnet was resuscitated, and then only by Milton, who did love a challenge. It may be that the vogue for sonnet sequences after Sidney's *Astrophil and Stella* did more than anything else in English literary history to solidify the idea of form as a fixed, intrinsic set of poetic rules. No wonder Donne, Jonson, and others rebelled by writing in whatever forms they could make, revivify, or find lying around on the street, or that Shakespeare decided in his plays that the most radical form of dramatic poetry was *prose*. For Renaissance writers, when a form became fixed — became a rule *rather* than a generative set of possibilities — it was time either to rewire it or to ditch it.

All Renaissance poems had their initial existence not in printed books but, of course, in manuscripts. Rather than single-author works, many of these manuscripts were produced by a coterie of like-minded people who wrote, circulated, and annotated them collaboratively.* One of the best-known and most important of these is the so-called Devonshire Manuscript, now housed in the British Library.

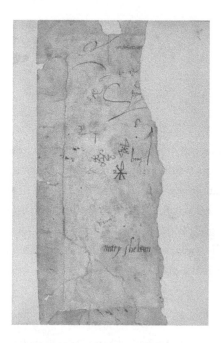

---

* On the Renaissance practice of coterie publication, see, for example, Harold Love and Arthur F. Marotti (55–80); Arthur F. Marotti; and Wendy Wall.

The manuscript, which was compiled in the 1530s and 40s, centred on Anne Boleyn, Henry VIII's infamous and ill-fated queen. The manuscript includes sixty-six poems by Sir Thomas Wyatt found nowhere else, as well as numerous poems by his contemporaries, including Henry Howard, the Earl of Surrey. Most strikingly, it provides the first sustained evidence of men and women writing together in the English tradition, and many of the poems are related to questions of gender and love.[*]

One of the most curious is identified by its first line, "all women have vertues," and attributed in the manuscript to the poet Richard Hatfield.

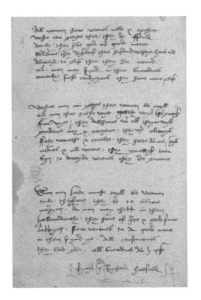

Although the manuscript poses challenges both in terms of legibility and handwriting style (it is written in a sixteenth-century hand called Secretary, which includes several features that have long since dropped out of English script), at least one remarkable feature of the poem stands out even to the modern eye: although it is lineated, there are occasional slashes in the midst of the lines, as well as extra-grammatical periods and other odd forms of punctuation. What is the poet up to?

---

[*] The best ongoing work on the Devonshire Manuscript, including a facsimile and a thorough bibliography of its critical context, is to be found in *A Social Edition of the Devonshire MS (BL Add 17,492)*.

Read carefully, the meaning of the backslashes quickly becomes apparent. The poem is structured so that it can be read in two ways: one respects the line breaks of the manuscript, and the other respects the internal punctuation. Here are two transcriptions of the poem, both with modernized spelling, the first printed as lineated (with added punctuation to clarify syntax), and the second as dictated by the internal backslashes:[*]

> All women have virtues noble & excellent.
> Who can perceive that they do offend?
> Daily they serve god with good intent,
> seldom they displease their husbands to their lives' end.
> Always to please them they do intend.
> Never man may find in them shrewdness;[**]
> commonly such conditions they have more & less.

> What man can perceive that women be evil?
> Every man that hath wit greatly will them praise,
> for vice they abhor with all their will.
> Prudence, mercy, and patience they use always;
> Folly, wrath, and cruelty they hate, as men say.
> Meekness and all virtue they do practise ever;
> sin to avoid, virtues they do procure.

---

[*] Transcription and modernization mine, based on the facsimile provided in *A Social Edition of the Devonshire MS*.
[**] Shrewdness: shrewish behaviour.

Some men speak much evil be women —
truly therefore they be to blame.
Nothing a man may check in them,
abundantly they have of grace and good fame,
lacking few virtues to a good name.
In them find ye all constantness;
they lack perde* all shrewdness as I guess.

Or:

All women have virtues noble & excellent?
Who can perceive that?
They do offend daily,
They serve god with good intent seldom,
They displease their husbands to their lives' end always —
To please them they do intend never.
Man may find in them shrewdness commonly;
such conditions they have more & less.

What man can perceive that women be evil?
Every man that hath wit.
Greatly will them praise for vice:
they abhor with all their will prudence, mercy, and patience.
They use always folly, wrath, and cruelty;
they hate, as men say, meekness and all virtue.
They do practise ever sin.
To avoid virtues they do procure.

Some men speak much evil be women truly.
Therefore they be to blame nothing.
A man may check in them abundantly.
They have of grace and good fame lacking.
Few virtues to a good name in them find ye.
All constantness they lack, perde,
all shrewdness as I guess.

* Perde: by God.

The procedure, as we see, produces two antithetical poems, each nestled within the other. The first poem is a rousing, if formulaic, protofeminist defence of women's constancy and wisdom, while the second is an equally formulaic misogynist attack upon women's behaviour. Neither of the poems in themselves would be interesting; conjoined by a creative procedure, they produce a complex commentary on gender relations in the court of Henry VIII, in which Anne Boleyn and her fellow queens are alternately seen as the pinnacle of beauty and nobility, or as whores, with little in between. Circulated within a mixed-gender coterie which without doubt included Boleyn herself, the poem further comments upon how gender operates in courtly poetry, with women acting both as authors and objects — sometimes revered, sometimes reviled — in social and literary contexts.

There is a great deal more to say about the social ramifications of both the poem and the manuscript in which it appears, but my interest here is in what this poem and its context tell us about Renaissance poetic form.[*] It's a surprising poem in many ways:

- It uses not a received form but an invented one.
- It is generative, producing discourse through the fact of its constraint.
- It is *also* rule-bound, in the sense that it imposes a rule inseparable from the poetic construction.
- It is rhythmically structured, and is written — the first version at least — in the rhyme scheme of rhyme royal, but neither version is metrical. In other words, the fact that it is a form does not mean that it automatically corresponds to the mathematics of metre: it conforms to a principle of measure, but not to the principles of alternating accents and fixed syllable count that we usually attribute to most English verse between Chaucer and Thomas Hardy.

Such a poem seems to contradict most descriptions of form as conceived historically. It is not received, it is not a conveyor of abstract rules, it is not associated with a particular metric, and its relation to its content is utterly inextricable. We might say, by way of objection, that it's a pretty mediocre poem, long on cleverness and short on art, and we might point out that it

[*] On the social valences of the manuscript, see the article by Elizabeth Heale.

was never published. But in doing so we would be judging the poem by anachronistic standards. The Renaissance placed a very high value on cleverness (Shakespeare's sonnets are full of witty wordplay), and many poets — including Wyatt, Sidney, Donne, and Herbert — withheld their poems from publication. (The facts that this poem is found in three other manuscripts, and is one of the few poems in the Devonshire manuscript carrying an authorial attribution, both imply significant popularity).* The point of the poem is not to turn a beautiful phrase, but to use a poetic procedure to explore a linguistic phenomenon that comments, in turn, upon the procedure.

Lest we consider this poem an exception that proves the rule of an otherwise unitary conception of form, let us turn to the period's most important theorist of poetic practice, George Puttenham, whose 1589 *Arte of English Poesie* was the first full-scale poetry-writing manual in the English language. Puttenham begins his book with a thumbnail history and description of formal verse patterns. At moments he ascribes, as did most theorists of the period, intrinsic meanings, subjects, and emotions to specific verse forms: he describes the Roman funeral elegies, for example, as "placing a limping *Pentameter* after a lusty *Exameter*, which made it go dolourously more than any other meeter" (39). But when it comes to contemporaneous practice, he rejects these distinctions in favour of a more fluid relation between form and content. Love poetry, for example, "requireth a forme of Poesie variable, inconstant, affected, curious and most witty of any others," suggesting that one must construct one's verse organically, in tandem with the fleeting emotions one is trying to capture — a notion that mixes the Black Mountain Poets with the Oulipians (36).

The second book of Puttenham's treatise, "Of Proportion Poetical," treats the technicalities of practice. It begins (as does Jacques Roubaud's introduction to the *Oulipo Compendium*) by relating poetic procedure to mathematics. Puttenham's discussion of metre emphasizes experiment and innovation over traditional rule-following, and indeed he shares both of these qualities — viewing metre as a kind of math, and poetry as an innovative practice — with the two major poetic theorists who follow his work, Thomas Campion and Samuel Daniel. (This continuity is all the more remarkable for the fact that Campion's treatise may be read as a reaction

---

* On the issue of authorial attribution, see David Carlson's "The Henrician Courtier Writing in Manuscript and Print (Wyatt, Surrey, Bryan, and Others)." On the poem's appearance in other manuscripts, see *A Social Edition of the Devonshire MS.*

to Puttenham's, and Daniel's is an explicit retort to Campion's.) Having admitted, for instance, his preference for lines with even numbers of syllables, Puttenham nevertheless allows that lines with an odd syllable-count, "if they be well composed … are commendable inough …" and offers an example (N7v).* Nor does Puttenham address forms in the sense that we teach them — as discrete concatenations of metre, line- and stanza-length, and rhyme scheme to which a single label is affixed. Nowhere is the sonnet mentioned in either Puttenham's or Campion's treatises, and Puttenham invokes Petrarch — the great innovator of the sonnet — only in order to vaguely discuss his "canzoni," which might refer either to a particular form or generically to his vernacular poetry, and his "seizino," which seems to be a garbled term for sestina (72).** The single common modern form discussed is an Oulipian favourite, the anagram. Puttenham devotes the majority of his discussion to a minute analysis of different sorts of feet and line-lengths, interleaved with a disquisition on visual poetry. He encourages his writer to try different stanza-lengths, according "to the makers phantasie and choise," illustrating them ocularly to show some different possible shapes.

---

74   OF PROPORTION. LIB. II.

and that is by one whole verſe running alone throughout the ditty or ballade, either in the middle or end of euery ſtaffe. The Greekes called ſuch vncoupled verſe *Epimonie*, the Latines *Verſus intercalaris*. Now touching the ſituation of meaſures, there are as manie or more proportions of them which I referre to the makers phantaſie and choiſe, contented with two or three ocular examples and no moe.

Which maner of proportion by ſituatiō of meaſures giueth more efficacie to the matter oftentimes then the concords them ſelues, and both proportions concurring together as they needes muſt, it is of much more beautie and force to the hearers mind.

To finiſh the learning of this diuiſion, I will ſet you downe one example of a dittie written extempore with this deuiſe, ſhewing not onely much promptneſſe of wit in the maker, but alſo great arte and a notable memorie. Make me ſaith this writer to one of the companie, ſo many ſtrokes or lines with your pen as ye would haue your ſong containe verſes and let euery line beare his ſeuerall length, euen as ye would haue your verſe of meaſure. Suppoſe of foure, fiue, ſixe or eight or more ſillables, and ſet a figure of euerie number at th'end of the line, whereby ye may know his meaſure. Then where you will haue your rime or concord to fall, marke it with a compaſt ſtroke or ſemicircle paſſing ouer thoſe lines, be they farre or neare in diſtance, as ye haue ſeene before deſcribed. And bycauſe ye ſhall not thinke the maker hath premeditated beforehand any ſuch faſhioned ditty. do ye your ſelfe make one verſe whether it be of perfect or imperfect ſenſe, and giue it him for a theame to make all the reſt vpon: if ye ſhall perceiue the maker do keepe the meaſures and rime as ye haue appointed him, and beſides do make his dittie ſenſible and enſuant to the firſt verſe in good reaſon, then may ye ſay he is his crafts maiſter. For if he were not of a plentiful diſcourſe, he could not vpon the ſudden ſhape an entire dittie vpon your imperfect theame or propoſition in one verſe

---

OF PROPORTION. LIB. II.   75

verſe. And if he were not copious in his language, he could not haue ſuch ſtore of wordes at commaundement, as ſhould ſupply your concords. And if he were not of a maruelous good memory he could not obſerue the rime and meaſures after the diſtances of your limitation, keeping with all grauitie and good ſenſe in the whole dittie.

CHAP. XI.
Of Proportion in figure.

YOur laſt proportion is that of figure, ſo called for that it yelds an ocular repreſentation, your meeters being by good ſymmetrie reduced into certaine Geometricall figures, whereby the maker is reſtrained to keepe him within his bounds, and ſheweth not onely more art, but ſerueth alſo much better for briefneſſe and ſubtiltie of deuice. And for the ſame reſpect are alſo fitteſt for the pretie amourets in Court to entertaine their ſeruants and the time withall, their delicate wits requiring ſome commendable exerciſe to keepe them from idleneſſe. I find not of this proportion vſed by any of the Greeke or Latine Poets, or in any vulgar writer, ſauing of that one forme which they cal *Anacreons egg*. But being in Italie conuerſant with a certaine gentleman, who had long trauailed the Orientall parts of the world, and ſeene the Courts of the great Princes of China and Tartarie. I being very inquiſitiue to know of the ſubtilities of thoſe countreyes, and eſpecially in matter of learning and of their vulgar Poeſie, he told me that they are in all their inuentions moſt wittie, and haue the vſe of Poeſie or riming, but do not delight ſo much as we do in long tedious deſcriptions, and therefore when they will vtter any pretie conceit, they reduce it into metricall feet, and put it in forme of a *Lozenge* or ſquare, or ſuch other thing, and ſo in graum in gold, ſiluer or iuorie, and ſometimes with letters of ameriſt, rubie, emeralde or ropas curiouſly cemented and pieced together, they ſende them in chaines, bracelets, collars and girdles to their miſtreſſes to weare for a remembrance. Some fewe meaſures compoſed in this ſort this gentleman gaue me, which I tranſlated word for word and as neere as I could followed both the phraſe and the figure, which is ſomewhat hard to performe, becauſe of the reſtraint of the figure from which ye may not digreſſe. At the beginning they wil ſeeme

---

* I employ the folio number here, as the page numbering throughout the section is incorrect.

** Daniel's treatise, however, addresses the sonnet briefly on F7r-F8v.

Then he suggests a variety of shape poems, each of which observes a metrical scheme devised by Puttenham in keeping with the exigencies of the shape's required line breaks, and nearly all of which somehow describe or enact their shapes.

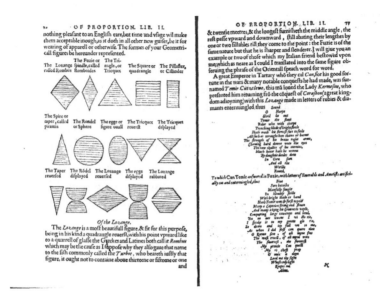

They are, in other words, nearly indistinguishable from Oulipian forms, like the snowball. In fact, one of the most frequently anthologized Oulipian poems, Harry Mathews's lozenge snowball "Liminal poem," employs a constraint much discussed, under the same name, by Puttenham.

Throughout the section on proportion, Puttenham's attitude is that of a craftsman or scientist. Given a range of tools and strictures — syllable, accent, caesura, line — how does one construct a workable, harmonious verse? The emphasis on construction and materiality (Puttenham, like Sidney and every other Renaissance poet, reminds his reader straight off that *poet* comes from the Greek *poiein,* to make) gives the lie to any notion of form as received or fixed vessel.* Puttenham's goal is to make his readers into good builders of poems, giving them an arsenal of equipment and then setting them to work creating beautiful, intricate patterns. Puttenham isn't too

---

* On poem-making as a kind of artisanal and material knowledge, see especially works by Rayna Kalas and Pamela H. Smith.

far from Jacques Roubaud's definition of an Oulipian author as "a rat who himself builds the maze from which he sets out to escape" (41). Likewise Robert Duncan's definition of poetry in "Often I Am Permitted to Return to a Meadow" as "a scene made-up by the mind, / that is not mine, but is a made place / that is mine" (lines 1–3).

We might object that these poems clearly do not belong to mainstream Renaissance writing, since our anthologies are not exactly littered with shape poems. Perhaps they were seen as mere ditties, as are the "posies" Puttenham describes that were commonly painted on plates, to be revealed as a kind of epistemological palate cleanser at the meal's end (47). Yet we know that a great part of Renaissance social life expressed itself through ephemera, ornamentation, and triviality. The Renaissance was a culture of fragments, "a cosmos," to quote Patricia Fumerton, "in which even central historical configurations seemed broken apart and marginalized in incoherence, and where self was thus fixed in fracture" (1). These trivial fractions of verse helped give structure to both public and private life. Puttenham presents them as survival tactics for courtier-poets, and as glittering linguistic constructions that achieve a social function, and potentially, — though not necessarily — a literary one. Poetic form — for Puttenham, Richard Hatfield, and most of their contemporaries — consists in using the material tools of language to construct lyric and narrative objects with a range of purposes — political, cultural, linguistic, literary. The *Arte of English Poesie* — both Puttenham's book and the art itself — provides a workshop for the writing of *potential* literature. Those shape poems do, by general agreement, become literature when George Herbert, whose "The Altar" and "Easter Wings" were likely influenced by Puttenham's manual, elevates them to that status. In the meanwhile, they are still made objects, are still forms. As Roubaud again writes, "It is clearly in the resort to complex systems of constraints, to strategies of progressive demonstration, and to ceremonials of revelation and dissimulation that the distinction is created between the 'five-finger exercises' of elementary pieces written according to constraints and creation that is truly literary" (qtd. in Mathews and Brotchie 42). The art of Renaissance English poetry is a procedural art of potentiality. It makes things out of syllables, words, lines, and shapes, and those forms bring content out of and through themselves — sometimes as revelation, sometimes as artifice, sometimes as expression. At best, as all three.

The idea of "poetic form" as received vessel or static structure no doubt recurs in various places and times, attached to particular kinds of writing, as it does in our own. Once certain procedures harden, they may inevitably start to become forms. This is one reason why Oulipians and other proceduralists, from Puttenham to Roubaud, emphasize the importance of the new. "The constraint," writes Christelle Reggiani, "is a rhetoric of invention which owes its powerful effect precisely to the fact that it exceeds the cultural expectation defined by the rule" (qtd. in Andrews 224). As Chris Andrews argues, speaking of Reggiani and other theorists of procedure, "The constraint is implicitly defined as a new and/or little-imitated rule" (224). But for the late sixteenth century, a period of tremendous poetic experiment and transformation, the power of metrical and other prosodic units lay in their power both to organize and surprise — to describe and advance the ways in which language builds a world both cognitive and material, a lived world.

To acknowledge that Renaissance formalism is far more avant-garde — even in the contemporary sense — than we usually give it credit for may change us as writers, for when we return to that time for inspiration, we may find it altogether richer and stranger, and more like our own experiments, than we care to admit.

Acknowledgements
I wish to thank Jennifer Summit, who introduced me to the wonders of the Devonshire Manuscript. An earlier version of this essay was given as a talk at CCWWP 2012, and I am grateful to the audience of that panel, especially Christian Bök, for insightful comments and questions that helped shape subsequent drafts.

WORKS CITED

Andrews, Chris. "Constraint and Convention: The Formalism of the Oulipo." *Neophilologus* 87 (2003): 224. Print.

Braid, Kate, and Sandy Shreve, eds. *In Fine Form: The Canadian Book of Form Poetry.* Vancouver: Raincoast, 2005. Print.

Campion, Thomas. *Observations in the Art of English Poesie.* London, 1602. Print.

Carlson, David. "The Henrician Courtier Writing in Manuscript and Print (Wyatt, Surrey, Bryan, and Others)." *A Companion to Tudor Literature.* Ed. Kent Cartwright. Chichester: John Wiley & Sons, 2010, 161–62.

Daniel, Samuel. *Defence of Ryme.* London, 1603. Print.

Duncan, Robert. *The Opening of the Field.* New York: New Directions, 1973. Print.

Eisenstein, Elizabeth L. *The Printing Press as an Agent of Change.* 2 vols. Cambridge: Cambridge UP, 1979. Print.

Fumerton, Patricia. *Cultural Aesthetics: Renaissance Literature and the Practice of Social Ornament.* Chicago: University of Chicago Press, 1991.

Heale, Elizabeth. "Women and the Courtly Love Lyric: The Devonshire MS (BL Additional 17492)." *Modern Language Review* 90.2 (April 1995): 296–313. Print.

James, Alison. "Meter, Constraint, Procedure: Some Problems of Form in American and French Poetry" (presented at *La forme et l'informe dans la création moderne et contemporaine,* Cerisy, France, 2009). Web.

Johns, Adrian. *The Nature of the Book: Print and Knowledge in the Making.* Chicago: U of Chicago P, 1998. Print.

Kalas, Rayna. *Frame, Glass, Verse: The Technology of Poetic Invention in the English Renaissance.* Ithaca: Cornell UP, 2007. Print.

Love, Harold, and Arthur Marotti. "Manuscript Transmission and Circulation." *The Cambridge History of Early Modern English Literature.* Ed. David Loewenstein and Janel M. Mueller. Cambridge: Cambridge UP, 2006. Print.

Marotti, Arthur F. *Manuscript, Print, and the English Renaissance Lyric.* Ithaca: Cornell UP, 1995. Print.

Mathews, Harry, and Alastair Brotchie, eds. *Oulipo Compendium.* London and Los Angeles: Atlas, 2005. Print.

Perloff, Marjorie. *Differentials: Poetry, Poetics, Pedagogy.* Tuscaloosa: U of Alabama P, 2004. Print.

————. *Radical Artifice: Writing Poetry in the Age of Media.* Chicago: U of Chicago P, 1991. Print.

Puttenham, George. *The Arte of English Poesie.* London, 1589. Print.

Roubaud, Jacques. "The Oulipo and Combinatorial Art." Reprinted in Mathews and Brotchie, *Oulipo Compendium*, 41.

Smith, Pamela H. *The Body of the Artisan: Art and Experience in the Scientific Revolution.* Chicago and London: U of Chicago P, 2004. Print.

A Social Edition of the Devonshire MS (BL Add 17,492). Wikibooks. Web. 10 Nov. 2013.

Steele, Timothy. "Tradition and Revolution: The Modern Movement and Free Verse." *Twentieth-Century American Poetics: Poets on the Art of Poetry.* Ed. Dana Gioia, David Mason, and Meg Schoerke. New York: McGraw-Hill, 2003. Print.

Wall, Wendy. *The Imprint of Gender: Authorship and Publication in the English Renaissance.* Ithaca and London: Cornell UP, 1993. Print.

Spoken Word:
A Gesture Toward Possibility

Andrea Thompson

We die. That may be the meaning of life.
But we do language. That may be the measure of our lives.
— Toni Morrison, Nobel Lecture, December 7, 1993

In 2011, during my second year studying creative writing through the University of Guelph's MFA, I was assigned a reading that deeply affected the way I thought about spoken word, an art form I had been practising and teaching for close to twenty years. The reading, Toni Morrison's lecture for the 1993 Nobel Prize for Literature, served as an antidote to an incident that occurred during an evening at the program's reading series, when two class-mates openly snickered about the fact that I write poetry that rhymes. Though I had found the program's administration and instructors to be supportive of my performative background, this incident did not completely take me by surprise. While audiences of spoken word have been growing in Canada at an exponential rate, I knew some still viewed the form with suspicion and distain.

Once upon a time. It is these words, spoken aloud, that so often mark the beginning of our experience of literature. Through stories we are initiated into the world of metaphor, language, and symbols used to convey the values, traditions, and history of our society. In this way, oral lore becomes cultural artifact; transitory in its transmission, yet serving as the thread of know-ledge passed from generation to generation. On the day she spoke before the

Swedish Academy, the narrative Morrison chose to share was a folk story of a blind old woman who, in spite of her physical handicap and her station as solitary outsider, had been granted the position of wise elder. Morrison's story begins as a group of children approach the woman, seemingly to test the breadth of her knowledge. They stand before her, telling her that they have a bird in their hand, and posing the question: Is the bird alive or dead?

All stories are an invitation to explore a personal specificity of meaning behind the symbols and narrative presented. The information these stories impart is a facet of our understanding of culture, as well as our understanding of who we are as individuals at our particular stage of development on our life journey. Morrison said that for her, the old woman represented a practised writer, while the bird she viewed as language. Though this key to the story's semiotic meaning serves to clarify Morrison's subsequent interrogation of the uses and abuses of language, we must each view the narrative through the lens of our own perceptions and experiences in order to fully unlock its mysteries. Rather than a metaphor for language in general, for me, Morrison's story reflected the journey of spoken word towards claiming its place in the national canon as oral literature.

Spoken word is enigmatic. An umbrella term that refers to a hybrid genre that includes forms such as performance poetry, dub, jazz, and hip-hop, each branch of spoken word has its own historical lineage. While some spoken word artists use traditional elements of literary verse (or "page poetry," as it is often referred to in the spoken word community), this adherence to poetic norms is not required in order for a spoken word piece to be successful. Many spoken word artists draw inspiration from a different well — blurring the lines between poetry and performance art, theatrical monologue, standup comedy, sermonic rhetoric, and storytelling. Most spoken word artists use a blend of varied influences, creating their own unique aesthetic — the common denominator being that each artist writes and performs pieces that are focused on creating a sense of engagement with an audience through a combination of sound-play, word-play and an unlimited range of other perfomative techniques.

Spoken word is a paradox. While some audiences are just beginning to become acquainted with this dynamic "new" oratory, spoken word is one of our oldest forms of creative expression. A natural evolution of the oral tradition, with an ancestry deeply rooted in pre-print literature, spoken word is as primordial as cave painting. In English literature, it can be traced back past the European troubadours of the eleventh century, to *Beowulf* and the Homeric epics. In other literary traditions the role of spoken word is closely related to the poetic oratory of cultural figures, such as the African griot, or the traditional song, storytelling, and chanting practices of aboriginal people around the world.

In the early nineties, as Morrison joined the ranks of Nobel laureates, the spoken word movement in North America was undergoing a flourishing revival. In the United States, many marked the emergence of oral forms into popular culture as being rooted in a renewed interest in the Beat Poets of the fifties and sixties, and their rejection of the norms of both the literary establishment and society as a whole. Allen Ginsberg commented on the similarity between the Beats and the growing spoken word movement in an article that appeared in a 1995 issue of the *New Yorker*: "This movement is a great thing: the human voice returns, word returns, nimble speech returns, nimble wit and rhyming return."

This growth of spoken word in the United States prompted a similar wave of interest north of the border. Poets such as Black Cat and Jill Battson stirred up the scene in Toronto, while others such as Sheri-D Wilson, Adeena Karasick, and Kedrick James and his performance troupe AWOL Love Vibe lit up West Coast stages with their unique brand of spoken word play. In the book *Impure: Reinventing the Word*, spoken word practitioners Victoria Stanton and Vincent Tinguely document the theory, practice, and oral history of the thriving spoken word scene in Montreal at the time. One of the results of this momentum was the creation of the first Canadian poetry slam in Vancouver. From this lively, weekly performance event organized by James P. McAuliffe and Graham Olds, the first national slam team emerged. The team, consisting of Cass King, Justin McGrail, Alexandra Oliver, and myself travelled to Portland, Oregon, where we reached the semi-finals in the 1996 National Poetry Slam Championships and witnessed a new brand of vibrant spoken word as practised by artists from across North America.

The history of slam in the United States goes back to the mid-eighties, when poet and activist Marc Kelly Smith created the form of competitive performance poetry, as a method to inspire poets to share their work in a way that was engaging, and to integrate the audience into the process of determining literary merit by appointing them as judges. In a 2009 article in the *New York Times*, Smith declared that his intention was to challenge the current literary establishment with a form of poetry that was both democratic and subversive. Slam was, and continues to be, a popular art form with youth and, as such, often represents a microcosm of youth culture. As the thoughts, feelings, and perceptions of its practitioners express a direct reflection of the experiences and preoccupations of their generation, slam pieces often gesture toward themes of disenfranchisement and social justice.

Despite its vibrancy, the spoken word scene of the late nineties lacked self-definition. Many of us called ourselves performance or action poets. Spoken word was just one of the new terminologies used for this form of orature. While the phrase "fusion poetry," first put forth by Todd Swift in 2002 through his anthology *Short Fuse: The Global Anthology of New Fusion Poetry,* successfully captured the hybridity inherent in spoken word, it did not become common terminology. At the time I believed that categorization was essentially irrelevant. Like many spoken word artists of the time, I was more interested in exploring the parameters of the form, as I began to move beyond the staging and time restrictions of slam into experimentation merging poetry with elements of music, theatre, and the new electronic media that were beginning to open up even more doors of possibility.

While the spoken word community continued its creative exploration and self-definition, a palpable rift began to form between those who practised the oral presentation of poetry and those who focused on the written word. Many of us who came to the stage from the page felt pressured to declare allegiance, with spoken word portrayed at best as a cheap trick of theatrics, and at worst a toxin to the body of poetic culture. Through a proclivity toward performance, spoken word artists became literary other and, as the other, many experienced anxieties of marginalization and self-representation as we practised a form viewed by some of our peers to be terminally transgressive.

By 2003, the voices of protest against this new wave of spoken word had moved beyond barely audible grumbling at poetry events to a full frontal attack. Due to the sudden growth and popularity of slam in Canada and around the world, many detractors collapsed spoken word and slam into a single entity, and viewed the entire genre, not as an evolution of oral tradition, but as a substandard poetic, the creation of which was indefensible. Shortly after George Bowering's appointment as the first Canadian Parliamentary Poet Laureate in 2002, a reporter from the *Globe and Mail* asked Bowering if he thought there were any connections between the success of B.C. poets in the award circuit that year and the growing proliferation of spoken word in the province. Bowering replied, "Horseshit," adding that spoken word artists and slams were "abominations" that were "crude and extremely revolting."

This public lambasting of spoken word has not been merely a Canadian phenomenon. Jonathan Galassi, honorary chairman of the Academy of American Poets, referred to poetry slams as "a kind of karaoke of the written word," and literary critic Harold Bloom declared them "the death of art" in the spring 2000 issue of the *Paris Review*. Condescension toward, and positioning of, spoken word artists as inferior has furthered the conceptualization of spoken word artists as literary other, and has also helped to perpetuate the page versus stage dichotomy.

But who does not know of literature banned because it is interrogative; discredited because it is critical; erased because alternate? And how many are outraged by the thought of a self-ravaged tongue?
— Toni Morrison, Nobel Lecture, December 7, 1993

Some artists in the Canadian spoken word community began to volley their own criticism in response, many viewing traditional page poets as out of step with the times. In a 2010 blog post entitled "The Living Language of Spoken Word," poet and activist Chris Gilpin noted, "Each old guard tries to expel the work of the avant-garde before inevitably embracing it," citing early criticism of Ginsberg, and Robert Frost's dismissal of free verse as "playing tennis with the net down," as historical examples. Gilpin goes on to chastise poets, "entangled in academia and its publish-or-perish credo," for creating work "so insular and cryptic, so divorced from broader society that they have alienated a generation from their brand of poetry." South of the border, poet and critic Victor D. Infante stated in an essay in *OC Weekly*, "[The death of art] is a big onus to place on anybody, but Bloom has always had a propensity for (reactionary) generalizations and burying his bigotries beneath 'aesthetics,' insisting — as he did in his prologue to the anthology *Best of the Best of American Poetry* — that the 'art' of poetry is being debased by politics." Infante goes on to say, "The irony, of course, is that denying politics a place in the poetry canon is itself a political position, one undeniably born of class and privilege."

Critics of spoken word on both sides of the border have overlooked the sociopolitical implications of the genre's roots. The impetus for its creation, as well as many of the performative techniques currently used by spoken word artists, is reminiscent of one of the form's precursors, the Black Arts movement of the 1960s, which was based on an imperative to create a representation of the realities of Black people, while unearthing racial inequities in American culture. This manifested itself through an assortment of techniques designed to use art as a vehicle toward the creation of community — where accessibility of language and commonality of cultural reference are reflected in both content and delivery. Didacticism, a dirty word in most contemporary poetry, was openly encouraged as an extension of what Gwendolyn Brooks referred to as "preachment," a sermonic oracular style rooted in the history of Black sermons, gospels, and spirituals. Didacticism also served the purpose of furthering a political agenda. The immediacy of performance was often punctuated by a call-to-action or the use of call-and-response or dialect to further the imperative of audience engagement and accessibility. Idioms, slang, and profanity served to challenge traditional syntax, spelling, and grammar, while representing the rhythmic patterns of Black vernacular.

Rap (most commonly believed to be an acronym for "rhythm and poetry"), dub, and jazz poetry all use the technique of "signifying," the practice of using homonyms to explore the complexity of allusion that arises from the use of common vernacular to imply a deeper meaning, or what Louis Henry Gates calls a "verbal strategy of indirection that exploits the gap between the denotative and figurative meanings of words." In his landmark book *The Signifying Monkey: A Theory of African-American Literary Criticism*, Gates investigates the roots of signifying that go back to the days of slavery and the development of a communally based language that allowed slaves to communicate to each other without their meaning being deciphered by their overlords. Gates summarizes the confluence of these sorts of historically based speech patterns with the evolution of its speaker's literary aesthetic by stating, "A vernacular tradition's relation to a formal literary tradition is that of a parallel discursive universe." As Modernist poets of the early twentieth century experimented with fragmentation and a desire to, in Ezra Pound's phrase, "make it new" rather than emulate traditional forms, the poets and writers of the Harlem Renaissance were creating a written aesthetic that strove to bring the traditions of the past forward. In his book *Afro-American Poetics: Revisions of Harlem and the Black Aesthetic*, Houston A. Baker calls this impulse Afro-American Modernism, which "was concerned pre-eminently with removing the majority of the black population from the poverty, illiteracy and degradation that marked southern, black, agrarian existence in the United States.... Rather than bashing the bourgeoisie, such spokespersons were attempting to create one."

While the influence of Afro-American literature on spoken word is significant, it is only one of the streams feeding the form. Contemporary spoken word in Canada has also been influenced by poetry that emerged in of the sixties, seventies, and eighties: the experimental poetry of bill bissett and the Four Horsemen (bpNichol, Paul Dutton, Rafael Barreto-Rivera, and Steve McCaffrey), De Dub Poets (Lillian Allen, Clifton Joseph, and Devon Haughton), and the Tish collective (which included Frank Davey, Daphne Marlatt, Fred Wah, and others). In *From Cohen to Carson: The Poet's Novel in Canada*, Ian Rae tells us that the name of this groundbreaking group came about as a playful reference to an anagram for "shit," adding that "the scatological connotations of *Tish* underscore the collective's anti-establishment irreverence." Ironically, George Bowering was a key member of this radical youth movement, disenchanted with the current state of Canadian poetics and driven by a desire to move beyond the conventional parameters of the literary establishment.

✎ ⌨ ☼

> You trivialize us and trivialize the bird that is not in our hands. Is there no context for our lives? No song, no literature, no poem full of vitamins, no history connected to experience that you can pass along to help us start strong?
> — Toni Morrison, Nobel Lecture, December 7, 1993

Spoken word is a hybrid animal and, as such, must be evaluated in terms of the particularities and genealogy inherent in the dialect of spoken word being experienced. Some pieces clearly emphasize theatricality, musicality, comedy, or sermonality. Each spoken word practitioner is attempting to master their own language, their own unique expression of the creative influences that inspire them. Judging spoken word on its use or misuse of traditional poetic devices is as useful as judging a poem printed on the page based on its ability to explore the full range of performative possibilities. One cannot judge a page poem for its lack of audience engagement; neither can one judge a spoken word piece by its ability to survive and thrive within the confines of the printed page. The concept of an oral literature that is different yet equal was encapsulated by Ugandan linguist Pio Zirimu in the early seventies when he coined the term "orature" in response to the growing sentiment in African literature that the oral traditions were inferior, less evolved forms than their printed counterparts.

As the controversy over the legitimacy of spoken word as a literary form continued, most artists practising under the auspices of this incarnation of oral tradition moved on from the debate. No longer children at the feet of their elders, begging for validation, spoken word artists moved the genre forward on their own terms. Over the last two decades, Canadian scholars such as Corey Frost and T.L. Cowan have conducted extensive research in the area of spoken word as part of their graduate theses. In addition, spoken word artists have taken their work into the areas of community building and youth engagement, using the form as a tool for empowerment and the development of literacy skills. Spoken word artists are often invited to perform and speak at community centres, libraries, literary festivals, high schools and post-secondary institutions across the country, and spoken word components have been a part of several university creative writing courses for years.

In 2010, spoken word artist Brendan McLeod began teaching the form at Langara College — opening the way for spoken word to be taught at a post-secondary level. Yet the genre remains marginalized, with only a few designated credit courses on spoken word theory, history, or practice currently offered at Canadian universities. Lillian Allen, who teaches a fourth-year Dub, Spoken Word, and Performance Writing course at the Ontario College of Art and Design University, states that one of the problems in academic circles is that spoken word seems like too much fun to be taken seriously. "Spoken word artists also have an unapologetic appreciation of media and multimedia technologies, and the methods they afford to further creative expression," she says. "The book isn't quite dead, but it's no longer the only train leaving the station." Allen also sees the dichotomy created between the stage and page communities as artificial. "It's a spectrum," Allen states, adding that the need for people to reduce the issue to a polarity is due to the urge to categorize, define, and marginalize what they don't understand or perceive to be "other."

It is this literary marginalization that Morrison alluded to in her Nobel lecture. In the book *What Moves at the Margin: Selected Nonfiction,* Toni Morrison and Carolyn C. Denard elaborate on the motives of the children in the tale Morrison shared. They were not attempting to humiliate the old woman; rather they were offering her an invitation to impart some of her wisdom — an invitation that Morrison refers to as "a gesture toward possibility." The silence the old woman offers in response is indicative of neither indifference nor condemnation: it is offered as a sign of respect, and a willingness to learn and listen. "It's quiet again when the children finish speaking, until the woman breaks into the silence. 'Finally,' she says, 'I trust you now. I trust you with the bird that is not in your hands because you have truly caught it. Look. How lovely it is, this thing we have done — together.'"

Perhaps the best strategy to bridge the gap between spoken word artists and the literary establishment is to aim for mutual appreciation and respect through creating events that provide the opportunity for cross-pollination. Through both his Mashed Poetics series and his role as organizer for the Vancouver slam, veteran spoken word artist RC Weslowski has included writers from outside the spoken word community in his programming for years, as has Warren Dean Fulton with his series, Twisted Poets. In Toronto, the ArtBar (the longest-running literary series in the country) regularly features a mix of page and stage writers, and the Toronto Poetry Slam has showcased literary writers such as George Elliott Clarke (who featured at the slam shortly after his appointment as Toronto Poet Laureate).

After reading Toni Morrison's Nobel lecture, I was inspired to find that Morrison also had a history with slam, when in 2006 she organized a performance event in Paris while serving as guest curator at the Louvre. This event centred on the theme of "The Foreigner's Home" and investigated the concepts of identity, exile, and belonging. Moved to action by the anger and alienation felt by youth in Parisian suburbs, which had sparked violent rioting in the predominantly working class immigrant communities that live there, Morrison wanted to give the youth a venue for free creative expression.

In an interview in *Libération*, Morrison stated that "from my experience in the United States, I know that the music of outsiders, those who are discriminated against, have historically become very powerful.... I have come here to listen to the young people; it is not for me to tell them anything."

Spoken word artists are the town criers of the world: our subject matter is as old as human emotion and as new as the most current regional and global events. The national spoken word scene in Canada has blossomed from coast to coast. From Calgary, home of Canada's first International Spoken Word Festival and the Banff Centre of the Arts Spoken Word residency program, to Montreal, where innovative artists like Cat Kidd and Alexis O'Hara are pushing multimedia performance into realms reminiscent of eighties Laurie Anderson, and musical fusion performances by Ian Ferrier, the Kalmunity Vibe Collective, or Les Filles Electriques, artists are redefining the parameters of the genre. On the East Coast, Shauntay Grant, El Jones, and the Word Iz Bond collective continue to create work that inspires, ignites, and reflects Halifax's complex social climate. Nationally, the slam scene has grown from its roots in Vancouver to a flourishing movement, with over thirty regional venues (including four youth slams) in cities across Canada. Spoken word is and will always be the voice of the people, rooted in community at a grassroots level. Each year, spoken word events across the country draw crowds in the hundreds, who come in order to listen to a form of orature that is both old and new, and fed by a variety of cultural and artistic streams. At its heart, spoken word is a fluid, ever-evolving form of guerilla literature, a verbal transmission of culture — from performer to audience — word by word.

WORKS CITED

Morrison, Toni. "Toni Morrison — Nobel Lecture." *Nobelprize.org.* Nobel Media, 7 Dec. 1993. Web.

Two Dots Over a Vowel

Christian Bök

THE INTENTIONAL IN CONCEPTUAL LITERATURE

Modern social trends in computing (as seen, for example, in digitized sampling and networked exchange) have so thoroughly ensconced piracy and parody as sovereign aesthetic values that not only do the economic edifices of copyright seem ready to collapse, but so do the romantic bastions of both sublime creativity and eminent authorship seem ready to dissolve into a morass of protoplasmic textualities, all manufactured at a prodigious, industrial scale by means of plagiaristic appropriation and computerized recombination. Varied pupils of the avant-garde at the listserv UbuWeb (including, among others, Derek Beaulieu, Craig Dworkin, Robert Fitterman, Kenneth Goldsmith, Simon Morris, Nick Thurston, Darren Wershler, and I) have all striven to respond to these trends by conceiving of an innovative literature that, for lack of an apter title, critics have seen fit to dub "conceptual." Such poets disavow the lyrical mandate of self-conscious self-assertion in order to explore the ready-made potential of uncreative literature. They resort to a diverse variety of anti-expressive, anti-discursive strategies (including the use of forced rules, random words, copied texts, boring ideas, and even cyborg tools), doing so in order to erase any artistic evidence of "lyric style."

Works by members of UbuWeb have often confronted the intentionality, if not the expressiveness, of such lyric style by offering alternatives to this normative condition of writing — alternatives inspired by such variegated precedents as the formalist writing of Perec, the aleatoric writing of Cage, the readymade artwork of Warhol, and the axiomatic artwork of LeWitt, among the work of many other writers and artists, all of whom have suppressed their subjective experience on behalf of otherwise demeaned concepts of literary activity. Poets who write conceptual literature often parody the principles of sublime egotism. Such writers might observe the self and examine the self, but they do so with such exactitude and with such detachment that the act of reportage itself borders upon a kind of fanatical obsession. Such writers might in turn generate unscripted recordings of the self, speaking, verbatim, in a kind of stream-of-consciousness, improvising without editorial revisions. Such writers might also go so far as to generate exhaustive structures for the self, pushing the fulfillment of formal rigour to the most athletic extremes. Such writers might even delegate their creativity to a diverse variety of prostheses, all of which might compose work without intervention from the self at all.

Works of conceptual literature have primarily responded to the historical precedents set by two disparate movements in the avant-garde: first, the systematic writing of Oulipian pataphysicians (like Queneau, Roubaud, et al.); second, the procedural artwork of American conceptualists (like Kosuth, Huebler, et al.) — precedents that, in both cases, reduce creativity to a tautological array of preconceived rules, whose logic culminates, not in the mandatory creation of a concrete object, but in the potential argument for some abstract schema. Ideas that we conceive for works now become systemic "axioms," and the works that we generate from these ideas now become elective "proofs." The concept for the artwork now absorbs the quality of the artwork itself. The idea for a work supplants the work. The idea renders the genesis of the work optional, if not needless. For the proponents of conceptual literature, a writer no longer cultivates any subjective readerships by writing a text to be read, so much as the writer cultivates a collective "thinkership"* — an audience that no longer even has to read the text itself in order to appreciate the importance of its innovation. The text no longer begs to be read clearly for the quality of its content, but rather begs to be seen blankly for the novelty of its concept.

Works of conceptual literature constitute what Dworkin might call "the writing of the new new formalism," insofar as such literature imposes

---

* Kenneth Goldsmith has remarked that "conceptual writing is ... interested in a *thinkership* rather than a readership," and for him, "conceptual writing is good only when the idea is good; often, the idea is much more interesting than the resultant texts" ("Conceptual Poetics").

arbitrary, but axiomatic, dicta upon the writing process, doing so in order to extract an otherwise unthought potential from this structural constraint. The self-conscious attention paid by a lyrical poet to the life of the self now gives way to the self-reflexive attention paid by a radical text to the form of its idea. All aspects of both intentionality and expressiveness now find themselves governed, not by the whim of a poet, but by the rule of a game — a "language-game," like the kind discussed by Wittgenstein, who argues that, when playing such a game, "we look to the rule for instruction and *do something*, without appealing to anything else for guidance" (86e, 228). The poet subordinates all subjectivity to this rule, replacing an act of volitive expression with an act of negative capability. The poet constrains the cognitive functions of the self on behalf of other aesthetic functions in the text (be these functions automatic, mannerist, or even aleatoric). The poet thereby expands the concept of writing beyond the formal limits of any expressive intentions, doing so in order to conceive of hitherto inconceivable preconditions for writing itself.

Since the reign of the New Critics (like Wimsatt and Beardsley, for example), the values of both intentionality and expressiveness have come to represent recurrent "fallacies"* of aesthetic judgment — fallacies that have served to ignore the traits of the poem itself in order to attach the merits of the work to the genius of a self. When judging a work, based upon its intentionality, the critic evaluates the emotional "origins" of the work in the mind of the writer, doing so by asking: "How successful are the lyrical motives of the poem — and does the poet exert an authentic control over the self?" When judging a work for its expressiveness, however, the critic evaluates the emotional "results" in the mind of the reader, doing so by asking: "How persuasive are the lyrical effects of the poem — and does the poet voice an authentic message from the self?" No poem can easily answer such questions on its own — and thus critics have since sought to detach the merits of the text from the genius of the self, doing so in order to account, not only for the work's autotelic coherence,

---

* W.K. Wimsatt and Monroe C. Beardsley discuss the "intentional fallacy" in the discourse of literature by arguing that "intention of the author is neither available nor desirable as a standard for judging the success of a work" (3), because "the poem ... is detached from the author at birth and goes about the world beyond his power to intend about it" (5). Likewise, Hal Foster studies the "expressive fallacy" in the discourse of aesthetics by arguing that "even as expressionism insists on the ... interior self, it reveals that this self is never anterior to its traces," and thus "'the artist' is less the originator of his expression than its effect" — a condition that such expression both reveals and rejects (62).

but also for the work's technical innovation. No longer is the author an actual person who might precede a text and certify its aims so much as a "function"* — operant, as a concept, through each reading of the text.

Poets who have produced conceptual literature have replaced the expressive intentions of such a self with a whole array of apparently impossible poetic values, arguing for the viability of work that skeptics might dismiss as uncreative, unoriginal, unengaging, unreadable, uninspired, uneventful.... Even though a poet like Kenneth Goldsmith, for example, might describe his own acts of poetic tedium as nothing more than a banal brand of data management or word processing,** in which the poet becomes a kind of monk, doomed to recopy only the most leaden genres of boring speech in some nightmarish scriptorium; such work, nevertheless, still creates surprise and engages interest. Lest we dismiss these tactics of Goldsmith as nothing more than the mere symptoms of a creeping, literary necrosis, occasioned by the murder of the author at the hands of such postmodern theorizers as Barthes, for example, or perhaps Foucault*** — let us consider that conceptual literature might strive to accent the disjunction between intentionality (*what we mean to mean*) and expressiveness (*what we seem to mean*). If the lyric voice, for the sake of an authentic sincerity, yearns to repair this breach between what we intend to say and what we appear to say — then conceptual literature, by contrast, accentuates this discrepancy.

THE CONCEIVABLE IN CONCEPTUAL LITERATURE

What if both intentionality and expressiveness do not represent "fallacies" of formalist criticism, but instead represent the vectors for specific concepts of writing? The lyric style, for example, might thus be what I call "cognitive" in

---

* Michel Foucault notes that, among its many traits, the "'author-function' ... does not refer, purely and simply, to an ... individual insofar as it simultaneously gives rise to a ... series of subjective positions that individuals of any class may come to occupy" (131) — and in fact, "we can easily imagine a culture where discourse would circulate without any need for an author" (138).

** Goldsmith notes, "I am a word processor.... The simple act of moving information from one place to another today constitutes a significant cultural act" ("A Week of Blogs" 143–44).

*** Roland Barthes notes that "the removal of the Author ... utterly transforms the modern text ... or — which is the same thing — the text is henceforth ... read so that the author absents himself from it at every level" (51–52). Michel Foucault also notes that "to know the writer in our day, it will be through the singularity of his absence and in his link to death, which has transformed him into a victim of his own writing" (117).

its aesthetics, insofar as it demands that the author be both self-conscious and self-assertive at the same time — but other relationships between intentionality and expressiveness might also be conceivable, and the poet who must "think up" novel modes of conceptual literature does so by rethinking other less studied, if not less exalted, relationships between self-consciousness and self-assertiveness.* When teaching poetry to my students, I strive to convey the diverse variety of aesthetic attitudes that can define the value of a given style — and I usually begin by asking questions about what kind of game a student might wish to play. I argue that, if we accept that all poetry involves both an attitude toward intentionality (i.e., the act of needing to tell) and an attitude toward expressiveness (i.e., the act of telling a need), then there are only four ways to play the game of poetry itself: cognitive, automatic, mannerist, and aleatoric. I believe that such a "quadrivium" defines the limit-cases for all the ways of conceiving both intentionality and expressiveness together.

A. Cognitive Writing

Works that embody as values both intentionality and expressiveness I might describe as "cognitive." These works aspire to be both self-conscious and self-assertive. Their authors profess to exert control over both what they "will" in the text and what they "tell" in the text. They do so in order to minimize any discrepancy between what the self might intend and what the text might convey. Such authors embrace both voluntary self-control and voluntary self-exhibit. We might, of course, recognize this "cognitive" impulse, for example, in the tradition of Romantic lyricism, which has come to represent the style of writing aligned with autobiographic investigations like the kind seen in *The Prelude* by Wordsworth. We see this impulse at work in poetic

---

* We wish to emphasize, of course, that despite the professed attitudes of any author about being either self-conscious or self-assertive during the process of writing, authors can never exert perfect control over what they will and what they tell — and indeed, critics nowadays spend much of their time "deconstructing" the disparity between what the author means to say and what the author seems to say, showing the degree to which the self reveals more about itself than it might, otherwise, claim to show or deign to hide. We do not wish to repeat "fallacies" of either intentionality or expressiveness in our own discussion, but we do want to show that, during the process of writing, authors can only ever choose from among a limited variety of vantages about their own self-consciousness and their own self-assertiveness — and in turn, these vantages make available to the author only a limited variety of possible concepts about the very process of writing itself.

genres as diverse as the imagistic poetry of William Carlos Williams and the divulgate poetry of Elizabeth Bishop — poets who strive to articulate themselves in a plainer, sincere form, equal to the tranquil emotions of retrospection. An author adopts a lyrical persona to represent the subjective experience of the self, and the reader in turn judges this persona for the mimetic realism of both its originary being and its authentic voice. We witness the self thinking to itself, alone and aloud, about itself, bearing witness to the intimacy, if not to the quietude, of its own thoughtful confession.

B. Automatic Writing

Works that embody as values less intentionality and more expressiveness I might describe as "automatic." These works aspire not to be self-conscious but to be self-assertive. Their authors profess to exert control, not over what they "will" in the text, but only over what they "tell" in the text. They do so in order to maximize what the text might convey at the expense of what the self might intend. Such authors forfeit voluntary self-control, but embrace potential self-exhibit. We might recognize this automatic impulse, for example, in the kind of Surrealist outpouring that has come to represent the style of writing aligned with graphomaniacal psychoneurosis, like the kind seen in *The Immaculate Perception* by André Breton. We see this impulse at work in poetic genres as diverse as the rhapsodic liturgies of Kurt Schwitters and the rapturous diatribes of Allen Ginsberg — poets who strive to articulate themselves in a complex, baroque form, equal to the ecstatic feelings of deliriousness. An author avoids conscious, editorial censorship of the self in order to give vent to an unexpurgated stream-of-consciousness, and the reader merely judges the quality of vertigo in this flow. We witness the self speaking to itself without thinking about itself, bearing witness to the outburst of its own irrational exuberance.

C. Mannerist Writing

Works that embody as values more intentionality and less expressiveness I might describe as "mannerist." These works aspire to be self-conscious, but not to be self-assertive. Their authors profess to exert control over what they "will" in the text, but not over what they "tell" in the text. They do so in order to maximize what the self might intend at the expense of what the text might convey. Such authors embrace potential self-control, but forfeit voluntary self-exhibit. We might recognize this "mannerist" impulse, for example, in the kind of Oulipian elegance that has come to represent the style of writing aligned with formalistic constraints like the kind seen in *A Hundred Thousand Billion Poems* by Raymond Queneau. We see this impulse at work in poetic genres as diverse as the programmatic alexandrines of Raymond Roussel and the anagrammatic translations of Unica Zürn — poets who strive to articulate structures in a precise, orderly form, equal to the rational precepts of scientificity. An author wilfully enslaves the self to a rule in order to excavate a newfound liberty from such a test of will, and the reader merely judges the quality of triumph in these results. We witness the self as it subordinates its own subjectivity to a rigorous procedure, thereby bearing witness to the outcome of a formalized experiment.

D. Aleatoric Writing

Works that embody as values no intentionality and no expressiveness I might describe as "aleatoric." These works are neither self-conscious nor self-assertive. Their authors profess to forfeit control, both over what they "will" in the text and over what they "tell" in the text, doing so in order to maximize the discrepancy between what the self might intend and what the text might convey. Such authors forfeit both voluntary self-control and voluntary self-exhibit. We might recognize this "aleatoric" impulse, for example, in the kind of Dadaist anarchy that has come to represent the legacy of Tristan Tzara and his *poésie découpé*. We see this impulse at work in poetic genres as diverse as the "mesostics" by John Cage and the "asymmetries" by Mac Low — poets who strive to articulate structures in an uncanny, vagrant form, equal to the oracular surprise of synchronicity. An author delegates authorship to the otherness of chance (often doing so through the replicated pretexts of readymade poetry, the randomized cuttings of respliced poetry, or the programmed machines of googlized poetry), and a reader, in turn, judges the uncanniness of these results. We witness the self as it subordinates its subjectivity to an arbitrary procedure, thereby bearing witness to the outcome of a stochastic experiment.

Cognitive, automatic, mannerist, aleatoric — this "quadrivium" of literature exhausts every means of permuting the relationship between intentionality and expressiveness. Each relationship constitutes a "language-game"
subject to its own rules of engagement — and hence we might consider
the degree to which these games might in fact conform to the celebrated
categories first conceived by the poet Roger Caillois, who classifies games
according to four sets: *mimesis* (games of mimicry), *ilinx* (games of vertigo), *agon* (games of prowess), and *alea* (games of fortune).* Cognitive
writing (with its demand for a realistic depiction of subjective experience)
might thus be a game of *mimesis*; automatic writing (with its demand for a
delirious depiction of subjective experience) might thus be a game of *ilinx*;
mannerist writing (with its demand for a virtuosic overthrow of a procedural constraint) might thus be a game of *agon*; and aleatoric writing (with
its demand for a receptive deference to all stochastic exigencies) might
thus be a game of *alea*. If conceptual literature has already explored each
concept of writing beyond the "cognitive," perhaps such literature must
now imagine unthought varieties of writing beyond these four categories
in order to imagine a new way of "playing" at literature.

Michel Foucault notes that "writing unfolds like a game that inevitably moves beyond its own rules and finally leaves them behind" (116).
My four concepts of writing itemize all ways of permuting intentionality
and expressiveness. The two categories of expressive writing ("cognitive" and
"automatic") constitute the domain of, what I might call, a "Wordsworthian
subjectivity," concerned with the sublime affirmation of a self on behalf of
some poetic "identity," whereas the two concepts of non-expressive writing
("mannerist" and "aleatoric") constitute the domain of, what I might call, a
"Keatsian subjectivity," concerned with the extreme sublimation of a self on
behalf of some poetic "alterity." The avant-garde has colonized three of these
four domains (the "automatic," the "mannerist," and the "aleatoric") —
and while any poet might traverse all four with ease, playing with multiple

---

* Caillois notes, "I am proposing a division into four main rubrics, depending upon whether,
in the games under consideration, the role of competition, chance, simulation, or vertigo is
dominant," and hence, "I call these *agon, alea, mimicry,* and *ilinx*" (12).

concepts of writing, switching from one to another, perhaps even doing so within the same work, no poet can play in more than one domain at the same time. I suggest that, ultimately, poets who write conceptual literature must now begin to probe the limit-cases of this "quadrivium" in the hope of imagining more neoteric concepts of writing situated elsewhere, far beyond this potential playfield.

TABLE OF CONCEPTS FOR WRITING

COGNITIVE

INTENTIONAL

EXPRESSIVE

(poetic game of mimicry)

MANNERIST

INTENTIONAL

NON-EXPRESSIVE

(poetic game of prowess)

AUTOMATIC

NON-INTENTIONAL

EXPRESSIVE

(poetic game of vertigo)

ALEATORIC

NON-INTENTIONAL

NON-EXPRESSIVE

(poetic game of fortune)

WORKS CITED

Barthes, Roland. "The Death of the Author." *The Rustle of Language*. Trans. Richard Howard. New York: Farrar, Straus, and Giroux, 1986. 49–55. Print.

Caillois, Roger. *Man, Play and Games*. Trans. Meyer Barash. New York: Free Press of Glencoe, 1958. Print.

Dworkin, Craig. *The UbuWeb Anthology of Conceptual Writing*. 2003–. Web.

Foster, Hal. "The Expressive Fallacy." *Recodings: Art, Spectacle, Cultural Politics*. Port Townsend: Bay Press, 1985. 59–77. Print.

Foucault, Michel. "What Is an Author?" *Language, Counter-Memory, Practice: Selected Essays and Interviews*. Ed. Donald F. Bouchard. Trans. Donald F. Bouchard and Sherry Simon. Ithaca, N.Y.: Cornell UP, 1977. 113–38. Print.

Goldsmith, Kenneth. "Conceptual Poetics: Kenneth Goldsmith." *Harriet*. Poetry Foundation, 9 Jun. 2008. Web.

———. "A Week of Blogs for the Poetry Foundation." *The Consequence of Innovation: 21st-Century Poetics*. Ed. Craig Dworkin. New York: Roof, 2008. 137–49. Print.

Wimsatt, W.K., and Monroe C. Beardsley. "The Intentional Fallacy." *The Verbal Icon: Studies in the Meaning of Poetry*. Lexington: U of Kentucky P, 1954. 3–18. Print.

Wittgenstein, Ludwig. *Philosophical Investigations*. Trans. G.E.M. Anscombe. Oxford: Basil Blackwell and Mott, 1974. Print.

Bastards, Pirates, and Halfbreeds: Playwriting in Canada

Yvette Nolan

In the twenty-five years that I have been writing plays, I have been invited to participate in dozens of conferences, symposia, panels, and gatherings. Usually, I am the only playwright. For many years, organizers did not quite know what to do with me. Playwrights are the bastard children of letters; the thing we do is not quite literature, most people never read a play, many people do not know how to read a play. Most plays are never published, because the thing that playwrights do exists in the air, in the mouths of actors. Production is more important than publication, and very few plays get published until they have been produced. In 2011, only 39 plays were submitted for consideration for the Governor General's Literary Awards in Drama, as opposed to 238 books of fiction and 170 books of poetry. One doesn't even have to be literate to receive a play: for millennia, plays have been used to teach, to educate, to edify, to illuminate the often unwashed, uneducated, illiterate masses.

In 1981 we battled our way into the Governor General Literary Awards, forty-five years after they had been established. Drama was eligible before that in the category of Poetry or Drama, which I suspect really irritated the poets, even though the playwrights never won. The closest we came to victory was in 1962, when James Reaney's *Twelve Letters to a Small Town and The Killdeer and Other Plays* took the prize, but I suspect the drama snuck in under cover of the poetry of *Twelve Letters*. And while there is no shame in being beat out by Leonard Cohen, Michael Ondaatje, Milton Acorn, Gwendolyn MacEwen, Dorothy Livesay, Earle Birney, Margaret Atwood, P.K. Page, Irving Layton, Al Purdy, and Alden Nowlan, the category was never a particularly good fit. We all know what poetry is, and yet it is hard to define. An assemblage of words that evokes an emotion, a rhythmic composition, an art form that elevates human expression … As I once heard the brilliant poet Ken Babstock say, *extempore*, "Who is able to say that this column of words is approaching the state of being a poem?" Drama shares some things with poetry — an economy of words, for instance — but really, plays are about voice.

I am the daughter of two people who understood the power of words. My mother was a polyglot: her first language was Algonquin, her second French, her third English. One of the reasons she survived residential school was because her command of French made her a favourite of the nuns, a French order. My father was an immigrant from Ireland who had won a medal for being the best speaker of Irish when he was in high school. Both of them knew the power of mastering English, which was, for both of them, the oppressors' tongue.

I became a playwright by accident. I loved the theatre, had always loved the dressing up and imagining a better or more exciting or more dangerous life. Seeing into other people's lives, walking in someone else's shoes for a short time. I was a theatre rat, making props, hanging lights, coordinating costumes, anything to keep me working near or around the theatre. I thought I wanted to be an actor, but an actor does not have very much control over what she gets to say. Working as an administrator at the inaugural Winnipeg Fringe Festival in 1988, I watched a lot of plays, and thought, *Surely I can do better than that.* I have been trying ever since.

I wrote my first play at my computer after hours at the Winnipeg Fringe Festival. *Blade* is the story of a young woman killed by a man who was killing prostitutes and was thereby transformed into a prostitute by the media. The story was inspired by events at that time in Winnipeg, and although the murder and disappearance of young Aboriginal women is now so common as to have its own shorthand — "missing and murdered women" — in 1990, the world had yet to recognize a pattern. Canadians had yet to meet Robert Pickton or hear the term Highway of Tears. My heroine, Angela, got to speak her truth after her death, and in speaking her truth, called into question the "facts" about all the young women killed before her. Angela, a young, white university student, gave voice to the young Native women who had been silenced in life and in death.

I produced the play in the 1990 Fringe Festival, and the response was immediate and transformative. I was twenty-nine years old and I had discovered the power of giving voice.

From 2003 until 2011 I served as the artistic director of Native Earth Performing Arts in Toronto, where I had the opportunity to read hundreds of plays by Indigenous artists, and the power to produce a few of those every year. The Native scripts that compelled me were the ones that gave voice to individuals who had been marginalized and who had disappeared. The first major work I chose to produce was Marie Clements's epic *The Unnatural and Accidental Women*, which she wrote in reaction to "the Boozing Barber," Gilbert Paul Jordan, who for decades stalked Native women on Vancouver's Downtown Eastside, paying them to drink with him. After the women passed out, he continued to pour booze down their throats. The women's impossibly high alcohol levels lead the coroner to deem their deaths "unnatural and accidental." Jordan was linked to the deaths of at least ten women, but was only ever convicted of manslaughter, for the death of one of his few non-Native victims.

Struck by the fact that the media coverage was all about Jordan, with very little written about the women he victimized, Marie gave the women voice in her play. The audience gets to see a little of the lives of these women whose deaths did not even arouse curiosity in the public. Throughout the first act, we are introduced to the women, we see them battle demons of loneliness, poverty, and addiction. We learn their names, that they had children, and lovers, and friends. At the end of the act, the women who have been hunted and felled by the Barber are summoned by the formidable Aunt Shadie:

> Aunt Shadie calls to them in song, and they respond, in song, in rounds of their original language.

> The women in the Barbershop call to each fallen woman, in each solitary room. The women respond and join them in song and ritual as they gather their voice, language and selves in the barbershop.

Throughout, the song floats in and out of each scene, sub-merging under some, and taking over others, flowing like a river. Each call and response a current. It grows in strength and intensity to the end of Act One where all their voices join force.

Aunt Shadie
Do I hear you sister like yesterday today
Ke-peh-tat-in/jee/ne-gee-metch
Das-goots/o-tahg-gos-ehk
Ahnotes/ka-kee-se-khak (57–58)

The women, once victims, are resurrected, gathered into a community, and given voice.

The playwright Erik Ehn once said that theatre was "uncovering the dead and constructing a history for a community." If there is a people whose history has been buried, it is the first people of this land, so it is no wonder that there are so many plays that work to unearth those hidden histories and make them visible for the population. Marie Clements, Daniel David Moses, Melanie J. Murray, and Turtle Gals Performance Ensemble have all dragged our stories onto the stage and illuminated them for our consideration. They are often uncomfortable stories, stories that challenge the viewer's notion of who they are as Canadians. But if, as the *New Yorker* theatre critic John Lahr has posited, "the most profound function of theatre is to disenchant the citizen from the spell of received opinion," much of the work of First Nations playwrights in the past decade has sought to shake Canadian citizens from their comfortable assumptions about their nation: that its people are polite and tolerant people, its society a just society, that all who live within its borders can achieve equality and prosperity.

Marie Clements gave voice to the missing and murdered women in *The Unnatural and Accidental Women* and *The Road Forward*, and in *Burning Vision* literally unearthed the history of uranium mining and its effects on the Indigenous communities in northern Canada from where the uranium was first dug up, to the impact it had as it was dropped on Hiroshima and Nagasaki. Her *Tombs of the Vanishing Indian* begins in the tunnels under-neath Los Angeles, where a mother is killed trying to keep her daughters with her, the shot propelling each of the three young women into very different journeys, each a possible outcome for a seized Native child, none completely successful or whole, because of the lack of roots.

Daniel David Moses's seminal play *Almighty Voice and His Wife* offered audiences several ways of looking at the history of Canada. The first act is a deceptively simple rendering of the courtship and marriage of the Cree warrior Almighty Voice and his wife, White Girl, so named because of her time spent in residential school where she learned to fear the white god. The marriage leads to the death by cop of Almighty Voice, who had killed a cow for his wedding feast, making him a fugitive. The act ends with Almighty Voice's death at the hands of the Northwest Mounted Police and their big cannon.

The second act is vaudeville, enacted in whiteface, in an abandoned industrial school a hundred years later. White Girl is now the Interlocutor and the Master of Ceremonies in a macabre minstrel show, in which she demands that the Ghost re-enact his death for the entertainment of the gentle audience, who want to be titillated by stories of savages, from the safety of their seats: "These fine, kind folks want to know the truth, the amazing details and circumstance behind your savagely beautiful appearance. They also want to be entertained and enlightened, and maybe a tiny bit thrilled, just a goose of frightened" (31).

Almighty Voice's story and White Girl's identity have been buried by the tools of colonization — the Church and the residential school system — and the narrative imposed by the dominant culture, of savages who once roamed this land, but have disappeared, except on the stages (and screens) where they are allowed and even encouraged to perform their Indian-ness. This performance invites audience members to both recognize their own role in the making of the stereotype, and to participate in the dismantling of it. As the players wipe the whiteface off their faces in the final moments of the play, exposing the authentic Aboriginal person underneath, the audience has the opportunity to consider their own response to the representations of First Nations that they are offered on a daily basis.

There is little comfortable about "disenchant[ing] the citizen from the spell of received opinion." People often prefer to remain under spells, to believe that they are powerless, and therefore not responsible for any number of things: missing and murdered women, the death of a Cree warrior, a people who live on the margins of society. The playwright who suggests otherwise, that the individual has power, can make a difference, who shows how we are all connected, wakes the sleeping at his or her peril.

Playwriting can be a dangerous business. Ask Christopher Marlowe, who wrote plays about revenge and ambition and massacres, who was suspected of being a spy, and was stabbed to death in an argument over the reckoning — the bar bill. Ask Ken Saro-Wiwa, the Nigerian playwright whose battle with Shell over the Ogoni homelands led to his hanging. Vaclav Havel, whose plays got him banned from the theatre, which in turn provoked him to make more plays, which transformed him into the former Czechoslovakia's leading dissident. Here, in polite and comfortable Canada, Michael Healey's *Proud*, a satirical play about a prime minister, cleverly named Prime Minister, was not banned from Tarragon Theatre, where Healey had been playwright-in-residence for eleven years, but rather it was just not going to be produced, allegedly because members of the theatre feared legal repercussions from the Conservative government.

Plays are — can be — dangerous. They are powerful because they say things into the air, and the very act of saying things into the air can make them so. Plays can make people mad. The only death threat I have ever received was over comments I made about a play, not even my own damn play, but David Mamet's *Oleanna*. The play is about a university student who accuses her professor of sexual harassment, thereby ruining his chance at tenure. I had written to the artistic director of a theatre that was producing the play, expressing my opinion that the play was a backlash play, weighted unfairly against women and feminism, and every production inevitably ended with audience members yelling "Kill the bitch!" at the stage. The artistic director responded publicly in a daily newspaper, using my discomfort to illustrate the relevance and impact of theatre. He suggested his *Oleanna* would be a balanced and fair examination of power, and the final line in the article was his assertion, "I think this will be an *Oleanna* that even Yvette Nolan can approve of." I took the bait, agreeing to do a post-show panel with three others — a journalist, a feminist academic, and someone else — but the night before the panel, I received the death threat. The theatre was forced to pepper the audience with undercover security in order to proceed. Dangerous stuff.

When I was in university I had a lover whose mother hated me because I was a "halfbreed." I never met her, but the lover told me that his mother thought of a halfbreed as a kind of pirate, someone "with a knife in her teeth, climbing up the ropes of a ship." This was not the first time in my life someone's mother didn't like me because I was a halfbreed; my friend Robert Klein in grade school was not allowed to consort with me for the same reason. This image has stuck with me for twenty-five years, and to a certain extent informed the way I engage with the world. Putting it into the air makes it so.

My status as a halfbreed, a formerly derogatory term that Maria Campbell reclaimed for us with her 1973 memoir, conferred upon me a gift of unbelonging. Not white enough for my friend Rob's family, or my former lover's mother, never quite Native enough to represent First Nations issues, told that I didn't "need to do that — that Indian thing," because I could "pass," I found myself just outside enough to have some perspective on my communities.

The pirate is a great image for a playwright, who is so often the outsider, rarely welcomed in the hallowed halls of literature, except of course for the big kahuna, the one and only Master Will. As Annie says in Tom Stoppard's play *The Real Thing*, "Shakespeare out in front by a mile and the rest of field strung out behind trying to close the gap." (There is a delicious irony in the fact that the damn-with-faint-praise comment one hears about all kinds of writing is "It ain't Shakespeare.") The pirate is a plunderer, plucking the choice bits from other people's lives for her own use. My mother could never come to a play of mine without accusing me of putting pieces of her life onstage. One of my theatrical heroes, Judith Thompson, wrote her *Crackwalker* characters so clearly that she was, for years, not welcome in Kingston. Perhaps that is an apocryphal story, but what do I care? Yo ho! Yo ho!

Harold Pinter, one of our theatrical elders, upon receiving the Nobel Prize for Literature talked about the responsibility of the writer to seek truth: "The search for the truth can never stop. It cannot be adjourned, it cannot be postponed. It has to be faced, right there, on the spot." Pinter asserted that as a writer "you find no shelter, no protection — unless you lie — in which case of course you have constructed your own protection and, it could be argued, become a politician." So affecting was Pinter's Nobel speech, titled "Art, Truth & Politics," that English PEN (Poets, Playwrights, Editors, Essayists, Novelists) established a prize in his name to honour a writer who "casts an 'unflinching, unswerving' gaze upon the world and shows a 'fierce intellectual determination ... to define the real truth of our lives and our societies.'"

With great power comes great responsibility.

In 1996, I wrote a play called *Annie Mae's Movement*. It's about Anna Mae Pictou Aquash, a Mi'kmaq woman from Nova Scotia, who left her family to go to the United States to work with the American Indian Movement. In 1976 her body was found on the Pine Ridge Reservation in South Dakota. Initially, the authorities said she had died of exposure and she was buried as a Jane Doe. When her family had her body exhumed and another autopsy done, it was discovered that the cause of death was actually a bullet in her head.

When I sat down to write the play, twenty years after her death, no one had been arrested for her murder, and many of us, many of us women in Indian Country, believed that no one ever would be.

I wrote the play because I was afraid that Annie Mae was going to be forgotten.

The play was produced in 1999 in Whitehorse and toured to Winnipeg and Halifax. In 2001 it received another production at Native Earth in Toronto. Then one day in March 2003, I was in a hotel in Calgary and the phone rang, and it was a *Globe and Mail* reporter wondering if I had a comment about the fact that John Graham had been indicted in Annie Mae's murder. I went to my hotel door and there was the *Globe* with the news. After twenty-seven years, someone was finally going to be charged with her murder, and it turned out to be John Graham, a Yukon resident who was living in Whitehorse when the play premiered there.

I had, like most playwrights, done my research diligently and then set it aside and written creatively. I gleaned what facts there were in the literature (and in 1996, the World Wide Web was still a new and spotty research tool), and set out to articulate some kind of truth about Anna Mae Pictou Aquash, warrior, mother, martyr. As Pinter pointed out in his Nobel speech: "Truth in drama is forever elusive. You never quite find it but the search for it is compulsive. The search is clearly what drives the endeavour. The search is your task."

The penultimate scene in the play is the rape and murder of Annie Mae. One of my pieces of research is the autopsy report, and there is no naming of rape in the report (mind you, there is no bullet in the first autopsy report, either, which doesn't mean it wasn't there). But I know that Anna Mae died in a war, and men rape women in war, and that is a truth I know. Much later, I spoke with Denise Maloney Aquash, Anna Mae's eldest daughter, and I sent her a copy of the play at her request. Denise became the executive director of Indigenous Women for Justice in 2004, a public figure herself, and in interviews I have heard her refer to the rape and murder of her mother. And I wonder, did I make it so by saying it?

On Christmas Day in 2011, I received an email from a lawyer in Massachusetts who had represented Leonard Peltier from 2002 to 2007 and Arlo Looking Cloud — one of the men convicted of shooting Anna Mae — since 2008. And he wanted to read the play.

I thought, oh oh, I am in trouble. I told him it was available from Playwrights Canada Press, Amazon, or Powell's.com. I explained that it was a work of fiction, "a piece of art, an imagining of the time between Anna Mae's decision to go to Wounded Knee and her death a couple of years later. It can also be seen as the moment from the time the bullet leaves the gun until it kills her."

Five days later, I got another note from him, saying he got the book on Amazon, read it, and I was "right on." He confirmed for me some of the facts that I had invented, and affirmed my ending, my truth about who was responsible for Anna Mae's death. The exchange had me shaking my head, realizing again what I already know about this work I do.

There is an Adrienne Rich line that bounces around in my head a lot (if I were a tattoo kind of pirate, I might have it inked on my skin): "But there come times — perhaps this is one of them — / when we have to take ourselves more seriously or die." This *is* one of them. I believe it is. I feel that we live in dangerous times.

Governments are in the process of dismantling our history. I cannot help but think that cutting funding to archives, the film industry, Statistics Canada, anyone who advocates on behalf of environmental issues is a way of erasing our memory, our mythologies about ourselves as who we are as Canadians, as denizens of Turtle Island. If they can make us forget who we are, and where we came from, how we got here, why we got here, then they can move forward without regard to who we thought we were.

This is why artists are so important, why writers are so important. Playwrights, who say things out loud, are more important now than ever, and more dangerous. Playwrights who strive to "disenchant the citizen from the spell of received opinion" are especially dangerous, and because we are pirates, we have little fear, and little concern for society's rules.

I love my pirate relations, and there are many, young and old, established and emerging: Daniel Macdonald, whose play *A History of Breathing* forces us to look at our role in genocide and reinvent the world in love; Colleen Murphy, who howls with outrage at who we have become as Canadians in her Governor General's Award–winning play *The December Man* and her upcoming *Pig Girl*; Anthony MacMahon, who shows us how easy it is for a people to be divided by showing us the Irish Troubles in *The Frenzy of Queen Maeve*; Donna-Michelle St. Bernard, who is dismantling colonialism country by country with her *54-ology*; Tommy Taylor, who was transformed into a playwright by his arrest at the G20; Judith Thompson, now in her fourth decade of playwriting, who is tackling everything from the right-to-die movement to the Dove-commissioned play *Body & Soul*, starring non-professional actors.

As I was writing this, I was thrilled to hear that Tom Stoppard had been awarded the PEN/Pinter Prize. I was amused to hear him identified as the man who co-wrote the screenplay for *Shakespeare in Love* and the play *Rosencrantz and Guildenstern Are Dead*. (It ain't Shakespeare, except it kind of is.) Stoppard has been a guilty pleasure of mine since I saw (five times) the 1985 Manitoba Theatre Centre production of *The Real Thing*, a play about love and the power of words. Stoppard's hero in *The Real Thing* is Henry, a playwright. Explaining to his new wife the power of and responsibility of the writer, he says, "I don't think writers are sacred, but words are. They deserve respect. If you get the right ones in the right order, you can nudge the world a little or make a poem which children will speak for you when you're dead."

WORKS CITED

Clements, Marie. *The Unnatural and Accidental Women.* Vancouver: Talonbooks, 2005. Print.

Moses, Daniel David. *Almighty Voice and His Wife.* Toronto: Playwrights Canada Press, 2009. Print.

Rich, Adrienne. "Transcendental Etude." *The Dream of a Common Language: Poems 1974–1977.* New York: W.W. Norton, 1993. Print.

Stoppard, Tom. *The Real Thing.* London: Faber and Faber, 1986. Print.

PART III

WRITING THE CREATIVE
WRITING PROFESSOR

Teaching, or Not Teaching, Creative Writing

Aritha van Herk

I cannot resist thinking of the writing life as a condition that occupies the writer, a low-grade viral state, with flu-like symptoms. Much has been made of this writing life, with dozens of books and blogs proclaiming its habits and discouragements, with tips and tricks and guidelines and recommendations, all seasoned with the condiment of the particular author's experience. Similarities can inevitably be tracked. Pain should make an obligatory appearance and nature must enjoy at least a cameo. Walking and woods and wildness serve as integral conditions, but none so furiously that they upstage the central mystery: the conundrum of how to write.

This is the ice rink of hubris, to imagine teaching this slippery ritual to any audience of captive chairs, to think that there are ways to hand out skill or distill its conspiracy of mechanism and magic, when what is required is not so much a translation of inspiration, but of the quotidian, of patience, of the uses of distraction, of the carpenter tools of claw hammer and level.

Students of creative writing used to clutch the work to be discussed close, holding pages against their chests as if to keep the words warm, or to warm themselves with the heat of the words on the page. Now they keep pages and words alike at arm's length, even pens and pencils alien instruments, and the shaped plastic of the keyboard, the cool glass of the screen, where their words embark. I fear this interval as a fracture, a dead space separating their fingers and their words, but they happily ignore the carnal knowledge between their writing and its evocation. All is reduced to words, those slippery conceptual units that beguile and baffle, that escape and elude their intrinsic work. In the dubious pedagogy of creative writing, cartography begins with words.

Meditating on words is one method by which to instruct an impossible-to-teach pursuit. Words themselves argue the complexity of what they suggest. For example, it is useful to negotiate the plurals of all that is grammatically singular: sugars, snows, stupidities, sands, and, not least, singulars. Ah, the way that language trips and skips, inviting this play. Activities that might be individually very different in their specifics but similar in some general aspect will sometimes be *plurale tantum* or in plural form, *pluralia tantum*. These are words used for objects that actually operate in sets, like scissors or glasses or pants. I am particularly fond of the Dutch plural for brains, *hersenen*. Uncountable nouns indulge in shenanigans, heroics, or hysterics, and sometimes all three together. Thus arises the challenge of unitary objects and how they can work in writing, the weight of mass nouns and whether they can be measured or counted, the terrible thicket of plural logic. Dodging, too, misery words that lurk around the margins of a page: luggage, despair, money.

Words can plumb the abyss of the body, the blood and bone the young occupy and yet ignore, too confident of their lives to imagine betrayals, how experience will fall on them, a heavy book from a shelf or the sudden force of a bag of oats in a pantry, sliding from above to administer a thump that should include roughage. I quote Simon Winchester's reflection on *set*, that perfectly innocuous word, too short to be a missile, but too intricate to be discounted:

> I include this simply as an aide-mémoire: there are more meanings for this innocent-looking trinity of letters than there are for any other word in the English language — fully 62 columns' worth in the complete *Oxford English Dictionary*, and which naturally include such obvious examples as: the condition of what the sun does each evening; a major part of a game of tennis; what one does if one embarks on a journey; what one does if one puts something down on a table; a collection of a number of items of a particular kind; and a further score, or more, of other disparate

and unconnected things and actions. Set is a term in bowl-
ing; it is what a dog (especially a setter, of course) does
when he is dealing with game; it is a grudge; what cement
does when it dries; what Jell-O does when it doesn't dry; a
form of power used by shipwrights; what a young woman
does when she wants to secure a man's affections; the direction of a current at sea; the build of a person; a kind of
underdeveloped fruit; the stake that is put down at dice …
need I go on? In the search for a synonym it is worth pointing out, and only half in jest, that it is quite possible that
one or other meanings for set might fit the bill, exactly, and
will have you all set, semantically, and quite neatly, without
nearly as much effort as you supposed. (799)

And so, we loop toward what the next sensory event will bring, indulging in
a writerly eagerness for detour and its temptations, the pleasure of research
as digression.

In fact, a writing class can become a unit of measurement, a yardstick,
a cup, a salt-lick, a boot, eluding the contours of its expectation like vapour,
the faint murk of water hanging in the air but not containable, merely a
miasma, a ghost. I want to dote on the lengthening light of February, how
blithe it is to have escaped winter's lockdown, dark at four, too pitiless to
allow even a fingernail of moon to eclipse its thick authority. But writing
students are determined to find something to give themselves the impression
they exist and can write. And though I might talk about the ablative absolute, its participle ferocity, they stare at me blankly, preferring not to know
the name of the adze they wield or the hammer head that will bruise their
collective thumb. Even if I shift to punctuation, and how Beckett declares
the semi-colon hideous, they laugh. Afraid of its railing, the teeth inside its
footprint, they simply avoid the mark.

Is writing then design, the sentences siren songs that ask to be heard and
followed? Is it arrangement I teach or is it, Houdini-like, how to escape George
Orwell's "familiar dreary pattern" ("Politics and the English Language"), how
to resist premeditated words in their ant-trail path across structure?

The. That damned article. The bear went over the mountain. Sanctified
now, the story reversed to Alice Munro's "The Bear Came Over the Mountain."

The sentencing confusion of article noun verb, iambic pentameter plod resisting its own interruption.

Writing students yearn to be slovenly, to let their pants drool around their hips, to spill over the edges of the lines in a colouring book. They stuff every idea and object into the gunnysack of "thing," as if that noun will cover the bases, the territory, the spread, the camel's hump and all its alternatives. I have come to detest "thing's" smug laziness, its distance from its own provenance, its automatic door introducing an excuse or retribution, its appetite for abstraction, its colloquial evasion, its bloggish faux-intimacy, its lack of specificity, its infernal refusal to commit, its thinginess as offensive as injury. Thing is durable and remorseless and ubiquitous, rather like a battered purse filled with wrapped mints and shredded tissues, hoarding comfort.

And yet, behind the casual is a desire for aesthetic purgatory, that wish to have some object to stare at, if not hold onto, more comforting than the wind that flings itself against the windows of our patience. Little do writing students know how a candlestick or a fringed shawl will outlive words without even digesting the essence of their own thing-ness. Omelettes lie shivering with fat on a plate and wait to congeal. They insist on being eaten hot, steaming with their own coagulation. Eggs, my home economics teacher explained to us, coagulate. Like blood, whispered one of my classmates.

Writing students are sometimes bellhops, officious and obsequious at once. Just try to get them to talk about the body. Camel toe and penis line, the onslaught of scent, the obligatory pungency of flesh in active decay.

I try to persuade them that the malodorous aspects of writing are most interesting, but they resist, don't like to think of smells and their provenance, or the cause of such smells, the stink of death, the promise of age. They want to write a story that is squeaky clean, repelled by soil, sprayed with aromatic gel. Dirty diapers, the reek of sewage, the raw wind melting gasoline-soaked snow, unidentifiable slime. The drive-by body of the struck skunk in full black and white repose beside the road. The high smell of a salesman anxious to close a deal. Tousled sheets.

I am teaching not only finesse and content but architecture, the struts and bearing walls of structures that need to hold within their frame a narrative. From a two-by-four studded world comes a yearning for the curve of balconies and balustrades, the rock of verandas and the projection of bay windows. It is the window seat we all imagine, inside but soaked with light, a cushioned bench where one can draw up one's knees and read.

The gift of literature, its sheer expanse, an open prairie of books like whispering stalks of grass, drenched with plenitude. In the sere landscape of pragmatism, the one we're condemned to live in now, such wealth simply waits, sentences unspooling like floss, silently reciting promise. That lovely dart from line to line, page to page, the ripe wait of the next and the next and the next.

Involute: a complex experience that cannot be disentangled.

How then to charm the process, seduce it into co-operation? Not the classroom or the students but the stew of practice, how to make praxis accomplish more than its habit and desire, how to make it tremble every once in a while, tremble and wonder. Onslaught, although not assault, subtle enough to perform as persuasion.

Offer rules but waive them immediately when useful. Let the wild follow the wild, hope that transgression will lead to surmise and risk. Always happy to meet a malapropism, its charming dimensions signalling that language can still play with our expectations. Can still irritate. There's a grail. And recondite, a word to wield in a workshop. Cryptic. Impenetrable. For those who expect me to perform miracles, make the process translucent, an application like those we download on smartphones.

But their impatience with detail! They are not born to be philatelists or seam checkers (does that occupation still exist?), pharmacists, or dental-orthotic technicians. They are eager to drive Olympic-sized graders, cutting huge swaths through open fields and not thinking to look behind. Avoiding the callow suburban street, they step onto the ferris wheel of fantasy, a spin above the ground that pretends it is not of this world. Making me yearn for scientists, for the training of lab reports as antidote to Tolkien and his incessant inheritance.

Fear is still useful. Squelch that desire to shore up the ego, mine or theirs, to measure excellence against effort. Every time I walk into a workshop, the chairs hedging the classroom table, I am afraid, not of failing but of succeeding too well, persuading the eager chins lifted there that they can slaughter dragons and make a fairy tale out of that corner cupboard where the cookie-tin crouched, waiting to satisfy a sudden crave for sugar, to reward tears. Supposing the cheap therapy is true, that all goes back to childhood, its tension and thirst, its scars and retributions. I shudder at that, don't want to play therapist of any kind, not suited and not trained, and even worse, repulsed by the confessional.

I want perversely to encourage the rude and unwieldy but in the end I desist, let them choose their own temptations — murderers and bad men, those who never wear ragged underwear. Still, they yearn to baffle, to confound the reader, to raise their words to the level of multiple meanings, the density of suggestion and its after-effects. My taste for the unstated, the inexplicable, will never be sated. I'd rather not know how the key fits in the lock, but, of course, I'll insist that detail be present, even if not on the page.

I am the reader/teacher who wants to savour the content and read in a gulp, not despoil its margins with pencilled (truth to tell I use red ink — for I am inclined to shouting) comments that record dissatisfaction. I want them to exercise their own disdain, disdain for the impeccable bland, the tailored suit, the sleek upholstery of television sets, and all the upright dullness sold by chains.

And encourage their reading, tipping at books as if they were birds at a puddle, but perhaps better than were they to devour the *oeuvre* of those published writers they admire en masse. Reading is a way of looking for love, finding contentment among the thicket of sentences. Desire is all poetry, but reading is that embrace of aloneness that leads to conjunction. And there is so much to read, so much that reads the reader, the arrangement of words always seductive.

I want to know what books litter the floors of their writing rooms. I want to know if their mess is like mine, a mixture of unsent thank-you cards, travel guides, aged magazines long past their publication dates, a mugful of thumb drives that hold different drafts of different efforts, and three staplers — now why is that necessary? Surely one would do?

They mock my injunction against death. Snowmobilers do die in avalanches, they declare. Hikers are mauled by bears. Nuns are struck by cement trucks. Nouns can be slaughtered by verbs. Even good politicians can be assassinated. The poor are eliminated by poverty. We dispatch 115 million chickens a day, in the service of food. That's death on a grand scale, they shake their fingers at me, while I stubbornly resist the ease of death, how it can be brought to bear with a shameless deftness, the laziness of a writer refusing to administer mouth to mouth or lifesaving surgery. What is so tempting about death, I demand? The subsequent quiet, or the grotesque pleasure of the extinguishment?

Thanatology, I insist, is the price to be paid for a character conveniently eradicated. Let us at least see an autopsy, the slime of disintegrating tissue and the gnaw of maggots. But no, students want a clean death, quick and painless. They'll settle for blood, its dramatic spill, its bright shine against grey pavement, but they don't want to think about the cold steel of a cadaver dissecting table, the rubber brick that arches the chest upwards for ready access to the knife's evisceration. While they are inclined to death and its temptations, they resist disclosure, look away.

And what about, they ask, famous suicides? Hart Crane and Diane Arbus, Cleopatra and Virginia Woolf? They are interested in the lives of writers and the augury of their deaths, which they deem to be "romantic," but they focus on the stone in Woolf's pocket and not the soggy mass of her fur coat after she had been rolled by river water for twenty-one days. It is more important, I remind them, that Hart Crane's father invented Life Savers and sold the patent before they became the ubiquitously popular roll of candy that they are now. They look at me with disbelief, are far more inclined to remember him lost at sea and stung by his short stint in Paris's La Santé prison.

Still, dangerous conditions fascinate us all: Caracas and Cape Town, Rio and San Pedro. We recite with relish moments when we have encountered crime, eager to believe that we have been at risk. Subject matter is so fine a tool that it resists invention, even while the mantra that there is no new story is one that we carry in a pocket, knowing there is no new story, only a new rearrangement of words by which we do our best to convey rapture or deliquescence without falling into a pit of lachrymosity.

And then there are the illnesses, Palsy and Parkinson's, a tremor, a collapsing leg, a cast to the eye that nevertheless makes a character beautiful. A whisper not whispered, beautiful. And yes, we all steal from our grandmothers, their Eccles cakes, their fiercely guarded wrinkles. We hoick their old-world bicycles from the back of the shed and try to ride them. Sick days, I insist, are a luxury that no sick person wants to take. Only the well indulge themselves, wish for the soft table of bed to muse and mutter.

I watch their faces. A brow and eye socket, a thread vein and the upper frenulum, the notch of a lip, is what stays over time. A bang cut savagely short, allocating to its forehead bare declaration, a name curlicued with ancient origin. Those are the student narratives that stay.

The terrible dictates of plot outdoing dialogue or ritual. Until the plot goes submarine, runs quiet and deep. Plot itself interests me very little, and yet students are mesmerized by the enigma of what will happen next, the then and then and then and then. They try to outline plot until I resist, say that I would far rather hear the words than hear about what happens. I yearn for characters to slice a pear into slender pinwheels or to pare their nails (I am well aware of the homophone's seduction). It is not that I resist action in favour of contemplation, that I endorse the hurried lope of the vexatious. I am happy to observe characters at sleep just so that they are doing something instead of strolling benign and continent through the geography of their stories, waiting for some event to supervene, to provide meaning and impetus. I've over-told the story of how I was instructed to pay homage to greatness, especially in terms of "war and peace," when I was then and still am far more interested in the scandal of an orange, the missing salt in the spaghetti sauce, the chronic foreboding of a dripping tap, those small particulars capable of starting a war or reciting heats of madness. These are the legislators of discontent, not orphaning or tragic accident but the minutiae that bode a thicker cancer, a dread bankruptcy.

We must, of course, identify cheap tricks: withholding, suppression, the irritation of sunsets blooming at appropriate moments. The writers who don't want to give it away, the writers who want to be sure that the reader "gets it," the writers who overwork the mechanical pencil until its spring recoils. I remind them that mechanical pencils are prohibited for those writing the Law School Admission Test, surely because of some candidate clicking the mechanism and unaware of her tic as a periphrastic delay to all answers. What is the wooden sheath around the lead of a pencil called? A scene to inscribe the teeth marks of an unfortunate testee. Bite-mark analysis: more than one criminal has been indicted by leaving behind the gnawed stub of a pencil. Now, there is a mystery, why any character would test his teeth on pencils.

But oh, the extravagance of ideas in a writing class, their race and disposition, the way they will organize dinner parties and crowd scenes, the riot of accidental paradigms trapping desire in their netting without ever putting shoes to pavement, or making knives approach scattered peas on china plates.

And yet, they understand the need for profile. The character needing not only an address and a closet, but a job, a means by which to make a living, to fill, even if inadequately, the maw of a bank account. Can a woman running a shoeshine stand turn this head? Can a salesman sell? I remind them that characters need to have a horror of dentists, credit card debt looming over their shoulders, some reversal of fortune to make us care. They have to figure out how to give characters presence, to move them past John or Joe or Mary to the sweaty perfidy of Raskolnikov, the terror of Quentin Compson, the suave aura of Philip Marlowe. Or closer to home, the loneliness of Lou in *Bear*, the enchantment of Anne (of Green Gables), the recalcitrant stubbornness of Hagar Shipley in *The Stone Angel*.

What is important, and here is the one piece of advice I dare to offer, is that they take the time to avert their gaze, to be shy with their offerings, to allow their stories a little privacy, a chance to tuck a towel around their naked shoulders. They believe that, as writers, they are meant to expose, to lay bare, when in truth, the writer is a keeper of secrets, a key in the lock of one of those old-fashioned diaries. Those are surely locks meant to be picked, but an action carried out discreetly, the contents not flaunted for scrutiny.

And if they have yet to figure out the dubious contestation of connection, how we make forays toward one another and yet dodge away, wary of revealing too much, eager to disclose but wanting to be taken seriously, they are yet tender, inquisitive, and faithful to what is itself most faithful, the desire to make words count.

WORKS CITED

Winchester, Simon. "Reflection." *Oxford American Writer's Thesaurus*. Ed. Christine A. Lindberg. New York: Oxford UP, 2012. Print.

Inciting a Riot: Digging Down to a Play

Judith Thompson

To write a play is to incite a riot; to awaken the artist in a student is to inspire a personal revolution, to tear down the walls around their imprisoned minds, to let their beautiful, terrible souls grow, expand, and fully occupy their beings. To teach the writing of a play is to carefully un-structure the student's thinking, which can be perilous for the student, as the school system and academy reward highly structured, dry thinking with the high grades and hyperbolic letters of reference that can make a career with a steady income a possibility.

A student who chooses this un-structuring is taking a risk; once the freeing process has begun, there is usually no turning back. To be a real playwright, this process must happen and it must be a full revolution. For the revolution to begin, the student must unravel the Gordian knot, or as Shakespeare has Cleopatra express it, "this knot intrinsicate," that society, religion, and family have crafted in each and every individual, around the still-shimmering but suffocated soul. It is the beautiful obligation of the creative writing teacher to first motivate students to begin freeing their souls, and then, with various magic tricks, commonly known as writing exercises, to show them how.

In the academy, it is often very difficult for students, particularly graduate students, to shift away from the requirement of their academic courses to the freedom of thought and approach that is needed to create art. Students are often delighted at first by the idea of throwing off the ties of academia, but soon find even a small amount of freedom of thought frightening and dangerous. I tell them that frightening and dangerous are what good writing is, and that now they are ready to begin.

However, there is not and cannot be a formula for teaching creative writing; each method is as unique as not only each playwright is unique, but as every one of their plays is unique. Each group of students creates its own living, breathing organism, unlike any other. My aim as a teacher is to respond to that organism in the most sensitive way possible. Sometimes I am successful and sometimes I have felt that I have failed: for example, a few years back there was a student who would arrive very late, talk while I was talking, sit directly in front of me reading a huge hardcover book, which he held up, almost in front of my face, as I talked about my process, and tried to inspire the class. When I asked him to please put the book down, as it was distracting, he was furious. At the break, he asked me why I "hated him." I was mystified. He had no notion that I might be offended, or even just thrown off my lecture, by his clear message that he was not interested. That student was in dire need of the self-scrutiny that is critical to the freeing of the mind; how could he possibly create characters if he was incapable of empathizing with the teacher — of seeing me as a vulnerable human being? I regret that I was not able to impart this to the student; he became more and more hostile and his writing was less than mediocre. He was not ready, as an unformed identity, to hear what I had to say. He was full of rage that he clearly did not understand, and some of that rage was channelled toward me. I don't know if one can ever be prepared for a hostile student. The fifteen-year-old girl inside me, who was persecuted for having acne as well as opinions, bolts forward in these circumstances, and I find myself hobbled, though I do not show my feelings to anyone but my family. We accept that teaching any creative practice is going to be fraught; as in therapy, there will be transference, both positive and negative. Indeed, I have had the most wonderful responses to my teaching imaginable, as well as the few "haters," which seems to be the cost of what we do, especially for women.

In my humbler moments I decide that it is, in fact, my job to earn every-one's respect, even those who seem unwilling to give it. I tell myself to just try harder, knowing that I will not always succeed. Conversely, in discussion with colleagues and friends, I will conclude that my teaching has nothing to do with these attacks. The occasional hostile student is part of the game, like being tackled in football, and there is so much that is good about the job that I will just have to take the bad with all that good. After all, I have always received a few vicious reviews for my plays, as well as a truckload of praise. All that being said, teaching is like any art — endlessly perfectible but never perfect. There is a piece of folk wisdom I recently heard: your children show you who you are — an idea that is difficult to accept but probably true — and that leads me to believe that our teaching shows us who we are. We stay the same and yet we change every day, and we have triumphs and family crises and heartbreaks that will affect our teaching. And none of us will ever be perfect.

I never took a playwriting course, or any creative writing course; not in grade school or high school or at university or the National Theatre School. I was dimly aware that the mostly excellent Queen's Drama Department in 1975 offered a playwriting course. Most theatre departments and theatre schools in that era had their share of professors who had affairs with students, and Queen's was no different, as I learned years later in conversation with others who had been in the theatre program; a few of them, in my experience at Queen's and at the National Theatre School, were superb teachers as well as "players," and there were, miraculously, a handful that were true artists and gentlemen. The teacher as lecher dynamic proved deeply destructive to young artists: even if the affairs were ostensibly consensual, their integrity was violated, and they were robbed of the autonomy that artistic practice is all and only about. Agency, autonomy, identity. I believe that this sexual conquering revealed an unconscious fear of the creative power of the young; removing their agency was the fastest way to freeze the creativity of the students, and thus, remain dominant.

What does this rant have to do with the teaching of playwriting? Everything. To teach any artistic practice is, as I have said earlier, to pry open the heavy steel door that locks the unconscious life from the conscious mind. If a teacher regards the student as a sexual object, the student will consciously or unconsciously absorb that objectification, and the unique identity of the student, which creativity utterly depends upon, is temporarily obliterated.

When we are young, especially, we will take on almost any role thrust upon us by those in power, particularly those we respect. Recently, a student that I was mentoring shared that a previous teacher/mentor, who was forty years older than her, had, after many congenial dinners with his wife and son, declared his "love" for her. This declaration slammed her creativity shut and filled her with anxiety; if she saw him at a public event she would run away, heart pounding. And a couple of years later, when she was starting to almost feel sorry for the guy (a sad romantic?), she found a play of hers that he had made lurid comments on — along the lines of "You need to have SEX with this character, you need to take all of your CLOTHES off with this character." No wonder she was blocked! He had taken away her agency with his expressed desire, and two years later she is still fighting to regain it.

All great art is infused with erotic energy, and when that energy is diminished in the artist because of a violation, the art is diminished, unless the art is exploring that very violation. Erotic energy is the energy of the living body on the earth, in relation to other living bodies, and it must be in every play, whether a solo piece or multi-character. Eros is deeply connected to passion, which can only come from suffering (which is in the etymology of the word) — and where is suffering but in the body? Cliché that it is, I believe absolutely that art can only come from one who has suffered, and everyone will suffer eventually. Many of us transform the suffering into art in order to survive it. Many artists have sexual and/or physical abuse in their past, but they have worked through it in their art in order to reclaim their power.

To return to the playwriting class I did not take. I often wonder why I chose not to take it, and instead, unbelievably, took a design course for which I was totally unprepared. Why would I take a turn so wrong and at such a tender place in my journey as a person? I had always read as if I was starving for words and stories. I had been acting in plays since the age of eleven, so playwriting, even if just to learn more about acting, would seem to have been a wise choice. Was this the Trickster having his way with me, throwing me off my course as a test? In a way it was, for my self-esteem and sense of agency had been badly damaged by growing up in the Catholic Church (have faith, don't ask questions, women are for baby-making only and they must wear hats in church because sins will travel through their heads and into the minds of men), sustaining (again, apparently consensual) rape in a teen relationship with a university student, and difficult family issues, and therefore I had lost my agency. I did not know what I wanted, beyond being an actress, and I was only an actress in the most passive sense of the word. Give me a script and I will inhabit your character. I never for a moment dreamed that I could actually be the primary creator, the playwright, whose ideas and thoughts and soul would be expressed through the characters, through the play, which could live on for years, for decades, even, possibly, for centuries. Me? I was a girl, a very girly girl. I was apolitical, and I hadn't a clue who I was or who I would be. So I did not choose to take the play-writing course. Who knows what I would have written?

I sometimes wish I had taken it, as I have heard it was a fairly inspiring and rigorous class, and I would have written my first play earlier. However, upon reflection, I realize that I was not ready. One has to be ready to write a play — to force oneself to write prematurely usually means a terrible play, which might put a student off for life. I saw this happen in that class at Queen's. A troubled but fabulously brilliant friend of mine took the class and it seemed that writing was the perfect thing for his unbridled charismatic and dangerous energy. He was a procrastinator, like all of us, and he often missed class in order to entertain and intimidate the rest of us in the Green Room. The final assignment was a full-length play. A few weeks after the last class, our local high-school theatre teacher was sitting with the prof, chatting about the state of theatre in town. As he did, he leafed through the pile of plays on the prof's desk and came upon the play my friend had handed in. He was interested in what my dynamic friend, who had also been in his high-school class, might have written. But as he read, he realized it was his play, his own play that he had staged with us in high school. My friend, who could have written something very exciting, had just handed in a mediocre play written by a high-school teacher. Why? Laziness is the first answer, followed by outrageous risk-taking, very much in character for someone who shoplifted constantly. The true answer? The prof resented my friend always being centre stage, having the class enthralled and laughing while the prof tried to teach. He tried to squash that energy. So my friend absorbed the script he was given about himself by the prof and chose not to write anything. I know he could have written an amazing play had he been encouraged and empowered and given real freedom. On the other hand, my friend was very difficult to deal with in a classroom: he would sabotage the class at any turn. I understand the impulse to inhibit that kind of disruptive energy. What is a teacher to do? How do we balance our needs as teachers with the writing student's need for freedom and empowerment?

I urge my students to free themselves, to follow their instincts, to be bold, unafraid to offend, and to just write, write and write more. I also tell them that with freedom there must be strict discipline, rigorous self-criticism, constant rewriting, and never ever complacency. When a talented student embraces both the freedom and the rigour, the student is ready to walk the path of a playwright. Sounds grandiose? It is.

The magic tricks that are writing exercises are many, and every creative writing teacher has her or his own bag of favourites. Many of the writing exercises I use are about exploring the identity of each student, helping students understand the choices that make them who they are. Students tease me sometimes about my classes being "like therapy." While I never pretend to be a therapist or offer therapy of any kind, I believe that self-awareness is the key to creating character. We ask ourselves: What am I lying to myself about? and then tell ourselves a hard truth. It may mean the animal lover finally seeing the connection between the blood on their plate of roast beef and the suffering animal. It may be the vacationer at the Mexican resort seeing the connection between their privilege — and perhaps occasional cocaine use — and the poverty and suffering of the Mexican people. What do our habits and reflexes reveal about us? I ask students to scrutinize their beliefs and separate what was inscribed by family and society from what they have discovered: What is autonomous and what is scripted? They usually resist the idea that anything they think or feel is constructed, and so my job as a teacher is just to keep asking, but never push ... if only a few seeds are planted, they may sprout years and years later and clear the way for true artistic practice. I have had many students approach or email me years after they graduated saying, "Now I understand what we were doing. Thank you!"

I begin every writing class with an exercise that beautifully illuminates the person underneath the social persona. I ask students to scan their memories for one of the many moments that they know transformed them somehow, in the smallest or largest way. The stories are always, always breathtaking, jaw-dropping, and transformational for the listeners as well as the speakers. The storytellers are always perfectly connected as actors; their voices, bodies, and emotions all working together to communicate a moment that is an essential part of the unique mosaic that is the storyteller's identity. Another thing it does is to shake up the students' first impressions of each other, helping them understand that appearances are deceptive and that almost nobody is who they seem to be. Young writers — all writers — fret about structure. I urge them to listen carefully to the unique structure of each story — usually about twenty per class — and assure them that each of them has an impeccable sense of structure when the story they are telling is, for them, a deeply significant and pivotal moment. When they ask me how they will know if it's a "significant" story, I assure them that the mere fact that they remember the story and that they chose to tell it means it is the right story. And it means they need to tell it, although they might not know the reasons.

For example: a young man of about twenty told the class a story about killing a raccoon. He prefaced the story by telling us that his greatest joy was hunting with his father. He then told us of a night not long before when his mother woke him and said there was a terrible sound in the field behind the house, and that she thought a rabid raccoon might be attacking their dog. He went out to the field, picking up a big shovel on the way. The moon was full, so he didn't need a flashlight. There, in the long grasses, he found a sick-looking raccoon, cornered by his dog. After he sent the dog away, he attacked the raccoon with the shovel. As he told us this, he made a weak joke about not wanting to get the raccoon brains all over the shovel. He paused. He said he wondered if he should kill the raccoon, but "what the hell." He struck the raccoon, over and over, until it died. When he went back inside, his mother was delighted. He looked at us with a little grin and added that raccoons are pests and everyone hates them, as they get into the walls and the garbage. At the end of his story he admitted that he hadn't been completely sure if killing the raccoon was right, but "what the hell."

Most of the other students laughed, mainly because they sensed he needed them to laugh. I observed that it was a wonderfully dramatic story, a great example of dramatic storytelling, because his need to tell the story meant that the event for him, spiritually, was like a splinter. It was causing a sort of ethical inflammation, a throbbing, the way a finger with a splinter in it will throb until it is removed. The telling of the story is like the tweezers probing the finger for the splinter, but it is very painful to remove a splinter, and the finger will pull away. The student felt unconsciously guilty about killing the raccoon, which was weak and in distress, and he wanted reassurance, or an end to the nagging guilt: he wanted the splinter out. This was his dramatic action, as a character. He wanted us to laugh about the image of brains on the shovel because that would be reassurance that what he did was not wrong. And further, the story (I did not say this) was his way of shyly questioning hunting altogether. He would never acknowledge the twinges of regret he probably had when he killed an animal, as that would be seen as a betrayal of his father, but his way of expressing this was to tell the class this story. A brilliant example of how to write character: it is always stronger if the character does not understand his or her motivation, but his or her actions tell us everything.

My mistake as a guide was to tell him what he was not ready to acknowledge — that he was feeling guilty about killing the raccoon. Thereafter, I felt hostility coming from him. Nothing angers us like the truths we are not ready to face, but that is exactly what a great play does to the audience, and though some of the audience will be grateful for the awakening, some will hate us for it. This explains why so many plays that have been declared masterpieces, or historical treasures, were reviled by the critics at first. Works of art that shift our thinking, that challenge the expectations of the audience, are often reviled. It is the few forward-thinking critics or, usually, academics, that see the brilliance and the need for hard truths to awaken us, and it is they who teach these plays, which might otherwise be forgotten.

Another recent example came from a young man from a religious immigrant family who told my class of seventy an account of being raped by a taxi driver in Montreal. He bravely explained that though he never said no, and actually performed more than the taxi driver had asked for, he was frightened and confused, and afterwards felt thoroughly violated — he understood sexual politics enough to know absolutely that he had been raped. I was in awe of his courage, in telling the class; I reflected that this was similar to the situation of students having "consensual" sex with their theatre teachers or directors. And marital rape as well: an actress who was in a recent workshop of mine shared that she had been raped every night of her first marriage, to a highly regarded neurosurgeon. She had never told anyone this, because she had just realized it through playing a role in my play, which explored violence against women. Her desire or lack of it was never even considered; lying there like a starfish was her wifely "duty." So this young man's story applied not just to a shy gay man just beginning to come out but to all and any individuals who have felt violated despite having apparently consented. To tell the story was an act of revolution, and though there were thirteen writing assignments in this class, each inspired by a different play in the anthology I used, every piece of writing this young man handed in dealt in some way with sexual violation. He has tremendous talent and courage, and I know his work will be on our stages within the next ten years. I believe that all great writers — playwrights or prose writers — are working out a great big splinter, over and over. When the splinter is out, often the writer stops.

Students sometimes become frustrated with the way I work. They want the craft before the art: hard rules on structure, character, dialogue, story arc, climax, denouement, selling the play, copyrighting the play (I say, "Don't worry, no one is going to steal your play, you will be lucky if they even read it"), and getting an agent. I tell them that all of that means absolutely nothing if there is no art, and when there is art, or soul, in the play, that is what determines the craft. The craft must serve the art. I give them an assignment to write a short scene, and some of them, those who have not had any theatre training, will protest: "How do I write a scene? I have no idea!" I love this because the answer is twofold: You play scenes many times every day. For example, scene one: you ran into a friend on the way to class. You were trying to avoid her because she was so drunk the night before and said some strange things. She asked why you were avoiding her and you lied. This is a scene. It is a scene because something happened. There was a dynamic between two characters, both of whom wanted something. And it is part of the "play" of your relationship to this friend. The reality of your friendship may not be interesting enough to write a play about, so you would need to ask yourself what could happen that would make a play about this relationship powerful. I suggest she take a seed that is already there, such as jealousy, and amplify it, blow it up to operatic/Greek tragedy proportions. So then the student is writing about something universal, with her relationship to this friend merely the jumping-off point.

A second way to learn what a scene is, I tell them, is immersion. Read as many plays as possible, from all eras, and especially see as many plays as possible. There is no formula, and if you write to formula you will fail.

Many of my students whine endlessly about seeing the plays, even though four of the six assigned are on campus — they find every excuse not to see theatre — and I wonder why they are enrolled in theatre courses. They will protest: "I don't actually want to be a playwright, I just needed a course for my degree." What can I say to that, other than that playwriting is, other than my family, my reason for living, it is life and death, it is a legacy, and it is history? I exhort them to watch people. To listen to what they say. To write it down, from memory, as we must become tape recorders. To look at what was said and see what the tiniest verbal tics and repeats and loops and fracturing really mean. What are they really saying to each other?

A character exercise I love: Think of the most fascinating person you know and write concrete details about that person as fast as possible for five full minutes, a list — for example, wears red bangles, says *shit* in every sentence, wobbles when she walks, has a fat tummy and skinny legs, always looks surprised, has three dogs, loves ginger ale, and on and on for at least two pages. These are always tremendously entertaining, and they teach students that we know what is happening in the deep waters by what is happening on the surface. All these details are clues about the person underneath. A bad play will analyze its characters. For example: this person has always wanted his mother's love. A good play will show us through fantastic and unique detail, which a good writer, yes, can make up, but there is nothing as powerful and quirky and amazing as real-life detail.

I ask them to listen to the way each storyteller creates a full character with one verbal brushstroke. For example: "And my friend Roxy kept three huge poisonous snakes in her basement but was head cheerleader who baked shortbread cookies for the elderly and had a new hairstyle every three weeks." I suggest that they examine the three descriptions of Roxy, and think about what she craves and what her action in a play might be.

I try to incite a riot within each student. I hope that beyond the specific art and craft of playwriting, they begin to question everything, to look more closely at all behaviour, and what it reveals, and to believe that writing a play can make a difference in the lives of the audience.

But what about me? It is commonly believed that there is a sort of hex on teaching: if you teach what you do, it will corrode what you do, until your art is nothing but a pile of rust, and you are no longer an artist, just a teacher waiting to retire. Perhaps that is why I insist on being a playwright first and a teacher second. I think of my classes as workshops, in which I have the privilege of sharing my process. Every class is a performance, a solo show that sometimes becomes a play with twenty-one, or even seventy-one characters. Sometimes the play works, and sometimes it doesn't. It is always exciting, and always exhausting. Does it corrode my playwriting soul? It does not, because I have never reduced what I do to formula, to right and wrong. I still learn by having to put into words what I try to do, and each and every student's story is an unforgettable gift.

Teaching also shows us who we are: we stay the same over the years and yet we change every day, we will have surgery and we will get fat and we will become thin and have triumphs and family crises and heartbreaks and reunions and just bad days, which will all affect our teaching. None of us will ever be perfect teachers, but the greatest gift we can give our students is to practise our art, to never become complacent, never give up, to revel, as artists, in our flaws and inconsistencies, embrace each crisis and write, write, write, with the absolute knowledge that while death will have all of us, our plays will remain vital, the characters waiting for living, breathing actors to bring the soul to life again and again, long after our remains have vanished in the earth.

Writes of Passage: Women Writing

Lorri Neilsen Glenn

Your silences will not protect you. What are the words you do not yet have? What are the tyrannies you swallow day by day and attempt to make your own, until you will sicken and die of them, still in silence?

— Audre Lorde

I have since reconsidered Eliot
and the Great White way of writing English
standard that is
the great white way
has measured, judged and assessed me all my life
by its
lily white words
its picket fence sentences
and manicured paragraphs

— Marilyn Dumont

Northwest Territories, 1980s. Calgary writing consultants fly in to teach government employees, most of whom are Dene and Cree, how to write complete sentences and fix their punctuation. Two former English teachers in tottering heels and southern clothes flapping round an overhead projector at the front of a room of silent women. From the distance of decades, I can still see the neon on the consultants' foreheads: *Doofus môniyaw.* My god, the workers must have howled when the workshop was over.

In a small classroom, people sit behind tables in a U-formation. "I am here to help you with your writing," the instructor says, too chipper and upbeat. "To help you tell your stories so you can finish your GED." Silence. "Maybe we can start by saying a bit about ourselves? Would you like to start?" The woman at the back looks down. No one speaks.

That earnest instructor has been teaching writing since she faced a crew of motorcycle fanatics in Alberta, rowdy and rambunctious teens only a few years younger than her twenty-one years. And what she remembers from that wild classroom are those boys; she doesn't remember the girls.

I've spent decades consulting, teaching writing at a number of Canadian and international universities, researching women's writing, organizing workshops in community halls, supporting technical and business writers in corporate boardrooms, advising graduate students writing theses and dissertations, and coaching poets and creative non-fiction writers.

It wasn't until I was in my late twenties, however, that I began to look beyond women's and girls' silences and acquiescence to see them in the classroom. To hear what they weren't saying, and to learn how to listen. As they struggled with their "writes" of passage, I was undergoing my own.

WHO THE HELL DO YOU THINK YOU ARE?

She sat in my office, picking at her hands, her eyes red and teary.

"You've done enough," I assured her. "You've read almost thirty books for this one course. You understand the issues. It's time to write, to discover what you think."

It has happened again. A woman who has scaled emotional mountains, a capable worker, wife, mother, someone who may have survived abuse or chemotherapy or who wrestles with food insecurity, aggressive landlords, racism, and loss, enters university with a bundle of insecurities, little sense of agency, and a firm belief she has nothing to offer.

Of course, you say. It's obvious why. Patriarchy. Colonialism. The privileging of the English language and the values it inculcates. Years of hiding in classrooms where others — the more confident, or the louder voices — take centre stage.

We know this woman. We might even be her. As Canadians teaching writing we know the "who do you think you are?" reference, and we see it playing out daily. Joan Bolker says, "Writing is not only a metaphor for the problem, but the thing itself: women's inability to write their concerns out into the public realm both increases their powerlessness and arises from it" (185). She adds, "If those among us who have had the most advantages have had this much difficulty overcoming silence, what hope is there for the woman who has never known she is entitled to any power in the world?" (186).

I LOST MY TALK. YOU SNATCHED IT FROM ME

A 30-below morning and the school door is locked when I arrive. A young man in an open coat offers a little girl a chip from the bag he's carrying; I watch as they make their way to the bus stop across the road. A woman darts around the corner, smiling. She holds up a key.

"Holy crap, it's cold today, eh?"

The 2015 Truth and Reconciliation report includes the statement: "The preservation, revitalization, and strengthening of Aboriginal languages and cultures are best managed by Aboriginal people and communities."

Yet here I am. The threads of my own Indigenous ancestry are slender; I was raised and schooled into Canadian working-class and middle-class settler values. I've learned, to use Marilyn Dumont's words, "the Great White way of writing English." Like so many writers, I excelled in school and never left it; I simply worked my way to the other side of the desk. And like other writing instructors, I talk risk-taking, blowing open systemic structures that silence women and underrepresented populations, and yet find myself toeing the line in more ways than I can count.

"Our stories are what connect us to the world," I say to the women in the small classroom. "Let's start with our stories."

Right. Those of us soaked in conventional education practices assume everyone wants to say something about themselves to strangers, that speaking is the only way to participate. We enter a classroom expecting a group will trust us — and each other — without the passage of time, without working on relationships to support that trust. The old "lionizing lone wolves" approach to writing workshops.

In this room are women who have not written for years, if ever.

My instincts as an instructor are to focus on holistic approaches, to create a setting where experiential learning can take place, where people can make connections and come to believe they have something valuable to say. To believe in the power of their own story.

Those beliefs have flown in the face of conventional institutional expectations: write (or tell) on demand; work promptly, quickly, and on your own; conform to the implicit rules of the writing classroom: keep a journal, write multiple drafts, revise, revise, focus on the work (not the writer), expose your work to others' critique, revise again, publish. And ... go!

Months ago, working with Indigenous women in northern Canada, I arrived promptly at 1:00 p.m. for the workshop and found the room empty. As the women arrived, some of whom had brought their children, we dove into the coffee and snacks and began to talk. I set out empty journals for everyone and the books stayed unopened as the afternoon unfolded. One woman gave her journal to her daughter to colour in. We laughed, there were thoughtful silences, a few dark moments, as well as tears. The women asked me questions about myself and my children, told me about their children and their home communities. We made more coffee, stayed long after the allotted time. I learned a lot about listening that day.

It's an honour to hear others' stories. And I've learned there are many ways to tell them. I've often begun a workshop with novice writers — especially those whose voices have been muffled or silenced by the standards of the Great White ways of teaching and learning — by bringing out blank paper, coloured pens, and small paint pots. Words aren't the be-all and end-all.

"Let's start this way," I've said. "Draw a picture or a map of a place you remember from your childhood. A street, a place by the river, a favourite spot where you always met your friends, the old shed where you buried a treasure."

As I've stood in front of women whose early lives weren't Dick and Jane and Spot or the Canadian version of *The Brady Bunch,* I rub up against my own limitations and deeply embedded biases. Once, I told a group, "As children we are closer to the ground; those places become our body memories." Later, I caught myself. The very notion of a body memory (as if there were any other) is steeped in a (still) long-held Western belief in the separation of mind and body. My Great White way cultural foundations betray me again.

What I do recall from that workshop, however, was what happens when we get beyond words and use other sign systems. Recreating and acting out a conversation. Telling a story to a partner and having them sketch what they hear. Once people realize there will be no judgment, no expectation of being "a good artist," inventive and colourful images will quickly appear. Even better, conversations seem to open up. Not all have responded to the opportunity to create art; but many do.

YOU TOOK MY TALK

Mi'kmaq poet Rita Joe wrote years ago about the loss of her language. So many of the women I've worked with, including those who may speak Cree or Michif, are in a liminal place — their language has been systematically extinguished, either in their parents' generation or their own, and so writing in English is learning to abide by cultural norms they may not wish to take on. To work on your Great White way education is both necessary and problematic. How to keep your talk and yet take advantage of opportunities that may benefit you.

Regardless of the cultural or educational background of the writer, I have learned the importance of getting to the core, the heart of what matters. Even during the times I've been asked to sit by the writer and scribe her story as she narrates it, I can sense, as she does, the tremors of something moving. I always hope it's the beginning of belief.

THE HEART OF THE MATTER

Like most women, I've dealt with loss, sexual violence, invisibility, emotional abuse, and silencing. But I have reaped so many benefits from my Western and colonialist upbringing that I am able to draw upon cultural, social, and financial resources to support me. A good percentage of writing instructors I know have as well.

So many women I have worked with, however, have more scars than most of us can find on or under our skin. They might have been from low-income families, had abusive marriages, travelled from a war-torn country with nothing in their pocket, birthed babies at fourteen, become deaf from beatings, lost a sister or a cousin, dealt with men who run off and keep coming back. They might have made compromises for a drug habit or lived in a succession of foster homes. They might have been a farm wife for thirty years before returning to school, survived residential school, or been scooped up in the sixties, wrenched from their home communities. The colour of their hair or their skin may have caused them to be followed by store clerks or targeted on a bus. They are struggling even now with illnesses of the body and the spirit. And despite all this, they are strong. They persist. They want an education.

We don't fully take into account the devastating impact of women's experiences on their ability not only to finish school, but to learn when they are there. Jenny Horsman, who has studied literacy in the lives of marginalized women for decades, says that "the education system must recognize the impact of women's and girls' experience of violence on their attempts to learn." I would suggest, too, that it's not only physical or psychological violence in the home or in the local community women have experienced, but the violence inherent in the kinds of cultural collisions so many must overcome in order to step into a classroom at all.

The heart of it all is their stories. Stories, as Thomas King says, are all we are. They are what drive us, soothe us, give us strength. Tapping into those stories isn't fundamentally about technique or style or grammar, nor about —

> lily white words
> its picket fence sentences
> and manicured paragraphs

— those features we too-often emphasize when we work with women who've had little opportunity to pick up a pen. Writing is a way — one way — into the world, and when marginalized women have the luxury of time to begin to tell their stories, the nascent sense of agency that arises can be life-changing. We can see our lives — interdependent and mutually reflected — on Indra's net, alongside others'. We learn we are not alone. For so many women without agency or good fortune — women whose lives are done *to* them rather than composed *by* them, the truth of their lives is what matters. To be [*esse* — Latin] is to speak one's truth.

It's difficult to keep that in mind when conventional educational settings are sites of ongoing judging and assessing. Oh, we make an effort to de-emphasize the fact; we candy coat our words in a writing classroom: "This part works, but here you could ..." "Have you tried *x*?" "I love the part where ..." Yet in any setting where writers are unsure, feel intimidated, have been crushed by judgment, or worse, are surrounded by cultural values antithetical to their own, what matters is the germ of a story, the spark that can ignite connection and resonate with the curious person across the table who wants to know what happened. Corbett and Connors's *Classical Rhetoric for the Modern Student* or Strunk and White can't compete with the stirrings of an untold story ready to be released. Maya Angelou's comment about the agony of carrying the burden of an untold story speaks to us all, but especially to those who've never been supported in telling theirs.

On many occasions when I've sat in a church basement or a community hall listening to women pulling fragments from their past I have found myself thinking: dazzling prose that earns an A or a sigh from the creative writing seminar on my campus would pale against these tales of blood, bone, and sinew. I have so much still to learn. We all have so much to learn.

I think back now to the last century, to that naive consultant of the last century, a young woman in her fancy leather heels determined to impress upon northern government workers how important the difference is between the active and the passive voice, and I shake my head. The irony was completely lost on her. On me. What a dumbass. Classic *môniyaw*.

TO GIVE MY CHILDREN

> My stories are my wealth, all I have to give my children.
> — Bronwen Wallace

A few times, I've helped workshop members gather their writing into a booklet or on a blog. And on occasion, writers have brought their family members to the reading. We usually sit in a circle with their publication in hand. Always there are treats and flowers.

One writer will ask her friend to read on her behalf. She's too nervous. Another two will take turns reading lines from the other's. Children eye the cake and the cookies on the table; once I saw a young boy counting the number of soft drinks left in the box.

After the reading, we often stay around the circle, talking, laughing. The mood is celebratory. No one is rushed; there is nowhere else to be. A long afternoon stretches its supple legs like a satisfied cat. It looks back at us, knowing more than we all can know, with a glint in its eye and something close to a smile. Stories are in the air and in the minds of others, and something has happened that writing can never tell.

Acknowledgements and Author's Note

Thank you to the women in a range of settings across the Maritimes, Newfoundland, western and northern Canada who have taught me, and many others, about what matters in education. Your stories have the power to change education.

The workshops I've described here are ones I have been invited to or contracted to organize and lead, as a volunteer or for a small honorarium. The workshops were instructional, and not part of any research project. This essay is intended as a means of honouring the women writers who have helped me unlearn old patterns and see more clearly my own biases. In the interests of privacy, I have not named these women nor have I revealed any of their stories.

WORKS CITED

Bolker, Joan. "A Room of One's Own Is Not Enough." *The Writer's Home Companion*. Ed. Joan Bolker. New York: Henry Holt, 1997. Print.

Dressman, Mark. "Lionizing Lone Wolves: The Cultural Romantics of Literacy Workshops." *Curriculum Inquiry* 23.3 (1993): 245–63. Print.

Dumont, Marilyn. "The Devil's Language." *A Really Good Brown Girl*. London: Brick, 1996. Print.

Horsman, Jenny. *Too Scared to Learn: Women, Violence, and Education*. Mahway, NJ: Lawrence Erlbaum, 2000. Print.

Joe, Rita. *Song of Eskasoni: More Poems of Rita Joe*. Toronto: Women's Press, 1989. Print.

Lorde, Audre. Statement originally delivered at The Modern Language Association's "Lesbian and Literature Panel," Chicago, 28 Dec. 1977. First published in *Sinister Wisdom* 6 (1978) and *The Cancer Journals* (Spinsters Ink: San Francisco, 1980). Print.

Wallace, Bronwen. "Testimonies." *The Stubborn Particulars of Grace*. Toronto: McClelland & Stewart, 1987. Print.

One of These Things Is Not Like the Others: The Writer in the English Department

Stephanie Bolster

When a former creative writing graduate student of mine decided to apply for a PhD in English at several top American universities, she asked me for a letter of recommendation. I'd nearly finished the letter, praising her dynamic and articulate contributions to class discussion and the combination of solid research, startlingly original imagination, elegant prose style, and inventive conceptual approaches that distinguished her fiction, poetry, and critical writing — qualities I presumed would also be valued among doctoral students in literature programs — when she let me off the hook. An adviser at one of the doctoral programs had told her to instead request a letter from one of her professors from her previous master's degree, in history. That an English program would value a letter from a history professor over one from a creative writing professor housed in an English department was at once baffling and all too familiar.

Although I entered the University of British Columbia's MFA program with a vision of eventually teaching creative writing, I didn't realize that an MFA was considered a terminal degree, whereas an MA wasn't. What I knew was that I'd been forbidden from doing a double-major in creative writing and

English as an undergraduate, having been told by the arts adviser that an English major is granted a BA and a creative writing major a BFA, and never the twain shall meet. I'd made my choice, and over time absorbed this distinction. Although my transcript showed no difference between my abilities in the literature classes I'd taken as electives and my creative writing courses, I was less passionately, fully, and deeply engaged with the former. So I began a graduate program that consisted only of writing classes — plus a sole open elective, a class called College and University Teaching, perhaps the most useful class of my degree.

In it, I developed a poetry course, which I pitched to Continuing Studies at the University of British Columbia (UBC) soon after graduation. No matter that I was painfully shy, had given only a handful of public readings, and had hardly spoken in class during my entire university experience. I would talk when the class was mine to teach — and teaching would be a welcome counterpoint to my day job as a secretary in the Dean of Arts' office. It turned out that I could talk, and did, and that being a good listener made me a better teacher. I spent the next five years in Quebec City and Ottawa, applying for — and, fortunately, getting — grants, and teaching writing courses to adults through Continuing Education and to elementary and high-school students through the Ontario Arts Council's Artists in the Schools program.

In the fall of 1999, a year after my first book had won the Governor General's Award, I received by email a job posting for a tenure-track position in creative writing at Concordia University in Montreal. Despite the award and the publication of a second book, I hadn't expected a chance at a teaching job for another decade or so. My husband and I were living in Ottawa, where I was doing stable and stimulating contract work as assistant editor of the members' magazine at the National Gallery, and he was planning to begin his doctorate at the Sorbonne. But this was the first creative writing opening — the first that did not require a PhD and experience teaching academic courses — since I'd received my MFA. I couldn't not apply.

Although my mother cautioned, "But what if you get it?" the application felt like a long shot. Not only did I lack university teaching experience in a degree program, I lacked graduate coursework in English. Concordia's students were required to complete an equal number of literature and creative writing courses and to defend their theses before both creative writing and academic faculty. How could I prepare students for a defence — and participate myself as an examiner — when I'd never experienced one? How effectively could I teach students whose reading, in historical periods and in theory, would likely surpass mine? I looked up publications by the members of the hiring committee and wondered what kinds of questions an expert on Milton would ask.

In that College and University Teaching class, I'd learned about, and understood all too well, imposter syndrome. The personal nature of literary creation makes writers susceptible to such thinking. Unlike academics, who achieve recognition because of what they know, how they articulate what they know, what they do with what they know, and how much funding they can secure, a writer gets to where she is for blurrier reasons. So much of what writers, particularly poets, do comes down to us: to our perspective, our vocabulary, our imaginations, our idiosyncracies, and often our experience. Although, as Mark McGurl discusses in *The Program Era: Postwar Fiction and the Rise of Creative Writing*, "creativity" has been increasingly touted during the past fifty years, many claim to value it while remaining skeptical of the fictitious and the imaginative (19, 21). Although we writers must have sufficient confidence to believe our work worthy of our own time and the partaking of it worthy of readers' time, we are plagued by the need to justify ourselves, a need on which the university, with its protocols, evaluations, and paperwork, feeds. Who do we think we are? What's our methodology? Who supports what we've done? And are we good enough at what we do to presume to teach others how to do it, too?

Perhaps fortunately, I retain few memories of the interview. When asked how I would continue to write while teaching, I began by saying, "Well, in other jobs I've had ..." a response met by one committee member with, "This isn't just a job." That evening I said to my husband that I doubted I'd be hired, and that if I weren't, I would probably never be hired anywhere, as I didn't know if I'd have the nerve to go through such an experience again.

Over a decade later, having served on my department's hiring committee and noted the uniformity of most candidates' profiles, distinguished by a list of uninterrupted degrees and post-docs — even many of those applying for our most recent creative writing hire were already teaching at universities — I'm surprised and grateful that I was granted an interview at all. The following September, making the rounds at a welcome reception for new faculty, the university's vice rector asked, "And which university did you come to us from?" Upon hearing, "Actually, I was working in Publications at the National Gallery," he shook my hand, staring out the penthouse window into the distance, and moved on.

So here I was. But, to paraphrase Northrop Frye, Where was here? And what was the price of admission?

A writer in academe gives up making writing the focus of her life — sacrifices the freedom *to* write — in exchange for the freedom *from* poverty and perhaps obscurity. Although the comparative generosity of Canadian arts funding creates an environment in which it *is* possible to write full time, at least for a while — the length of that while depending on the success of one's work and grant writing skills, and on one's household circumstances, place of residence, and ability to live frugally — those of us disheartened or exhausted by the stresses of grant-to-grant, contract-to-contract living opt for the American model of seeking a teaching position. If poets south of the border, some of whom command $5,000 or more for a reading, hold institutional affiliations, how much more enticing, one would think, would be a stable source of income for Canadian writers, most of whom will appear almost anywhere in the country for airfare, hotel, a meal, and the standard $250 Canada Council honorarium (which has not changed since I began to do paid readings in 1996).

And yet, most writers here are more skeptical of institutional affiliation and less pragmatic than I was. Some harbour deep suspicions of teaching positions, equating them with the death of one's existence as a writer. While in the United States nearly every one of the thousands who annually complete an MFA or MA, and certainly those embarked on a creative writing PhD, aspires to teach, I've had students tell me, frankly, that they're not interested in teaching writing: they want to write. And so, despite Montreal's considerable draws, if recollection serves I was one of some sixty applicants for Concordia's position, not, as would be the case in the United States, one of several hundred.

In his essay "Poetry and Ambition," Donald Hall laments the fact that, for over half a century, writers in academe have been increasingly segregated in creative writing programs rather than participating in English departments.

The kind of English department writer he has in mind, though, is the writer/ critic — he mentions Yvor Winters, who, he claims, "entered the academy under sufferance, condescended to" (139). What about the writer who is sought for his or her profile as a literary practitioner, but whose departmental affiliation is the same as that of those whose engagement with the written word is of a markedly different nature?

At a Politics and the Pen dinner on Parliament Hill, a short fiction writer I scarcely knew advised, on learning that I'd been hired at Concordia, that perhaps it wouldn't be such a bad thing to not be a great teacher. A poet and fellow overachiever, my superior at the National Gallery, counselled me to cultivate an air of fragility, to indicate that my need to write was primary and that other tasks would get in the way of my fulfillment of that need. It would go without saying, then, that to ask too much of me would make me an unproductive, non-publishing writer, a poor teacher, and a miserable colleague. Another poet, who had chosen the route of editing, reviewing, and writing criticism — all of this, partly by choice, partly by necessity, outside the university — cited examples of writing faculty who had published little after being hired, or whose work had, he felt, markedly declined in quality. "Just tell me if you see that happening to me," I said. "Keep an eye on me."

But I didn't entirely believe that survival in the university required a strategy. My professors at UBC, whether out of a desire to protect their students' sensibilities from the tedium of much of academic life or a complete lack of interest in talking about anything unrelated to writing, hadn't disclosed the sheer weight of extra-literary, extra-pedagogical responsibility that an academic position entailed. One would think that two years of office work in various departments on campus would have opened my eyes, but I remained convinced that only those who became chairs or who chose (it didn't seriously occur to me that they might have been coerced) to edit journals or head major committees faced significant service demands.

My first suggestion of what lay in wait came midway through the summer of 2000, as I was packing up to move to Montreal. I received an email from a writer who said she'd been sent my way by one of my new colleagues on the understanding that I would be looking after the English department's reading series for the coming year. With a faint sense of doom, I queried the chair. As it turned out, my predecessor had coordinated the series and it had been decided that I would take over. He apologized for having forgotten to tell me, but couldn't, of course, apologize for assigning me the role; a writer himself, he had given so much to the institution that what was being asked of me felt paltry.

Not only was I unprepared for the service commitments of a university teaching position, I'd underestimated the difference between teaching a continuing education class to mature students and teaching a year-long graded course to undergraduates fresh out of high school or CEGEP. I soon realized that the method by which I had been taught — a sort of workshop immersion, in which we learned how to talk about writing by talking about writing — was woefully inadequate in a class of twenty-three students (close to twice the size of my own first workshop), many of whom had not written poetry before and most of whom had little experience of or interest in reading it.

When I learned that curricular logistics made it impossible to require students to take an Introduction to Poetry literature course concurrently with an introductory poetry course in creative writing, I built the literature course into the creative writing one. While I used to require students to submit their work to journals, now I require them to write craft-oriented book reviews. My students write essays, give presentations, do regular exercises (including some designed specifically to shake them up), and read essays on craft. While thought bubbles over their heads may say, "I'd rather be workshopping," I know the workshop discussions, when they happen, benefit from all the rest. Although there are seven of us with tenured or tenure-track positions in creative writing — a healthy number for a Canadian creative writing program — my colleagues and I remain just under 30 percent of the twenty-four total departmental faculty. My title, "Professor, Department of English" seems a misnomer, not to mention that in institutional correspondence I'm respectfully granted the honorific "Dr."

How not to feel like an imposter when asked to assess the comparative qualifications of various candidates for a medievalist position? How to voice my dismay that so few scholars seem to do close reading any longer — that theory has overtaken an interest in a work of literature as a made thing, assembled of words and punctuation marks — without sounding retrograde or simply naive? How to grapple with the absence of evaluative judgment among academics, for whom it seems anathema to comment on a work's aesthetic quality, so rife with political implications are terms like "good"? I don't have true insight into what it's like to teach a lecture course of eighty students with no teaching assistant, nor do my academic colleagues know what it's like to teach twenty students, from whom submissions of work are ongoing and often revealing, and for whom assessment always feels — and on some level is — personal. Only a stalwart few of my academic colleagues offer to serve as readers for creative writing theses. At many times, the two "streams" in my department are indeed, to use Hugh MacLennan's term, "two solitudes."

Before being hired, I'd heard of SSHRC. That was as far as my knowledge went; it was someone else's acronym. Had I not been part of an academic department in a university intent on augmenting its research profile, I would never have felt compelled to attend an information session on research grants shortly before teaching my first class. Joining me were two recently hired colleagues, one a novelist, the other a Renaissance specialist. The novelist and I took few notes, quickly realizing that the nature of our practice disqualified us from grants with a scholarly orientation; the Renaissance specialist, meanwhile, stayed up for nights on end and produced a successful application. For the next few years, I took solace in the fact that I was exempt from the fierce institutional demands to bring in funds; then SSHRC introduced its research/creation grants. Immunity lost, I began the process of writing the most epic application I'd ever completed, filling out CV forms online to list every poem I'd ever published, every reading I'd given, every prize or grant I'd received (in dollar value, of course), all using an elaborate, plodding multiple-choice system. For six weeks, this is how I spent my weekends. Soon after learning that my project had been funded, I began to understand a colleague's joke that the best thing about getting a grant was not having to apply for at least another three years.

To spend the money meant hiring research assistants. For the first time, I delegated aspects of my creative life, sending grad students off to gather material for poems I might write. Though I was grateful to be able to fund them, and no doubt they were happier doing this than waiting tables, I couldn't help thinking that I was missing out, since often it was the material on the facing page from what I thought I was looking for that *really* sparked a poem.

In order to ensure that the funded research assistants also had more meaningful work, I'd proposed as part of my application an anthology project that paralleled in subject the poetry manuscript I would write. While I wrote poems about zoos, the RAs and I would research, compile, select, and introduce poems by others on the same subject. This project, the metaphor of which began to apply disconcertingly to its impact on my life, occupied much of my non-teaching time for several years. While the grant paid for my travels to historic European zoos, it offered no teaching release. Not surprisingly, I wrote less than I would have written without funding. The resulting anthology, *Penned,* was published in 2009; my own book did not see print until fall 2011, by which time it was often misunderstood as an offshoot of the anthology rather than the other way around. On the official record, the grant was a success, but it confirmed that my own practice is, at least so far, one that requires time more than money.

And time is scarce. During my first year of teaching I wrote regularly, while each year since then I've written less and less from September to April until, now that I have two children, I have resigned myself to not writing more than a few lines of poetry during the teaching year. As August ticks to a close and department meetings and orientations begin, I feel my life as a writer, rejuvenated during the summer, shutting down. I make notes on ideas for directions I hope to follow when I begin to write in earnest again the following May. Before classes begin, I think, "I cannot do this again" — and then something happens.

A class discussion takes flight as a student encounters William Car[?] Williams's "The Red Wheelbarrow" for the first time and asks what mak[?] a poem. A student who's submitted only heartfelt, overly obvious anec[?]

in the guise of poems writes an elliptical, imagistic wonder. Another student follows up on a reading recommendation with transformative results. A digressive conversation during office hours reveals the ongoing mystery and complexity of these human beings whose consciousnesses and aesthetics I have the privilege of sharing week after week. A novel I read in thesis form wins the Giller Prize. A student I taught years ago contacts me not to ask for a letter of recommendation but to express her gratitude for the course, from which she's still learning.

Although there's no doubt that I would have been a more prolific writer had I not submitted my application to Concordia, the loss I have felt as a result of the job has been of time, not of creativity. Rather than being diminished, my imagination has been augmented.

In a typical creative writing classroom, I see a richer range of writing than I do in any one Canadian literary journal; the distinctiveness of individual imaginations and aesthetics, before they become shaped by a desire to please the professor, the workshop group, or the magazine or book editor, continues to astonish me. The best and most innovative of my students have taught me new approaches to syntax, while the weaker have forced me to articulate criteria for excellence that have raised my standards for my own work. Students' boldness in rising to the challenges I set inspires and requires me to do the same. I read essays on poetic craft with a seriousness that I'd have been unlikely to bring to the task were there not a pedagogical imperative. At the end of every course, I tell my students that I will miss them, and I do.

When I'm critiquing a really fine poem, time vanishes as it does when I write; I'm not plunged into the depths of myself as when writing, but I'm plunged, nevertheless, into poetry. I discover other aesthetics and sensibilities, an experience no less memorable or illuminating — and certainly more refreshing — than swimming around in my own. Louise Glück has written eloquently on the ways in which ego vanishes when working with another's poem, "to get [it] right" (17). And although I'm not interested in influence in power-centric terms, I realize that in many ways I can have more of an impact on writing as a teacher than as a poet. In my twenties, I could, given the opportunity, write all day, every day. I'm not sure I could do that now, that I'd want to. Increasingly, I'm aware that writing is but a part of life that this is something to embrace rather than lament.

We come to teaching through our love of the material but, once here, we find ourselves talking to others all the time — students, colleagues, staff. My grant-and-freelance years were marked by long periods of solitude — sometimes leaving the house only to look at paintings or buy groceries — punctuated by bursts of enforced sociability when I went to a reading or spent a week giving school workshops. In that solitude, I wrote some of my best poems. But could I have called myself happy?

Although I had not anticipated this, the security of a tenured teaching position has largely protected me from a futile and distracting focus on grants, prizes, the breakthrough "poet's novel," and other potentially lucrative aspects of a writing career, freeing me to deepen rather than broaden, to work at my own pace, and to listen to my own instincts in developing an aesthetic that, for better or worse, does not privilege audience. The novel that I'd begun writing before being hired was, in part, motivated by an agent's interest in the novel that I might write. That I have not completed it, I must also admit, is partly due to the demands of teaching, but also to my recognition that my approach remains driven by image, language, mood, and idea rather than by character and plot, and that I haven't yet figured out how to make my strengths serve the form of the novel. So I have been free to take my time with prose, and to let my poems become increasingly idiosyncratic.

That I rarely see the friend who warned me not to stray off course attests to the different paths our lives have taken. If he were to report to me on my trajectory during the past decade, I'm fairly sure of what he would say, and I would agree. That I have succumbed to the demands of teaching and service; that during the past decade I have edited three books — one of which arose from my grant and one of which I was approached to edit in part because I taught writing — and published only one. That to shepherd books along is, though valuable, not equivalent to writing one's own. But what can he know of the rewards? I would respond that, as with parenthood, life is different on the other side.

WORKS CITED

Glück, Louise. "Education of the Poet." *Proofs and Theories*. New York: Ecco, 1994. Print.

Hall, Donald. "Poetry and Ambition." *Written in Water, Written in Stone: Twenty Years of Poets on Poetry*. Ed. Martin Lammon. Ann Arbor: U of Michigan P, 1996. Print.

McGurl, Mark. *The Program Era: Postwar Fiction and the Rise of Creative Writing*. Cambridge, MA: Harvard UP, 2009. Print.

PART IV

WRITING CREATIVE
WRITING PROGRAMS

Can'tLit: What Canadian English Departments Could (but Won't) Learn from the Creative Writing Programs They Host[*]

Darryl Whetter

SAY IT AIN'T SO

English writer Philip Hensher fulfills a writer's first duty — truth-telling — when writing novels about the idiocy of invading Afghanistan in *The Mulberry Empire* or the challenges of monogamy in *King of the Badgers*, and again as a creative writing professor willing to blow the whistle on how vehemently some English departments and professors hate writers, writing, and writing educations. Profiled in the *Guardian*, Hensher laments, "I learnt that there are people employed by English literature departments who hate literature and would put a stop to it if they could. They talk about literature being subversive and questioning of authority, but once they have admitted creative writing into a department they find that it can't be controlled and they don't like it" (Wroe). Despite this palpable hatred, Canada's pedagogical *spécialité de la maison* is to house creative writing programs in university English departments — "the enemies of literature," according to Hensher (*King* 365). Examples from Canadian university programs, professorial hiring, national research funding, and my own decade of work as a Canadian creative writing professor demonstrate a similar "hatred" between Canadian professors of English and the creative writing programs under their majority rule. This national preference

---

[*] A shorter version of this essay first appeared in issue 22.7 (2014) of the *Literary Review of Canada* and was then anthologized in *Best Canadian Essays 2015*. A similar, full-length version appears in the Routledge journal *New Writing: The International Journal for the Practice and Theory of Creative Writing*, 11.1 (2017), 316–26.

for having those who write about writing managing the educations of those who write has negative aesthetic, political, and economic consequences in and beyond Canadian education.

Canada's art historians and musicologists don't design and manage the education of our visual artists and composers, but English profs (who have rarely published books of poetry or fiction themselves) routinely control the educations of our writers, and with obvious costs to national and personal truth-telling. As indicated in the table below, the number of graduate writing programs in Canada *doubled* within the 2000s, yet various factors within the Canadian academy (not the internationally popular discipline of creative writing), find most Canadian writing programs more devoted to the head than the heart and managed, not coincidentally, by English departments. Our writing grads are much more likely to be versed in Elizabethan celibacy or Victorian diarists than what William Faulkner so rightly describes as "the human heart in conflict with itself." I've taught writing for a decade now at four Canadian universities and am worried that — with English professors predominantly calling the shots — few Canadian creative writing programs teach or even entertain core writerly skills like social-emotional intelligence, revealing, engaged and accurate dialogue, dramatic tension, comedy, and, most notably, plot.

ENGLISH-LANGUAGE MASTER'S WRITING PROGRAMS IN CANADA

Pre-2000	Post-2000
MA in English and Creative Writing	
University of Calgary	University of Toronto
Concordia University	University of Regina
University of Manitoba	
University of New Brunswick	
University of Windsor	

MFA in Creative Writing

University of British Columbia   University of Victoria

University of Guelph

University of Saskatchewan

King's University (creative non-fiction only)

In his *Lectures on Literature*, Vladimir Nabokov writes, "Let us worship the spine and its tingle.… The study of the sociological or political impact of literature [is] for those who are by temperament or education immune to the aesthetic vibrancy of authentic literature, for those who do not experience the telltale tingle between the shoulder blades" (64). Canadian creative writing programs rarely share Nabokov's devotion to a spinal "tingle." The current practices of our writing programs and funding agencies generally ask writers to be scholars who simply drop the footnotes, while graduate creative writing education in all major anglophone countries of comparison values the unique fusion of personal and cultural truth available to the creative writer and her reader.

(WHY DON'T WE) "FOLLOW THE MONEY"(?)

Canada's globally unique lack of interest in the exponentially growing market for a creative writing education hurts Canada intellectually, culturally, and economically. Canada's English departments ignore what Mark McGurl's *The Program Era: Postwar Fiction and the Rise of Creative Writing* rightly describes as creative writing's "insatiable student demand — that simultaneously progressive and consumerist value" (94). McGurl's bar graph about the growth of creative writing education in the United States shows a supplier's dream: an exponentially growing market (25). The Victorianists and Miltonists who run the majority of Canada's writing programs disregard not just the Canadian and global demand for a creative writing education in particular, but also creative education in general. Daniel Pink's *A Whole New Mind: Why Right-Brainers Will Rule the Future* observes, "In the US, the number of graphic designers has increased tenfold in a decade; graphic designers outnumber chemical engineers by four to one. Since 1970, the US has 30% more people earning a living as writers.... Some 240 US universities have established creative writing MFA programs, up from fewer than twenty two decades ago" (55). The well-documented efficacy of arts funding should find Canadian creative writing grads who are creative problem solvers and polyvocal communicators with varied employment opportunities. The Canadian Conference of the Arts (CCA) observes that approximately $9 billion of (tri-level) government spending in culture yields, according to the Conference Board of Canada, roughly $85 billion or "7.4% of Canada's total real GDP" (4). Analyzing figures from Statistics Canada and the Canadian Auto Workers union, the CCA counts more full-time Canadian artists (140,000) than autoworkers (135,000) (*Useful* 3). It also observes that "the percentage of artists who are self-employed is six times the self-employment rate in the overall labour force" (*Useful* 4).* More specifically, Statistics Canada counts, "Total operating revenues for the [Canadian] book publishing industry amounted to $2.0 billion in 2010" (*Book Publishing* 4).

Canada's creative writing graduates may in fact be more employable than those Canadian English majors conscripted into professionalized anglophilia, yet they are continually given short shrift by the *Moby Dick* experts and other scholars of non-Canadian literature who manage their educations. The University of Windsor has one of Canada's older master's programs in creative writing. Its creative writing undergrads (and/or undergraduate English majors) are required to take one credit of *either* American or Canadian literature (compared to several of English literature). Can any reader imagine a Portuguese university allowing its literature majors to substitute a Spanish literature course for the national literature? In February of 2012, I did a Canada Council–sponsored reading at Nipissing University. Chatting with a student, I asked which of her literature courses were most stimulating for the novel she was sketching now and hoped to work on

---

* In Scotland, the synergistic combination of profitable arts funding and the creative adaptability of artist entrepreneurs has led, according to Cabinet Secretary for Culture and External Affairs Fiona Hyslop, to Scotland naming "the creative industries" as "one of the seven priority sectors in the Scottish Government's economic strategy" ("Scotland's Economy").

significantly following graduation ("A Conversation with"). She replied that her two remaining English courses, Restoration Drama and Prairie Realism, did not really pertain to her novel about a contemporary Canadian woman coming of age in a city. This student's education is not good value for her or her country.

"ONLY IN CANADA, EH? PITY"*

The uninformed or hostile managers of Canada's creative writing programs who ignore student demand, the cost-effectiveness of arts spending, and the enormity of Canada's book industry do so at national cost (despite their government funding). As demonstrated in Figure 1, Canada lags behind almost all Western countries in the number of PhD graduates aged twenty-five to twenty-nine per 100,000 people (*Public Education* 16). Canada's low per capita completion of PhDs is shameful considering our global record for the highest per capita undergraduate enrollment (Grossman). The institutional disregard for creative writing and/or the study of Canadian literature (including that produced by creative writing grads) is illustrated by the national lack of interest in capitalizing on our high interest in undergraduate education in general and our ballooning interest in creative writing masters' degrees in particular. Notably, the doubling of master's creative writing programs in Canada has not been met here — as it has in other anglophone countries — with attendant changes in the number of Canadian doctoral programs in creative writing. A database at the Australian Association of Writing Programs lists 10 PhD programmes in CW (Australian). Despite Canada's ballooning number of creative writing master's programs and, as noted below, federal scholarship funding for creative writing PhD students, Canada has just three creative writing doctoral programs (and only two in English). Why does Australia — with 85 percent of our anglophone population and a highly comparable post-colonial history — have five times the number of anglophone creative writing PhD programs?

The United States also shames our doctoral creative writing offerings. AWP Executive Director David Fenza counts thirty-six creative writing PhD programs ("A Brief History"). In round numbers, the United States has ten

* This phrase was the tagline in a Canadian series of tea commercials from the 1970s ("Red Rose").

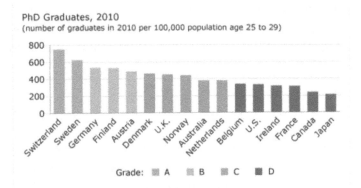

PhD Graduates, 2010
(number of graduates in 2010 per 100,000 population age 25 to 29)

Grade: ▓ A   ▒ B   ▨ C   ■ D

Reprinted with permission of author, the Canadian Federation of Students (*Public Education* 16).

times Canada's population yet twenty times the number of creative writing PhD programs. America's commitment to what Fenza calls "the art of writing as essential to a good education" has resulted, he claims, in "the largest system of literary patronage the world has ever seen" ("A Brief History"). Notably, this American patronage has evolved in an educational marketplace of both state-funded and privately funded universities. Unlike Canadian universities, American, Australian, and United Kingdom universities do not ignore the staggering student demand for graduate creative writing educations.

Unchecked discipline hostility appears to be one reason Canadian universities have not responded to the frankly insistent market for more Canadian creative writing PhD programs. In *Harper's*, American author and semi-reluctant writing professor Lynn Freed refers to graduate creative writing programs as "the cash cow of the humanities" (69). Fenza, too, knows that "creative writing classes have become among the most popular classes in the humanities." Amazingly (and at national cost), Canadian Humanities programs are uninterested in this cash cow. If the Canadian English professors who ignore the student demand for creative writing PhDs (to say nothing of the intellectual and cultural opportunities they afford) were wasting their own money, I'd be more forgiving. However, their cart-before-the-horse sales strategy insists on marketing a product students don't want to buy. McGurl contrasts the rapid growth of graduate creative writing with the minimal growth of graduate English degrees: "In 2003–04 there was a total of 591 US institutions offering either an MA (428) or a PhD (143) in English literature. In 1991–92 that number had been 549. This represents an increase of 7 percent, as compared to a 39 percent increase in the number of creative writing programs over the same period" (414). Countries with an abundance of creative writing PhD programs (such as the United States, the United Kingdom, and Australia) have much higher general completion rates for PhDs per capita (*Public Education* 16). As noted below, the Social Sciences and Humanities Research Council of Canada (SSHRC) is theoretically just as willing to fund a PhD thesis that *is* a Canadian novel instead of a disquisition *about* a Canadian novel. In the single most popular TED Talk ever, on the lack of creativity in schools, Sir Ken Robinson claims that "every education system on Earth has the same hierarchy of subjects.... And in pretty much every system too, there's a hierarchy within the arts. Art and music are normally given a higher status in schools than drama and dance" (Robinson). Canada's English professors perpetually hierarchize English literature over Canadian literature *and* all literature over creative writing.

DICK AND JANE VS. THE PALIMPSEST

Others who have taught in one of Canada's hybrid English–creative writing programs[*] have surely experienced that moment when a student, usually in third year and drunk on theory, discovers the word *palimpsest* and then writes a palimpsestic poem or scene of fiction. Palimpsests are undeniably interesting, but are they the appropriate focus for a writer's education? Before proceeding to evidence on *how* Canadian creative writing education promotes the head (palimpsests and rhizomes; England and the past) at the expense of the heart (love, humour, and plot), allow me to clarify the terms of debate. John Barth, high priest of both writing programs and, not coincidentally, postmodern fiction, utterly confuses the form and content of minimalism in his claim that "a language's repertoire of other-than-basic

---

[*] For reference, my creative writing tours of duty are: University of New Brunswick, 2000–01; University of Windsor, 2001–05; Dalhousie University, 2008–10 (as creative writing coordinator); Université Sainte-Anne, 2007–08 and 2010–present. All schools house their writing programs in English departments. My teaching load has varied from 50:50 creative writing and English (at Windsor) to 100 percent creative writing (Dalhousie) and has included graduate creative writing thesis supervision (Windsor).

syntactical devices permits its users to articulate other-than-basic thoughts and feelings" before going on to the utterly wrongheaded conclusion that "Dick-and-Jane prose tends to be emotionally and intellectually poorer than Henry James prose" (70–71). Given, amongst other facts, Canada's preference for making a creative writing education the smaller fraction in an English–creative writing degree, we routinely share Barth's preference for sesquipedalian pyrotechnics over social-emotional intelligence. Robert Olen Butler, a senior professor in Florida State University's influential graduate writing program and a winner of the Pulitzer Prize for fiction, knows, "We are the yearning creatures of this planet.... Every second we yearn for something. And fiction, inescapably, is the art form of human yearning" (40). Canada's national preference for a writing degree split — almost never equally — between writing workshops and English lecture courses combines with our national refusal to serve our own market for terminal degrees in creative writing and with institutional biases for scholarship over creative production to provide writing educations designed to produce clever and textually deft but emotionally underdeveloped writers.

I did the hybrid MA program at the University of New Brunswick and taught for four years in the one at Windsor. At their best, these hybrid programs combine the (crucial) peer learning of graduate-level writing workshops and creative theses with a good grounding in relevant literature. At their worst, the hybrid programs are like a military education that requires a tour of duty in literature seminars, where candidates will write scholarly essays, not stories or poems. Our national preference for argumentation and citation over emotion in creative writing pedagogy is manifest in the oral thesis "defences" required in these half-English MAs. The title and ritual of a defence suggest that a candidate can argue the merit of her collection of poems or stories, not simply present stories or poems that are their own argument. At Columbia, the largest and arguably most influential creative writing MFA program in the United States, a creative writing thesis passes or fails exclusively as a written document. If it passes, the committee then meets with the student at a "thesis conference" to discuss strengths and challenges ("Columbia Writing"; "Writing"). Canadian thesis defences are a clear hangover from the aped scientism of New Criticism (the zombie engine of English). McGurl's *The Program Era* warns, "With its penchant for specialized vocabularies and familiarity with the less-travelled regions of the library, literary scholarship is at least partly in sync with the scientism of its wider institutional environment, the research university. Creative writing, by contrast, might seem to have no ties at all to the pursuit of positive knowledge. It is, rather, an experiment — but more accurately, an exercise — in subjectivity" (405).

Canada's institutional fear of the inner life wants arguments, not poems, and rarely aesthetic arguments at that. English in Canada remains hostile or indifferent to evaluative criticism. This whistle-blowing from the academic snake pit should illustrate the kinds of people and priorities that govern the majority of creative writing educations in Canada. I spent two years as the coordinator of the creative writing program at Dalhousie University from 2008–10. Dal displays the national preference for a colonial ownership of creative writing by an English department to such a degree that the creative writing program had *no* permanent faculty from 2008 until 2015. During my two (limited-term) years at Dal, the English department professors strenuously debated whether or not they should reduce their teaching load from five courses over eight months to four. Such a reduction was ultimately endorsed by a nearly unanimous majority, but not before it was clarified to all stakeholders, including upper administration and most notably students, that creative writing professors would continue to teach a full third more than their English colleagues. If you wanted to study Russian, German, or Sanskrit at Dal, you could study with a prof who would be there next year and was paid to answer emails in the summer and who could compete for internal research funding, vote on major committees, and so forth. Not so for creative writing, even though, as the Writers' Union of Canada points out, Canada's cultural industries provide roughly twice as much GDP as the agricultural and forestry industries (*Pre-Budget*).

"NOBODY KNOWS ANYTHING"*

In the past two decades, creative writing in North America has shifted from the untutored ethos of rock and roll to the formal accreditation of a classical music education. Nonetheless, McGurl, Pink, and Fenza compellingly argue that we're long past debating whether creative writing can be

---

* Screenwriter and novelist William Goldman's famous description of the unpredictability of a movie's success (qtd. in Surowiecki).

taught (McGurl 24; Pink 27; "Brief History"). Twenty years ago, Canadian visual artists studied their craft at university, but writers largely didn't. Writers educated in the 1980s like Douglas Coupland, Lisa Moore, and Margaret Christakos actually majored in visual arts, not writing ("Douglas"; Christakos; "Lisa"). Now, graduate writing programs offer mentoring and peer critique (at a time when editors are busy marketing) as well as exposure to visiting authors, experience on literary journals, and financial assistance. Fenza notes, "Academic programs [in creative writing!] have mustered hundreds of millions of dollars to support the study, making, and enjoyment of literature." In Canada, creative writing should be a bridge between our multimillion-dollar industries in publishing and tertiary education.

In addition to our national preference for graduate writing degrees that must pay obeisance to codpiece poetry or radical textuality, crucial state institutions like SSHRC also prefer a junior writer's scholarly potential, not her creative output. In *Muriella Pent*, Russell Smith's satire of the culture of culture, an application form for a Toronto artistic residency overtly states "DO NOT ATTACH A WRITING SAMPLE" (106), and "Please note that support materials in the form of writing samples are no longer a part of the application process" (108). This same preference for explanations over art is funny in Canadian satire yet sad in public policy. The very real SSHRC does fund master's and PhD students (including creative writing students), yet its application similarly forbids a writing sample ("Eligibility"; Chaumont). SSHRC applicants submit a bibliography, but *not* a writing sample. SSHRC could be a significant patron of the Canadian arts. In 2008–09, SSHRC doled out more than $300 million in grants and fellowships to graduate students, faculty, institutions, and research projects, yet very little of that money went to storytellers and their traffic in social-emotional intelligence. The searchable awards database at the SSHRC site finds fewer than 5 fiction projects out of 121 projects in its Research/Creation Grants in the Fine Arts program for faculty ("Research/Creation"). Even the slash in the program title (always the hybrids!) shows our national refusal to respect art as art: English scholars and art historians could apply to this program *in addition to* other SSHRC standard research grants that would fund writing about novels but not the writing of novels. Write, and SSHRC had half a biennial program for you; write about, and it has several. I served on a SSHRC Research/ Creation jury in 2015–16, and nearly all the projects recommended for funding were exclusively scholarly and not creative or artistic ("Insight"). The same jury that was tasked with evaluating proposals for plays and novels also had proposals for exclusively scholarly articles or books on Shakespeare and Byzantine art in the same competition. The latter, not the former, received almost all the recommendations for funding. Not funding stories means not funding characters and, arguably, emotions and the inner life.

The political fallout of Canada's creative writing hostage-taking extends beyond where and what is studied by whom and includes, perhaps most significantly, what is written. Our national preference for arguments over art-making risks a hyper-rational ghettoization of graduate creative writing material. For almost half a century Susan Sontag's essay "Against Interpretation" has called for "in place of a hermeneutics ... an erotics of art," yet we keep steeping our writing students in hermeneutics, not aesthetics (7). University-trained (American) writer Sandra Cisneros states overtly that when she wrote her breakthrough novel *The House on Mango Street* she consciously used "a child's voice, a girl's voice" as an explicitly "anti-academic voice" (xv). The marginalization of emotional complexity within so-called humanities disciplines can additionally distance the marginal voices many profs claim to serve.

"UGLY WITH AN EXPLANATION"*

Canada's disregard for emotional complexity creates a creative writing pedagogy that denies students literature's fundamental work with empathy. Scottish writer Andrew O'Hagan's novel *Be Near Me* has the best, and shortest, definition of education I've ever read: "managed revelation" (32). Too often in Canada, a creative writing education involves conscripted decorum or endless reading lists from somewhere else, whether it be England, the past, or the developing world instead of "managed revelation" (32). Days after 9/11, Ian McEwan published a *Guardian* article that hinges on literature's stimulation of empathy: "Imagining what it is like to be someone other than yourself is at the core of our humanity. It is the essence of compassion, and it is the beginning of morality" ("Only Love"). Aesthetic theoreticians and cognitive psychologists also recognize the ways in which literature, especially

---

* *New Yorker* art critic Adam Gopnik distinguishes between art that is "Beauty Per Se" and "Ugly with an Explanation. Andy and Duchamp and so on" (83).

narrative literature, allow us to expand our minds by thinking like others. In a section of his *The Art Instinct* called "The Uses of Fiction," Denis Dutton argues that "of all the arts, [fiction] is the best suited to portray the mundane imaginative structures of memory, immediate perception, planning, calculation, and decision-making, both as we experience them ourselves and as we understand others to be experiencing them. But storytelling is also capable of taking us beyond the ordinary, and therein lies its mind-expanding capacity. To understand, intellectually and emotionally, the mind of another is a distinct ability that emerges ... [an] evolved adaptation" (119). Dutton goes on to conclude, "Fiction provides us, then, with templates, mental maps for emotional life" (122). Cognitive psychologist and novelist Keith Oatley summarizes human conversation as "verbal grooming" and suggests, "The primary function of conversation is to maintain relationships — a large number of relationships — and *to maintain intimacy in relationships*" (86; emphasis added).

The empathy-rich medium of fiction is not simply a font of emotion, but also intelligence. Creativity scholar and educational psychologist Howard Gardner observes that "many people with IQs of 160 work for people with IQs of 100.... In the day-to-day world no intelligence is more important than the interpersonal" (qtd. in Goleman 41). A national creative writing education that privileges literary analysis over literary production shuns interpersonal intelligence. George Eliot claims, "The greatest benefit we owe to the artist, whether painter, poet or novelist, is the extension of our sympathies.... Art is the nearest thing to life; it is a mode of amplifying experience and extending our contact with our fellow-men" (qtd. in Cooke 144). One can hear the phrase "rhizomatic poetics" in any Canadian university English department (including those that offer creative writing); one rarely hears the word "empathy" (or the excitement that attends to rhizomatism). We adore the fragmentary but disparage feelings. Harvard psychology PhD Daniel Goleman calls social-emotional intelligence "a meta-ability, determining how well we can use whatever other skills we have, including raw intellect" (36). In a land of methodology, thesis defences, bibliographies, and "uncreative writing," the crucial "meta-ability" of emotional intelligence fostered by literature is not meeting its maximum audience.

"THE GREAT GENEROSITIES"

As a university discipline, creative writing should be a thinking and communication tool, and it deserves a place at every institute of higher learning. Unacceptably, however, writing in Canada is managed (and sometimes even taught) by profs who have never published creative writing or have not published it in decades. Not even Canada would short-change its music or fine arts students in this way, yet we'll appoint unqualified English profs to direct or even teach story writing. Fenza knows: "In addition to advancing the art of literature, creative writing workshops exercise and strengthen the resourcefulness of the human will, and it is the exercise of will not over others, but for others, as stories and poems are made as gifts for readers and listeners." Henry James also attends to the "great generosities" of writing: "We trust to novels to train us in the practice of great indignations and great generosities" (86). In Canada, university after university has created a writing education that cheats its paying students of the great generosities of social-emotional intelligence.

WORKS CITED

"2010–2011 Course Offerings." Department of English, Home, Graduate. Concordia U. Web. 27 Jun. 2012.

"5000 Series 2011–2012." English, 2011–12 Course Timetable. U of Toronto. 22 Nov. 2011. Web. 27 Jun. 2012.

Australian Association of Writing Programs. 2016. "Writing Courses: Creative Writing, Doctoral." Web. 22 Sep. 2016. www.aawp.org.au/category/doctorate+creative-writing/.

Barth, John. "A Few Words About Minimalism." *Further Fridays: Essays, Lectures, and Other Nonfiction, 1984–1994*. Boston: Little Brown, 1995. Print.

Butler, Robert Olen. *From Where You Dream: The Process of Writing Fiction*. New York: Grove, 2006. Print.

Canadian Conference of the Arts. "Useful Statistics. Ottawa: Canadian Conference of the Arts," 13 Mar. 2012. Web. 22 Jun. 2012.

Canadian Federation of Students. Fig. 3.3. *Public Education for the Public Good*. Ottawa: Canadian Federation of Students, Oct. 2011. Web. 22 Jun. 2012.

Chaumont, Monique. "766-2013-A07 RE: Prof. Queries MA Requirements for Research." Email to Darryl Whetter. 7 Jun. 2011.

Christakos, Margaret. "Re: Q for mag: Vis. Art?" Email to Darryl Whetter. 7 Jun. 2011.

Cisneros, Sandra. Introduction. *The House on Mango Street*. New York: Vintage, 1991. Print.

"Columbia Writing Professor Sends World's Haughtiest Email to Former Students." *Gawker*, 29 Sep. 2010. Web. 27 Jun. 2012.

"Common Plants: Cross Pollinations in Hybrid Reality." Awards Search Engine. Social Sciences and Humanities Research Council of Canada. Web. 22 Jun. 2012.

"A Conversation with Darryl Whetter." *CCA Reads*. Nipissing U. 29 May 2012. Web. 26 Jun. 2012.

Cooke, George Willis. *George Eliot: A Critical Study of Her Life, Writings and Philosophy*. Boston: Osgood, 1884. Print.

"Douglas Coupland 'Welcome to the Twenty-First Century.'" Daniel Faria Gallery. Web. 27 Jun. 2012.

Dutton, Denis. *The Art Instinct: Beauty, Pleasure, and Human Evolution.* Oxford: Oxford UP, 2009. Print.

"Eligibility." *Joseph-Armand Bombardier Canada Graduate Scholarships Program Master's Scholarships.* Social Sciences and Humanities Research Council of Canada. 3 Nov. 2011. Web. 22 Jun. 2012.

"Faculty Listing — Alphabetical." Department of English. Queen's U. 2012. Web. 26 Jun. 2012.

"Faculty Members." Department of English. Dalhousie U. 20 Jun. 2012. Web. 26 Jun. 2012.

Faulkner, William. "Banquet Speech." Nobelprize.org. 2011. Web. 26 Jun. 2012.

Fenza, David. "A Brief History of AWP." *About AWP: The Growth of Creative Writing Programs.* Association of Writers & Writing Programs, 2011. Web. 22 Jun. 2012.

Freed, Lynn. "Doing Time: My Years in the Creative Writing Gulag." *Harper's Magazine* Jul. 2005: 65–72. Print.

"Full-Time Faculty." Department of English. U of Western Ontario. Web. 26 Jun. 2012.

Gardner, Howard. *Creating Minds: An Anatomy of Creativity as Seen Through the Lives of Freud, Einstein, Picasso, Stravinsky, Eliot, Graham, and Gandhi.* New York: Basic Books, 1993. Print.

———. *Multiple Intelligences: The Theory in Practice.* New York: Basic Books, 1992. Print.

Goleman, Daniel. *Emotional Intelligence: Why It Can Matter More Than IQ.* New York: Bantam, 1995. Print.

Gopnik, Adam. "The Children of the Party." *The New Yorker* 12 May 1997: 78–91. Print.

"Graduate Courses: 2012–2013 Course Offerings." Faculty of Arts, Graduate Programs, English. U of New Brunswick. Web. 26 Jun. 2012.

Grossman, Samantha. "And the World's Most Educated Country Is …" *Time.* Time Inc., 27 Sep. 2013. Web. 28 Sep. 2013.

Hensher, Philip. *King of the Badgers.* London: Fourth Estate, 2011. Print.

———. *The Mulberry Empire.* New York: Knopf, 2002. Print.

"Honours English Language and Literature." *Fall 2012 Undergraduate Calendar.* U of Windsor. 2010. Web. 26 Jun. 2012.

"Honours English Literature and Creative Writing." *Fall 2012 Undergraduate Calendar*. U of Windsor. 2010. Web. 26 Jun. 2012.

"Insight Grants Selection Committees: October 2015 Competition." Social Sciences and Humanities Research Council of Canada. Government of Canada. Web. May 18, 2016. www.sshrc-crsh.gc.ca/funding-financement/merit_review-evaluation_du_merite/selection_committees-comites_selection/insight_grants-subventions_savoir_oct2015-eng.aspx.

James, Henry. *Notes and Reviews with a Preface by Pierre de Chaignon La Rose: A Series of Twenty-Five Papers Hitherto Unpublished in Book Form*. 1923. Charleston: Nabu, 2010. Print.

"Lisa Moore BFA '88." *Alumni Gallery*. NSCAD U. 2008. Web. 26 Jun. 2012.

McEwan, Ian. "Only Love and Then Oblivion. Love Was All They Had to Set Against Their Murderers." *Writers on 9/11. Guardian*, 15 Sep. 2001. Web. 7 Jul. 2012.

McGurl, Mark. *The Program Era: Postwar Fiction and the Rise of Creative Writing*. Cambridge: Harvard UP, 2009. Print.

Morrissey, Donna. *What They Wanted*. Toronto: Viking, 2008. Print.

Musgrave, David. "Re: Cdn. CW Prof Double-Checks # of Aus. CW PhD Programs." Email to Darryl Whetter. 21 Jun. 2012.

Nabokov, Vladimir. *Lectures on Literature*. San Diego: Harvest, 1982. Print.

Oatley, Keith. *Such Stuff as Dreams: The Psychology of Fiction*. Chichester: Wiley-Blackwell, 2011. Print.

O'Hagan, Andrew. *Be Near Me*. 2006. Toronto: McClelland and Stewart, 2008. Print.

"People." Faculty of Arts, English. U of New Brunswick. Web. 26 Jun. 2012.

Pink, Daniel. *A Whole New Mind: Why Right-Brainers Will Rule the Future*. New York: Riverhead, 2005. Print.

"Project Zero." *Project Zero*. Harvard College. 2010. Web. 7 Jul. 2012.

"Red Rose 1977 TV Commercial." YouTube. Uploaded by robatsea2009, 4 Aug. 2011. Web. https://youtu.be/KAtDXOnmqiM.

"Research/Creation Grants in Fine Arts." Awards Search Engine. Social Sciences and Humanities Research Council of Canada. N.p., n.d. Web. 22 Jun. 2012.

Robinson, Sir Ken. "Schools Kill Creativity." *TED*. TED Talk. Jun. 2006. Web. 5 Jul. 2012.

"Scotland's Economy Thrives on Creativity." *Year of Creative Scotland 2012.* Creative Scotland, 28 Jun. 2012. Web. 9 Jul. 2012.

Smith, Russell. *Muriella Pent.* Toronto: Doubleday, 2004. Print.

Sontag, Susan. "Against Interpretation." *Against Interpretation and Other Essays.* New York: Farrar, Strauss & Giroux, 1963. Print.

Surowiecki, James. "The Science of Success." *The New Yorker* 9 Jul. 2007. Web. 27 Jun. 2012.

Statistics Canada. *Book Publishing 2010.* Book Publishers Ser. 87F0004X. Ottawa: Statistics Canada, 2012. Web. 13 Jun. 2012.

Wilbers, Stephen. *The Iowa Writers' Workshop: Origins, Emergence, & Growth.* Iowa City: U of Iowa P, 1980. Print.

Writers' Union of Canada. Pre-Budget Consultations for Budget 2010. Toronto: Writers' Union of Canada, 2009. Print.

"Writing." Columbia University School of the Arts: 2009–2010. Columbia U. 2009. Web. 28 Aug. 2012.

"Writing Courses." Creative Writing, Doctoral. Australasian Association of Writing Programs. Web. 21 Jun. 2012.

Wroe, Nicholas. "Philip Hensher: A Life in Writing." *Guardian*, 30 Mar. 2012. Web. 26 Jun. 2012.

The Low-Residency MFA: Coast to Coast and Across the Border

Lori A. May

Since the low-residency Master of Fine Arts (MFA) model was first developed in the 1970s, its proliferation has expanded to nearly sixty such programs. These are predominantly offered in the United States, with less than 10 percent offered by international institutions. Canada has just two low-residency MFA programs: the University of British Columbia (UBC) launched its optional-residency multi-genre program in 2005, and the University of King's College in Halifax launched its creative non-fiction program in 2013. Like the more traditional counterpart, a low-residency MFA is a terminal degree; students focus on craft and creative development, yet they also exit the program with qualifications to teach writing at the college level. The low-res model includes intensive workshops, assigned readings and analysis, exposure to publishing professionals, and the culmination of a creative thesis. The only difference in the low-residency MFA, then, is in how the program is delivered.

Low-residency programs offer a two-part model: term work is completed at a distance through packet exchanges with a mentor and/or in online or hybrid delivery, and programs range between two and three years of study; residencies, most often ranging between eight and twelve days, take place once or twice a year wherein faculty and students convene for intensive in-person instruction, workshops, and professional development sessions. Most programs begin each term with a residency to develop personal connections, as well as to inform and prepare students for the intensive term ahead. To continue the camaraderie established during residency, term work generally includes email and online forum discussions to allow for critiques, faculty mentoring, and peer interaction. Additionally, some faculty will consult with students over the phone or via Skype to enhance their mentor-student connection.

The appeal of the low-residency model is in its flexibility — for students and for institutions. Student-writers are able to benefit from the same level of intensive study as in an on-campus program without sacrificing their established lives, as relocation is not necessary. "Many writers simply cannot leave their homes, families, and jobs to take a full-time graduate residential MFA program," says Andrew Gray, founder of UBC's Optional-Residency MFA Program in Creative Writing.

While self-discipline is a must for the low-residency student, the challenge of balancing personal and academic activities provides solid preparation for the future writer. "There can be a temptation to treat distance education courses more casually since there is not a classroom where you have to be at a set time every week, and the distractions of the real world can be hard to ignore," Gray says. "Residential MFA programs are fairly artificial environments. In many ways, distance education students are more prepared for the continuing work required after graduation." After all, few writers rely exclusively on writing for their livelihoods; the ability to continue one's artistic pursuits amid a busy life of work and family is a skill honed in a low-residency program.

Institutions also benefit from increased flexibility with program delivery. The low-residency MFA uses campus space during off-peak times when residencies may utilize empty classrooms and dorms. "We're a small university with a small campus," says Stephen Kimber, professor in the School of Journalism at the University of King's College in Halifax and one of the low-residency program co-founders. "It would be very difficult, given our facilities, to add a new program that would require classrooms and labs during the regular school term. From a practical point of view we're making better use of those facilities in the summer season."

The model also allows for innovations previously unheard of in academia. For example, the Whidbey Writers Workshop MFA Program, formerly offered by the Northwest Institute of Literary Arts (NILA) in Coupeville, Washington, was the first program to be offered outside of a college or university and instead by a non-profit writing organization. NILA was nationally accredited by the Distance Education and Training Council (DETC), an agency recognized by the U.S. Department of Education. "Stepping outside the university had never been done before in an MFA program in creative writing," says former program director Wayne Ude. "We wanted to have a program designed by writers for writers."

Such flexibility is perhaps responsible for the proliferation of programs not only in the United States, but across the world. More and more programs are incorporating an international component to attract enrolment and heighten the student experience. New York University (NYU), for example, recently launched the MFA Writers Workshop in Paris, a two-year program that hosts residencies exclusively in Paris, while conducting the term work with NYU-based instructors. Arcadia University in Pennsylvania includes a study-abroad residency in locations such as Scotland and Italy, and Spalding University in Kentucky offers the option of taking part in international residencies held in France, England, Italy, and elsewhere.

Yet there are only two low-residency programs in Canada. Andrew Gray says he proposed the optional-residency program at UBC because he saw "the need for a low-residency program with greater flexibility than many of the existing programs out there." Stephen Kimber says the development of the new program in Halifax allows the university to capitalize on what it has historically offered. "Pedagogically, we're a liberal arts university that specializes in the humanities and journalism, which we believe is also an ideal combination for creative non-fiction." The University of King's College program focuses exclusively on narrative non-fiction, "including all its many and various offshoots — from memoir to literary journalism to travel writing to biography to historical non-fiction."

Considering the proliferation of low-residency programs across the world, it may be time for Canadian institutions to take advantage of the open opportunity. Xu Xi is a former chair of the Low-Residency MFA Directors' Caucus for the Association of Writers and Writing Programs (AWP). "I believe there is still potential for growth, especially for programs with an international focus. Canada is certainly a likely location, as are Australia and Europe and Asia," she says. "The MFA as a degree in creative writing is still relatively unknown outside of the U.S. Universities are cumbersomely bureaucratic by nature, and the larger the institution, the more difficult it is to introduce anything new."

To aid in the development and successful administration of a low-residency program, AWP recently established a resource, "AWP Hallmarks of an Effective Low-Residency MFA Program in Creative Writing," which — in addition to the "program directors' Handbook" — is free and accessible to the public on the organization's website (www.awpwriter.org). The document offers aspirational and best-practices information regarding curriculum, delivery modes, faculty selection and mentoring practices, student selection, student and administrative support, and supplementary infrastructure.

Administrators and approving bodies may find the delivery of creative writing distance workshops and courses unfamiliar, if not intimidating. Planning must include a reasonable outline of faculty and student expectations, for which the AWP Hallmarks can help in defining best practices. Gray says UBC wanted to ensure that they were able to serve the students while not exhausting instructors. "Online teaching ended up being more complex and more time-consuming than we'd originally presumed," he says, "and we've had to work to manage the workload of both students and faculty." A common misconception is that distance education is somehow less work for everyone involved; thus, new directors sometimes *over-program* to ensure students receive the education they deserve. While an on-campus class that meets three hours per week is contained within that timeframe, students and faculty in asynchronous online courses offered by low-res programs tend to carry on discussions beyond that perimeter. Trial and error indicates where some activities can be trimmed back while still offering a full academic workload. For online components, this means balancing the frequency of required peer interaction and forum discussion alongside creative thesis development.

"If there is one word that faculty and instructors need to remember regarding teaching and curriculum, it's flexibility," adds Don Sedgwick, co-founder and former executive director of the King's program. "We are teaching a form of craft, which has its many disciplines. But we are also teaching art, and this is where the learning becomes even more complicated. Like books, no two writers are alike. When you multiply this factor by the size of the entire class, you need to figure out when to add more content to a particular teaching module, or possibly to replace classroom time with reflective time for the students. They can get overloaded by information; they need time for processing. Similarly, the timing on a 'feedback loop' is always an approximation for a particular student — and possibly for an entire class. The amount of discussion needed for a group of memoirists versus essay writers is likely to be vastly different. For all these reasons, we need to expect change in the curriculum delivery, and be prepared to accommodate the writers' needs on the fly. In short, plan with care, and then be flexible enough to change as needed."

For any program, there are kinks and roadblocks to overcome, but Gray has found the work worth the effort. "The program has proceeded surprisingly close to our expectations," he says, "which, in looking back, were perhaps naively optimistic considering nobody had done one of these in Canada before, and since we were also breaking new ground in the way we ran the courses as workshops rather than mentorships. We are roughly where we expected to be in size and organization."

Size — pertaining to faculty, student enrolment, and course offerings — is a major point that determines the success of a low-residency program. Most low-residency programs pair up one faculty member for every two to five students for the term-long courses and mentorships. That number plays a role in ensuring student attention, but also determines faculty needs and, thus, acts as a guideline for maximum acceptance rates.

The residency experience is indeed what many students look forward to in their programs, as this is where close friendships first develop and intensive mentor consultations take place. Low-residency programs range between two and three years of full-time study, so the residencies that occur once or twice a year are important for bridging the time spent via distance communications. Yet it's the distance aspect that works for students and appeals to writers with other life commitments. Stephen Kimber says low-residency students "will probably be slightly older than your average grad student," which adds to the diversity of the student population; these are also likely writers who never imagined the ability or possibility of graduate studies, given their commitments elsewhere. Through online workshops and distance communication, students have the unique ability to participate any time of day and from the comfort of their home, office, or public library.

Gray says that "many of our students have become great friends without meeting in person. The online community is available for all students, and they continue to have access after graduation, as long as they want."

Programs may also consider what may give them the competitive edge over other institutions. Low-residency MFAs are becoming more competitive in offering pedagogical training and publishing internships for students who wish to use the graduate experience not only for their own writing development, but to increase job marketability. As an example, Spalding University in Kentucky offers a teaching curriculum, Wilkes University in Pennsylvania includes a mandatory publishing or teaching internship as part of its MFA program, and Oklahoma City University offers pedagogy and publishing strands. The optional-residency program at UBC recently added the Teaching Creative Writing course to meet student demand. In addition to discussion of theory and practice, students have the option of putting into practice their knowledge in a community-based teaching practicum. Students keep in touch throughout the practicum to share experiences, seek advice, and report on their completed work.

Even established authors often opt for a low-residency education: working writers most often do not have the time or flexibility to attend a full-time, campus-based program.

"On a similar note, many writers work in isolation," says Don Sedgwick. "It's the nature of the profession. At some point, often in mid-career, they need to step up their game and make deeper connections with the publishing industry. This is difficult to achieve without someone to open the doors to publishing houses, literary agents, and the host of other facilitators within the often closed-wall world of the media industry. The MFA at King's brings the student to — and through — the doors of the industry by delivering publishing professionals right to the classroom. Indeed, in the January residences in Toronto and New York, the students will literally be in the offices of publishers."

Most low-residency programs offer opportunities to make personal connections with editors and agents through their intensive residency programming. Guest speakers are brought in to discuss contemporary publishing concerns, and this is usually complemented by practice pitch sessions or one-on-one manuscript evaluations. During the term at home, students fine-tune their manuscripts with their faculty mentors so when the time comes to mingle with professionals, students are prepared to do so with confidence.

Such hands-on professional direction is hard to come by and, as Don Sedgwick says, is one of the reasons working writers pursue a low-residency MFA. Between residency sessions designed to prepare students for publication, and for the professional connections made in and outside of programs, writers who otherwise wouldn't be able to return to school are finding it possible to live out their dreams with the low-residency option.

With success stories and flexibility to its credit, why aren't more Canadian institutions embracing the low-residency MFA model? The geographic sprawl of the nation allows, even encourages, success with distance education. "There are many workshop models and different kinds of MFAs, but the expertise for faculty tends to be American trained and American," Xu Xi says. "But other countries have their own literatures." The proliferation of MFA programs is not only evidenced in the United States, though. Institutions in the United Kingdom and elsewhere are recognizing the opportunity — and ensuring it's not a missed opportunity for their domestic students.

"Based on my own conversations with students," Kimber says, "we are losing significant numbers of good students to creative writing programs in the U.S., and England as well. That's not to say some of them wouldn't have decided to study elsewhere anyway, but there should be more Canadian alternatives for them to consider."

Consider this: according to the AWP website, the number of MFA programs — low- and full-residency —essentially doubled in ten years. In 2002, there were 99 MFA programs listed as members of AWP, and in 2012 that number was 191. As of this writing, there are now 222 member MFA programs. Compare that to the mid-seventies, when the first low-residency program launched in the United States, and there were a mere 15 MFA programs in existence. The growth is staggering. Yes, there may be a cap on how far the model can expand, but there is certainly room for development in Canada.

"I think there's definitely a demand," Stephen Kimber says, noting his anecdotal evidence from student applicants. Andrew Gray agrees and adds that low-residency programs not only attract domestic students, but also "students from all over the world, and in some ways your competition is global when you create a program. New programs will have to differentiate themselves and make a compelling case to attract students. That said, international programs are expensive, and Canadians definitely appreciate the ability to study domestically with the funding, loan, and cost differentials that usually result."

Finances are a necessary consideration for everyone, but potential program developers may find relief in knowing the low-residency model is most often self-sustaining. Stephen Kimber explains that the salary of the director and the costs of writing mentors are covered by tuition revenues. The institution already has full-time faculty in place, so mentors that work one-on-one with students during the thesis are "hired on a sessional basis and remunerated based on the number of students they supervise per semester." Most low-residency programs in existence also bring in special guests and publishing professionals during residencies to offer workshops, panels, and informal talks, but the cost is minimal and generally offered as a flat fee for speakers. Residencies pose little additional overhead cost, Kimber adds, as "the program will utilize the university residences during a period when they would otherwise be idle."

Considering the minimal overhead, with no dedicated classrooms required during the year, a low-residency program may focus its finances more on delivering quality distance education and in hiring faculty who enhance marketability and student interest. "When we started the program," Andrew Gray says, "there was support for new programs at our university if they were self-supporting and operated almost like small businesses within the university. We were able to set our own tuition rates arbitrarily, based on our business case and the marketplace." Gray adds that the optional-residency program was viable quickly, but that was in part due to their large proportion of adjunct faculty.

In a challenging economic climate, graduate programs may not be a university priority as they provide smaller enrolment numbers than undergraduate classes. Yet, for those institutions eager to expand their offerings, the low-residency MFA program can prove a viable and self-sustaining choice, and one that perhaps helps retain Canada's writing students.

"The conclusion I kept coming to," says Xu Xi, "was that the low-res was actually a very sustainable financial model for, in particular, medium to large universities with a strong technology infrastructure." She adds that some programs actually result in profits — which may certainly attract administrators and approving bodies. "But the caveat," she says, "is institutional leadership and vision. Unless a university is progressive in outlook, the low-res model will come up against bureaucratic challenges that are more daunting than financial. In my mind, the financial viability is not the biggest challenge for low-res MFAs housed within an institution — unless of course the director is unusually extravagant."

One thing for certain administrators understand, however, is numbers. With the proliferation of low-residency MFA programs in the United States and across the globe growing to unprecedented numbers, isn't it time Canada takes advantage of this area of growth? For institutions looking for ways to enhance their program offerings and attract a new student demographic, the low-residency MFA may offer a viable and engaging solution. With brief residencies offered each year, and two to three years of distance mentoring, workshops, and peer development, student-writers are reaping the rewards across the border. Why lose domestic students to international programs when their needs and the demand may be met closer to home? The University of British Columbia and the University of King's College have paved the way and demonstrate the potential for success. Who will be next?

Engaged Practice: Coordinating and Creating a Community Within a Creative Writing MFA Program

Catherine Bush

The University of Guelph's Creative Writing MFA, originally conceived in the 1990s, was launched in 2006. In 2006 there was only one other MFA program in Canada, at the University of British Columbia in Vancouver, in addition to a number of programs where creative writing was taught as a concentration within an English MA. The latter remains the dominant mode for delivering creative writing at the graduate level in Canada. There was also, amazingly, no graduate creative writing program in Toronto, which has the largest and arguably most diverse writing community in the country, until the simultaneous arrival of the Guelph Creative Writing MFA and the University of Toronto's Creative Writing stream within its English MA.

Guelph MFA founding director Constance Rooke envisioned a semi-autonomous professional program that would take advantage of writers who were already on faculty in the English department. By locating the program in Toronto, on the suburban north campus of Humber College, where the University of Guelph offers courses and with which it has an administrative affiliation, Rooke aimed to take advantage of a range of Toronto writers and publishing professionals as faculty and visitors while providing students with access to the city's literary and wider arts communities. An MFA program, rather than a specialization within an English MA, would allow for greater professional concentration and enable the program to admit students without undergraduate degrees in English, since talented emerging writers come from a diversity of backgrounds. Some don't have university degrees at all but a level of professional accomplishment that facilitates admission into a graduate program.

After Rooke's death in the third year of the MFA, I took over as program coordinator. Key elements that Rooke promoted remain defining features of the Guelph Creative Writing MFA, including the individual study semester, or mentorship, which the students undertake with a professional writer of their choice in the summer of their first year, and the reading-based plenary courses, the program's two core courses, which I teach as coordinator and have further developed from Rooke's templates. The plenary courses bring together all twenty-four students in our two-year program and provide an issue-oriented forum for discussing writing craft and the writing life — the aesthetics and ethics of writing. The plenaries also provide a structured way of creating and consolidating an MFA community.

From its inception our MFA has situated the study of writing within an examination of what an engaged writing practice might be. Writing exists, first of all, in strong relationship to reading, and there are reading components to all our courses. But Rooke also wanted students to ask themselves: How should a writer live? The writer must look up from the page and consider the world. I might phrase the question a little differently: How should a writer attend — to the page and to the world, and how do we define and talk about that attention?

Students come to a graduate writing program for a variety of reasons. Some wish simply to intensify their study of the craft or, potentially, to expand their range within a genre or into another genre. Some are looking for training in the teaching of writing and accreditation that will help them find work teaching in order to support themselves as writers. What a graduate writing program offers all students is a community, which is another professed reason for attending such a program. The nature of the community creates a context for the creation of work, supports it, and shapes the conversation that enfolds itself around the work being created. It is useful to think about the nature of the community provided by a writing program and the nature of its engagement with other communities. In various ways, community engagement has also come to be a defining feature of our MFA.

Practicalities have had their influence on the current shape of the program. Original plans to expand the number of students and offer online delivery were curtailed by faculty resources, further depleted with retirement. In fact, the number of students was reduced to its current level of twelve to thirteen admissions a year. The initial plan to have a continually shifting series of sessional instructors (and thus employ a wide range of writers) couldn't be sustained because of sessional instructors' rights and seniority. However, Guelph boasts additional writers on faculty, both within the School of English and Theatre Studies and in other departments, who serve on our admission and thesis committees. We've had to strategically plan how to provide thesis supervision, given our lack of full-time faculty, and have been able to argue for the creation of a group of associated faculty, all professional writers based in Toronto, to help fill our supervision needs.

Our MFA does not currently have access to regular teaching assistantships. Yet students need and want opportunities to work, both because they require the income and because they desire teaching experience. As a result of our location at Humber College, students can fill a number of positions each year as tutors in the two Humber College Writing Centres on the North and Lakeshore campuses. This arrangement has had the added benefit of being a portal to ongoing hires of MFA graduates to teach rhetoric and composition at Humber College.

Community-based initiatives have become another way to offer students and graduates teaching experience. In Guelph itself, in collaboration with the university's Open Learning Centre, we have established Creative Writing at Guelph, a continuing education program whose instructors are MFA graduates and occasionally students with sufficient credentials. In Toronto, along with fellow Guelph English professor Michelle Elleray, a parent at Parkdale Public School in Toronto's downtown west end, I have initiated a six-week teaching practicum in which interested MFA students team-teach a weekly creative writing class to Grade 7/8 students. This program, now in its sixth year, has been supplemented by a second program in which MFA students teach their own two-day units within the Grade 12 Writers' Craft curriculum at nearby Parkdale Collegiate Institute.

Parkdale Public School is what's known as an inner-city model school, a program established to ensure that all children, especially those from low-income families or facing language barriers, have access to the skills and opportunities that will enable them to succeed. Both Parkdale schools have racially diverse student bodies; many students come from families of recent immigrants, even refugees, Tibetan and Roma in particular.

MFA students are responsible for developing their own teaching plans, aided by group discussions about pedagogy. They are given feedback on their teaching both by the MFA coordinator and the Parkdale teachers, who energetically support their work. Since many MFA students and faculty live in the downtown Toronto west end, this teaching takes place within the community that we inhabit as writers. While teaching, MFA students also have a chance to model themselves for the high-school students as emerging professional writers, to present this way of life as a possibility. The Parkdale programs end with the creation of booklets of student work and a combined assembly in which a selection of Grade 8, Grade 12, and MFA students read from their writing.

In the plenary class, I argue that students shouldn't take for granted the existence of a culture that will sustain literary art but should think as activists about what they can do to help create and maintain such a culture. They need to model themselves as readers and as writers, and as writers who read. The Parkdale Projects give us an opportunity to do this in a hands-on way while offering MFA students the practical experience of teaching creative writing in different educational settings.

Our two-year program attracts writers at various stages of development, from those just out of undergraduate programs to mid-career writers, and students are required to take at least one workshop (of three) in a second genre outside their area of specialization.

There are pedagogical challenges to our approach: highly developed poets may share a workshop with students who have little or no experience as poets, even though they have expertise in another genre. Instructors need to contend with this diversity of experience within the classroom. Still, our students write and think about writing with sophistication; conceptually, they are not beginning writers even if testing out another genre. The desire to gain experience in a second genre is one reason that mature writers return to school.

In the fall semester of each year, students come together for the plenary courses, Writers on Writing and Writers in the World, which are offered in alternating years. The plenary courses — called "plenaries" because they bring together all students in the program — are colloquia that combine the intellectual and the practical. Class discussion is interwoven with student presentations on a series of readings. Texts include works in the genres on which we focus as a program, along with hybrid texts that push the boundaries between genres and essays from the specific and wide-ranging literature of practising writers on their art, which is not necessarily encountered in literature classes. The breadth of the readings is global and ranges across time. Works by Yuri Herrera, Jan Zwicky, Etgar Keret, Binyavanga Wainaina, Mahmoud Darwish, Jeannette Armstrong, J.M. Coetzee, Kazuo Ishiguro, and Sheila Heti are among those encountered. The plenary courses provide a focus for a reading-based practice within the framework of a writing program while offering a forum for discussing writing through a series of issue-based inquiries.

Before I came to the Guelph MFA, I had, like many writers, mostly taught workshops, albeit with a strong reading component. The plenary courses present a different pedagogical opportunity, to develop twinned reading courses for graduate writing students that are simultaneously forums for lively, even contentious discussion. Astute students note thematic connections among the readings and between the two plenaries. The courses are structured to reinforce and bounce off each other, since one group of students will take one course first, the next cohort the other. The plenaries run one day a week and include a morning and afternoon session; the afternoons may involve smaller break-out discussions or visits from professionals (editors from traditionally published and digital magazines; publishers from conglomerates and independents; newspaper book section editors; agents; and writers). Visiting writers are invited with an eye to the different ways in which writing enters the world and is integrated in a wider life: Sina Queyras gave a talk on developing a voice and creating the online *Lemon Hound* literary magazine site and persona; Shyam Selvadurai spoke about the Write to Reconcile project that he has developed in Sri Lanka to teach creative writing skills to those who suffered trauma during that country's civil war.

Writers on Writing focuses on where the writer meets the page or screen, and examines how writers understand and describe their own creative processes and techniques. Our first week's discussion springboards from the framework of "What do you know? To write from what you know, or not, and, if so, how to determine what you know?" Developing writers are often told to write what they know. It seems useful to begin by asking students what and how they approach "knowing" as writers. What does it mean for a writer to know something? What does each of us mean by this? What is the place of experience in our writing, how do we each define it, and, conversely, what might be the role of "not-knowing" in our writing? Readings present varied points of entry into this quandary: an excerpt from Henry James's "The Art of Fiction," also from Annie Dillard's *The Writing Life*, Rainer Maria Rilke's "Letter One" from *Letters to a Young Poet*, Flannery O'Connor's "The Nature and Aim of Fiction," John D'Agata's introduction to *The Lost Origins of the Essay*, David Shields from *Reality Hunger: A Manifesto*, and a brief Harold Pinter essay.

In the second week we consider the question "Whom do you write for?" I'm careful to point out that we're not talking about the market but how we internalize the idea of a reader. Is it a version of the self, or a specific other, or others? What changes in the act of writing if we conceptualize it as an act of communication to another — or don't?

Writers on Writing also affords opportunities to interrogate terms that students might otherwise take for granted. One week, I ask them to articulate what they mean by realism, or what they mean when they say a piece of writing feels "real." Other weeks, we press up against definitions of what a story is, or a poem, or the nature of metaphoric language, or differing approaches to truth in creative non-fiction. We discuss the necessity of grappling with time in narrative forms, and ways to do so, and do a unit on constraint, expanding from formal Oulipean rigours to contemplate the place of constraint in all genres.

Writers in the World invites students to consider and debate how writers navigate, and choose to represent, the world around them. They are asked to consider both the assigned readings and their own writing practice in light of weekly themes. We begin with a discussion of how we give value to the act of writing and to literary works — spurred by readings from Lewis Hyde, Susan Sontag, Eileen Myles, Salman Rushdie, Ocean Vuong, and Li-Young Lee. We move on to consider various conceptions of place and land and our relationship to each, attempting to expand our spatial and temporal awareness and how we might collectively and individually describe our "here and now." Throughout the course we are continually engaged in a consideration of how we pay attention as writers. I want students to think about the fact that every choice we make about where to direct our attention has both ethical and aesthetic consequence. We take on some of the thorny debates about representing others who are not like us and the implications of racialized imaginings. During the course of the semester, we examine works by Dionne Brand, Judith Thompson, C.D. Wright, Roberto Bolano, and Caryl Churchill as responses to specific political and historical situations: the 2003 invasion of Iraq, the Pinochet years in Chile, the Israel-Palestine conflict at the end of 2008. We discuss differing forms that transgression may take on the page, literary strategies for depicting extreme experience or, conversely, leaving space for the unspeakable, the literary value of making absences of all sorts feel present. We consider practical issues such as the changing copyright climate (and debate whether and when we'd give work away for free), the effects of digitization on literary production and writers' professional lives, and the challenges of defining a national literature. I lead some of the discussions, as do students as part of their presentations, since the ability to generate class discussion is another useful pedagogical skill. Graduates describe missing the conversations of the plenaries, an intensity of dialogue that can be difficult to find elsewhere.

One of the challenges of teaching a class like the plenary is student diversity. Students come from a variety of racial and cultural backgrounds. Those just out of undergraduate programs may initially find it intimidating to speak in front of their older and more experienced peers. Some find the more rigorously intellectual offerings challenging and are most at home speaking from the pragmatics of their own practice. Some enter the program more politicized than others. Smaller break-out groups prove useful in giving the less assured room in which to speak; the mixture of first- and second-year students also helps. A graduate program shouldn't assume the "why" of what we're doing but should continually interrogate it, both at the level of individual artistic creation and as a practice. The creation of literary work asks students to encounter the world in its complexity and recreate an experience of complexity in literary form. Exposure to a diversity of voices in the classroom — those who speak Ojicree or Swahili or grew up with a rural Italian dialect in the home or have lived in the Philippines or served in Kandahar or whose fathers have vanished or who identify as queer or who write poetic drama or realist short stories or hybrid memoir — is a way to experience complexity and grow as a writer. At the end of the course, students submit a writing assignment in which they contend with one of the readings through the lens of an issue or issues raised during the semester, while taking their own writing practices into account. Encouraged but not compelled to respond creatively, some have submitted fictional interviews, lyric meditations, and hybrid narratives, others more formal papers.

The plenaries provide a framework for a course that in a scaled-down and less rigorous form could be offered to undergraduates, one that formally disrupts the dependence on the workshop model as a way to teach writing. The emphasis on debate keeps things lively.

Graduates of the Guelph Creative Writing MFA speak frequently of the unique opportunities provided by the mentorship undertaken during the summer of their first year. The mentorship provides an initial period of individual study prior to the thesis process, acknowledges the centrality of intensive yet guided solitary work in a writing practice, and gives students the opportunity to work independently with a professional writer.

Students are offered a list of potential mentors yet are free to suggest a writer/mentor with whom they'd like to work. Nor do mentors have to reside in Toronto. Students can communicate electronically with a mentor (if that suits them and the mentor), who responds to their writing in weekly meetings. As coordinator, I contact all potential mentors, set up the mentorships, and oversee schedules and reading lists. The amount of writing (and reading) that a student does will vary by project and writer. The arrangement affords great flexibility in terms of addressing students' varied needs and aesthetic sensibilities, and mentors have included American writers Francisco Goldman and experimental poet Charles Bernstein, Newfoundland-based novelist Lisa Moore, and then-Shanghai-based novelist Madeleine Thien, poet and hybrid prose writer Lisa Robertson, who lives in rural France, and closer-to-home writer Camilla Gibb and the poet Kevin Connolly.

During their last two semesters in the program, students concentrate on a thesis, a book-length creative project or full play script, which they have usually begun during the mentorship. Ideally, they leave the mentorship with a rough first draft or the major portion of a draft complete. Students are not required to work on their thesis project during the mentorship, but are encouraged to do so, particularly those writing novels or other long-form narrative. Students thus have two extended opportunities for intense, independent work on a writing project.

Thesis supervisors are drawn from either full Guelph faculty associated with the program or writers appointed to our Associated Faculty. Supervisors, unlike mentors, are required to work with students in person. Students defend their thesis — a work that has undergone significant revision and in some cases may nearly be ready to submit to publishers — at an oral exam in which they give a talk placing their creative project within a critical context that includes formal and conceptual challenges and supplementary readings.

It's sometimes charged that writing programs enforce aesthetic sameness on their students. This can happen, as can the over-workshopping of student writing in ways that merely emphasize competence. I see it as my responsibility as coordinator to be alert to such risks, to speak to them in the classroom and model their opposites, and explore formal and aesthetic possibility through a range of specific examples, by returning to that most crucial question. What makes a work of art feel alive? It's important to create a space in the classroom, and the program, in which a variety of voices and points of view feel safe to express themselves. The sense of safety is an essential element of community. It's not unusual for students' writing to be a response to personal trauma, and writers are often metabolically and psychologically sensitive.

Our extracurricular offerings are another way to approach the diverse forms that a writing life can take. I have organized a panel on writers and money (Sheila Heti spoke of loans among artist friends, poet Margaret Christakos to the financial insecurities of mid-life, playwright Colleen Murphy of using grant money to help buy a car). Madeleine Thien gave a talk on her personal engagement with the work of theorist Mikhail Bakhtin.

One of the advantages of our Toronto location is that students can make contacts with fellow writers, arts professionals, and organizations. We offer

Master Classes under the auspices of the International Festival of Authors at Toronto's Harbourfront, annual interviews in which students themselves have an opportunity to ask questions and meet the writers. Students have done internships at Toronto theatres; an MFA reading is part of the annual lineup at the Eden Mills Literary Festival outside of Guelph. We host a monthly program reading series in a Toronto bar that brings together students, alumni, and prominent local writers associated with the program.

What responsibility do we who teach and administrate graduate writing programs have to address how our students will make a living? Do academic programs generally have this responsibility? Arts programs? Students come to graduate writing programs looking for an intensive professional apprenticeship and, if they're text-based creators, portals to publishing. Giving students a realistic sense of the market doesn't have to mean depressing them with a torrent of difficulties. Students say as much: they don't want to be depressed. The fact is, lucky things happen to writers at all stages of their careers. Hope is a useful emotion. We had a recent graduate sell a short-story manuscript to a major publishing house in a week. Sometimes that happens; more often it doesn't. One year, six students in our program sold manuscripts within six months of graduation. In class, we debate the merits of digital publishing and self-publishing versus more traditional routes. The trans writer Vivek Shraya recently spoke to students about her own journey from self-publishing to a traditional independent press, all while she held down a full-time job. I speak to the ways in which my own writing process is slow and the decisions I've made to accommodate this, and about the challenges of maintaining an immersive writing practice while engaged in other work. I try to give a sense of how unstraightforward a writing life can be. Yes, students need to be given a sense of how they will make a living and tools that will help them do so. Yet a writing program also recreates a world, or a microcosm of the world, and within it, students should be encouraged to engage, in the broadest and deepest of ways, with questions of how to live as writers. This means grappling not only with how to create writing that lives but also how to navigate and embrace and respond to the world in which they and their writing live.

Selling It: Creative Writing and the Public Good

thom vernon

THE GOOD OF CREATIVE WRITING

If we think of pieces of literature as purpose-built spaces, we may gain a better understanding of exactly how literature serves those qualities we call the public good. We enter an author's literary spaces in order to transform raw perception and sensation into experiences of qualities that also happen to nourish the public good: recognition, trust, empathy, and so on. When we read a book or a story and have an *aha!* moment, it is very similar to walking into any new space such as a cathedral, an art gallery, or even a new friend's living room. Our senses register patterns, colours, and smells, and our brains organize this sensory data into what we call "experience." The construction of these spaces is, I would argue, a principal raison d'être of authoring. It is an activity that links private imagination to the communities in which we live.

Engagement with literature has a private side: we read and write alone. In these constructed literary spaces, our imaginations take flight. Our imaginative capacities, research has shown, are positively correlated with the reading of literature (for example). Invariably, then, we bring our private neurological, psychological, and emotional apparatus and experience back into the public sphere. One consequence of this private-public exchange among writers and readers is that our creative capacities increase our employment prospects. In fact, our creative capacities will soon provide our only economic security. Our world, the U.S. National Endowment for the Arts (NEA) advises, "is a world in which comfort with ideas and abstractions is the passport to a good job, in which creativity and innovation are the key to the good life, in which high levels of education — a very different kind of education than most of us have had — are going to be the only security there is" ("To Read" 77). Not surprisingly, then, reading rates are also positively correlated with social engagement as well as a sense of belonging. Hence, our private literary engagements dialectically shape, and expand, our public ones (86–93). The borders of our private imaginings bleed into public terrain.

Maybe it's true that "when we see or hear protests against the funding cuts, it is not ordinary Canadians protesting, but rather those who have made a career of living off government grants" (Lapajne). This argument, though, collapses with scrutiny — but probably not in the way its proponents might hope. The debate around public arts funding reveals a good that few other endeavours can claim.

Public arts funding certainly benefits the economy and generates media attention ("Rob, Doug Ford" 2013). At the same time, we value these creative activities precisely because of their contribution to the public and private good — not solely for their dollar return on investment ("How the United States Funds the Arts"). For instance, what exactly is the public monetary return on investment for a photograph in which a crucifix drowns in the artist's blood and urine? What is *good* about it may be more elusive than the value of the NEA award to the artist. Along with the work of four other provocative art works, Andres Serrano's *Piss Christ* became a symbol of government waste and sacrilege. Senator Jesse Helms took an ad hominem approach when he denounced the artist and his work on the floor of the U.S. Senate: "I do not know Mr. Andres Serrano, and I hope I never meet him. Because he is not an artist, he is a jerk.… Let him be a jerk on his own time and with his own resources. Do not dishonor our Lord" (qtd. in Koch). Perhaps Helms was not making the strongest argument, but the broader controversy did force many Americans to ask, What is art? and What is it good for?

If, for instance, money is not to be spent on the arts, education, and social welfare projects because it drains resources, then one wonders what we are spending our money on. In Canada and the United States there has been a shift away from the public funding of social welfare, education, and artistic investment toward an amplification of military expenditures (Vernon, "Selling It"). These expansions have relied on neo-liberal ideologies (market incentive, efficiency, etc.) to justify the privatization of military, education, health, criminal justice, and other formerly government-run activities. These strategic policy moves have facilitated, not the reduction in spending called for by many North American critics of big government, but rather a massive transfer of public wealth into private hands.

When Margaret Thatcher famously asserted that "there is no such thing as society," the neo-liberal project sought to neuter public support for the public sphere (Hussain; Duménil and Lévy). It's been argued that this move was strategic (Duménil and Lévy). Well before the most recent financial meltdown, analysts of class Duménil and Lévy argued that "the data are unambiguous. A particular class and a sector of the economy ... benefited from the crisis in amazing proportions.... The rising wealth of the wealthiest fraction can be easily documented. Households holding monetary and financial assets benefited from the change in policy." This move appears to have been as unproductive for our shared economies as it has been for our arts, education, and social democratic values. Further, the neo-liberal project did not fulfill its promise to ensure democratic rights and freedoms while expanding access to economic and personal self-determination. Neo-liberalism became the theoretical spine of the transfer of public wealth to the private sector. This policy move may have cost the public sphere much more than dollars.

In addition to its economic failure, the neo-liberal project has eroded many of the social ties that bind. As we work in jobs we hate to repay students loans we borrowed to earn the economic freedom promised by higher education, we are watched, tracked, and censored. There are, since the 1970s, far fewer people doing far better than everyone else. In 2000, the wealthiest 50 percent of Canadian families controlled 94.4 percent of the country's wealth, with the other 50 percent holding 5.6 percent (Brownlee 7). By 2005, according to Statistics Canada, the wealthiest 10 percent of families controlled 58 percent of wealth (8). It's no secret that a similar trend is playing out in the United States (Wolff 25). For instance, the Walton family (owners of Walmart) holds as much wealth as the bottom 40 percent of the population (Judt 14). One consequence of such drastic wealth inequality is a treacherous shift in allegiances. People's attention has shifted away from each other to the bottom line. Consequently, we are bound to our surveillance states and the meanings they deploy, perpetuate, and reproduce. "The problem with market economies," writes Terry Eagleton, "is that they erode the symbolic, affective dimensions of social existence" ("Reappraisals" 78).

The assertions and arguments that follow could be applied, arguably, to the entire North American arts and humanities project, which I will reference. However, my focus is creative writing. In a culture where meaning is being collapsed and narrowed to the bottom line, the demand and hunger for the indeterminacy of authoring has, as we shall see, risen.

While President Reagan and Prime Minister Thatcher led the divestiture of state investments in public goods (arts, education, income support, public infrastructure, etc.) through a long history of demonization, public policy moves, and nationalism, they were not the first. Neo-liberalism's "reduction of 'society' to a thin membrane of interactions between private individuals is presented today as the ambition of libertarians and free marketeers. But we should never forget," argues Tony Judt in *Ill Fares the Land*, "that it was first and above all the dream of Jacobins, Bolsheviks and Nazis" (119–20). Over the last thirty-five years, neo-liberal values (low taxes, less waste, government effectiveness and efficiency, etc.) have increasingly displaced the traditional social democratic values fostered by, say, literature. These values include the goods of access to health care and education, the right to organize labour, reproductive rights, and so on. A little further on we shall see exactly how art and literature helped victims of the Nazis, such as Walter Benjamin and Paul Klee, to articulate the collapse of meaning and the rise of fascism.

If our values do not bind us to each other, then we can only look to the state for meaning. Judt contends that the neo-liberal shift has "eviscerated society"; the privatization and bottom-line thinking in regard to public goods such as education leaves "nothing except authority and obedience binding the citizen to the state" (118). With the squeezing-out of public discourse of meanings other than those relevant to the bottom line and the state, we also diminish our capacity to recognize our unique self-conceptions and those of others. This is where fascism enters. But the arts — such as creative writing — could enter here, too.

For what it's worth, if one were to gauge the value of the arts based on economics, then the arts make a very strong case for themselves. In Canada, the Conference Board informs us that the contribution of the cultural sector to the nation's GDP is over 7 percent annually, with publishing leading the way in exports; and for every dollar invested in the arts, specifically, $1.84 is value-added to the economy. For its part, the United States is one of the top three producers and exporters of cultural goods (UNESCO). Even in the 2008–10 economic downturn, book sales declined only slightly (Milliot). So, the case for the economic benefits of the arts gainsays their historic demonization.

But even with all of the revenue generation and employment (1.1 million in 2007), there is something *inherently* valuable in the practice of, and engagement with, the arts — specifically literature (Conference Board). Very recently, it has been demonstrated that when one enters fictional narratives with an emotional stake in the story and its people, she is likely to practise empathy (Bal and Veltkamp; Kid and Castano). Roland Barthes asserts that we are born into a system of symbols, of which language is integral, and it is this "symbolic which constitutes the man" (*Grain* 93). Literature allows us to engage meaningfully with this symbolic order because it resists the collapse of meaning through amplification and refraction. "We become," Charles Taylor writes, "full human agents, capable of understanding ourselves, and hence of defining our identity, through our acquisition of rich human languages of expression" (32). Because our self-conception is inherently formed through dialogue and struggle with the society and symbols in and among which we live, we depend upon engagement with language to communicate and traffic socially.

Creative writing weaves self-interest (and exploration) into the public good through its construction of literary structures. It does this by positioning and deploying correspondences between the private experiences, perceptions, and sensations of author and reader. These privacies then reverberate as *experience* for the reader. The middle section of the final volume of Proust's *Finding Time Again*, for instance, offers one way to position such correspondences: "One can list indefinitely in a description all the objects that figured in the place described, but the truth will begin only when the writer takes two different objects, establishes their relationship, the analogue in the world of art of the unique relation created in the world of science by the laws of causality, and encloses them within the necessary armature of a beautiful style" (198). Proust, of course, is the master of these deployments. Very early in the first volume of *Finding Time Again* there is one example, a description of the reflections from "a magic lantern" placed in his room by his mother or grandmother to soothe the boy: "Golo would come out of the small triangular forest that velveted the hillside with dark green and advance jolting toward the castle of poor Genevieve de Brabant. This castle was cut off along a curved line that was actually the edge of one of the glass ovals arranged in the frame which you slipped between the grooves of the lantern. It was only a section of the castle and it had a moor in front of it...." (*Swann's Way* 9). The author's memories (real or imagined) prepare scaffolding, bound together by emotion, upon which the reader's imagination can climb. Reading just this section could allow a reader to experience ancient forests inhabited by a mysterious Lady, the frustration one can encounter as a child trying to make a mechanical thing work properly, remote castles to be conquered (and all things yet to conquer), and the soggy moors full of dangerous traps, pitfalls, and missteps. One can imagine being a frustrated and lonely boy like the narrator, put to bed too early and awaiting his mother's kiss. The very purpose of placing such scaffolding pillars is not to choose one or the other as correct, but rather to erect a structure into which a reader's imagination may enter.

As authors create these spaces, readers practise those values that let us cohere normatively. Editor Alana Wilcox puts it this way: "Reading and writing hone the imagination like nothing else, and imagination is the key to empathy, which is key to a successful, compassionate society. It's here, in this empathy, that literature contributes most to the public good." Recognition, empathy, and trust are the foundations of civil society. But, more precisely, Taylor holds that what has "come about with the modern age is not the need for recognition but the conditions in which the attempt to be recognised can fail" (35). Provocatively, in this same era where public support of the arts and humanities, and of education, has been drastically reduced, more and more people have turned to creative writing. In 1977 there were seventy-seven post-secondary creative writing programs in North America, while today there are almost nine hundred (Fenza). Perhaps because of the dialectical structures it employs, creative writing (for either producer or consumer) provides the spaces for empathy and recognition — upon which our social cohesion depends.

ARCHITECTURES OF EMPATHY

Elsewhere I have located the site of literary creation, metaphorically, in the debris pile of Paul Klee's *Angelus Novus* (1920). *Angelus* helped Walter Benjamin and Klee understand the distortions of the collective good, in their time, as fascism gripped the national German imagination. The angel can help us here, too, as we flesh out exactly *how* literature contributes to the public good through the multiplication of meaning.

For Benjamin and Klee, *Angelus* represented the progress of history. In it, an angel is caught in a storm. As Benjamin describes it, he beats his wings furiously, his curls wild, his eyes riveted on the right, the past. A "pile of debris before him grows towards the sky. What we call progress is *this* storm" ("Concept of History"). The storm is the storm of history and the debris is potent wreckage waiting for resurrection. The wreckage is composed of "traces": memories, experiences, perceptions, and sensations. Each "trace," and so the debris pile, too, is organized by original, organic impulses to desire, love, empathize, recognize, or trust (Kristeva 17–19). It is the foundation of the *organic* formalism that Klee offers in response to Martin Heidegger's *technological* formalism (Watson): "organic," because each perception or sensation, noticed by our awareness or not, organizes itself into what Freud (*Interpretation* 351) called "memory-traces," Benjamin called "trace" ("Baudelaire" 316–17), and we now call *neural networks*. Perceptions or sensations, and so "traces," carry with them original impulses and authenticities (auras), which makes them ripe for the author's picking. Benjamin advised that it is "the authenticity of a thing … that is transmissible in it from its origin on, ranging from its physical duration to the historical testimony relating to it" ("Work of Art" 254).

We authors, then, brood over "trace" in a psychological/emotional state of melancholy, and then craft that debris (some conscious, some not) into aura-bearing vessels such as allegories, narrative lines, short stories, or novels. Seemingly long-gone memories and experiences are revived and refracted through literary techniques such as multiple perspectives, tmesis, discontinuities, metaphor, and metonymy. Our melancholic engagement displaces aura into different points of view so that new meanings can surface. This dialectical relationship between past and present in a literary context casts the reader and author as messiahs.

The past is reified as humans narrate their lives into stories. When I tell you of my experience, organized from perception and sensation, it becomes your own. For example, my Aunt Sarah confessed to me, at ninety, that she still felt very guilty for setting the schoolhouse on fire in the little Arkansas hamlet where she was being courted by her future husband, Joe. Even at that age, she swore me to secrecy. Sarah's guilt rears its head, sometimes more or less consciously, every time I make an absent-minded misstep. The circumstances of my missteps are different than Sarah's, but her original impulses and auras traverse the decades and inform my contemporary experience — and my literature. So, when in *The Drifts*, Julie abandons Pity, a nine-year-old girl, in a storm-swept parking lot, I experience Sarah and her arson.

In "On Some Motifs in Baudelaire," Benjamin puts it this way: "Story does not aim to convey an event per se, which is the purpose of information; rather, it embeds the event in the life of the audience in order to pass it on as experience to those listening. It thus bears the trace of the storyteller, much the way an earthen vessel bears the trace of the potter's hand" (316). Our novels and allegories become these earth-bound vessels bearing their creator's aura.

These perceptions qua experience can be measured as electrically charged exchanges of sodium and potassium in brain cells. The charge is produced as brain cells (and other neuro-elements) emit energy, measured by frequency and amplitude (Hz/hertz and μV/microvolts, respectively). Such *aha!* moments are the brain's electrophysiological response to environmental stimuli, and it is a response that can be measured and recorded as *event-related potentials* (ERPs) (Moran). This energy is emitted, like the pulse of aura, when we have *experiences*. The sodium-potassium transfer reifies the past as it reconstructs it as the structures of allegory, metaphor, and experience.

Like neuroscience, chaos theory has something to offer this discussion. Allegories, as auratic vessels, cobble "trace" into story, much as subatomic particles create *strange attractors*: the unique, seemingly chaotic formations made by the collusion of subatomic particles moving over time (Bradley). Because the movement of subatomic particles seems random and fleeting, they do not, it seems, leave traces. But, tracked over time, elaborate structures are found to have been erected and organized as the particles are pulled toward and driven from one another. These are forces akin to the love that Kristeva cites. These attractive forces, acting as love, empathy, recognition, trust, and so forth, are the material ties that bind when it comes to "trace" (Benjamin, "Concept of History" 389–90).

Writers inscribe, disrupt, and deploy "traces" like magic spells. It is authenticity that sustains "trace" over time. And if clustered into neural networks,
or "trace," original authority becomes food for the progress of history. But
not so fast. There is a "whore" who casts the spell called "once upon a time,"
according to Benjamin ("Concept of History" 396). Hitler and his follow-
ers, for instance, invoked the mythical *Volk* in order to embody Germany's
past in himself and the Third Reich. "The Führer himself and he alone *is* the
German reality," Heidegger told his students (Evans 421). This embodiment
was deployed by Nazi culture as an instrument of historical and philological
paralysis. In his "On the Concept of History," Benjamin works out how, if
we can cut loose from the spell of "once upon a time," the past endows us
with a "weak" messianic power (390). We must, through dialectical engagements (such as authoring, reading, baking) "wrest tradition away from the
conformism that is working to overpower it." The love, empathy, and trust
that become our own experience during and after our engagement with
these "traces" erect the ceiling and walls of what we come to recognize as
our experience (Kristeva 21). These impulses also act as the organizing and
motivational principle for our social behaviour, according to Jane Jacobs and
others (qtd. in Judt 67).

The difference between writing and authoring is the "good" of writing.
In *The Grain of the Voice*, Barthes distinguishes between *writing* (writing
without polyvalence) and *authoring* (writing that provokes a multiplicity of
meanings); between *matte* (*sans* echo) and textured writing (94). If a piece
of work lacks dimension (i.e., lacks echo) it risks its ability to resonate as literature. Authoring, though, is a deliberate placing of "trace" on the margins
of linear time so that "a logical framework for the countless flashes, con-
densations, plots, and meditations" moves the reader beyond into a grand
cathedral of her own making (Kristeva 189). These "traces" then interrupt
chronological story-time so that a reader's imagination can enter (Chatman
406). Here, socially cohesive qualities can be experienced and practised. The
reader steps inside the literary space and into the pulsing, textured vibra-
tion emanating from each, her senses perceive the pulse of authenticity and
then she, herself, becomes an encoder (Kristeva 232). An East Los Angeles

university fiction student emailed me that "creative writing helps us learn what it means to be human from a variety of perspectives in time and place" (Ariel). She is alluding, I presume, to the multiplication of meaning that comes from engaging with creative writing. Our allegories enslave objects in meaning as they disturb aura — and so meaning — into new codes and meanings (Eagleton, *Walter Benjamin* 20). The virtue of this authoring, then, is that these codes are situated in the text, without instruction; the word, liberated, disrupts signs into a new architecture of meaning(s) and *experience* — and so, empathy, trust, and so on. This sort of writing is the blood of our literary *aha!* moments and our liberation.

And so, perhaps, here lies the reason that so many creative writers are enrolling in post-secondary programs. Authoring has the ability to interrupt the chronological temporality of a story so that a reader can expand the picture imaginatively (Chatman 406). Barthes's organic accidents of meaning take guidance, practice, and skill. The whole literary project is passed from generation to generation, writer to writer. In the neo-liberal era, these hand-offs are happening more and more in post-secondary creative writing programs.

WHY STUDY CREATIVE WRITING?

Although tuition is expensive, the Association of Writers and Writing Programs (AWP) confirms what was certainly true in my case: writing classes demonstrate the desire to direct energies toward what is aesthetically, socially, and politically positive (Fenza). Her experiences with literature provoked Karen McD, a practising lawyer working with battered women — and a creative writing graduate student — to give a client Stephen King's *Rose Madder.* "It had changed her life.... The novel had helped her more than the legal process." (McD). Karen then began to study creative writing.

Tuition for post-secondary writing programs runs from approximately $1,500 at a community college to upwards of $40,000 for some private graduate school programs. Adult creative writing classes are big money-makers, while creative writing classes for traditional students are regularly the most popular classes, supporting a variety of less-attended programs, such as comparative literature (Fenza). Since there are, it seems, fewer and fewer public avenues to form or reform the world, the AWP writes, enrollment become justifiable. We will pay big bucks to learn to contribute positively to other people's experiences.

Studying creative writing allows students to become more astute thinkers, producers, and consumers. As writers, we are constantly interrogating our thoughts and beliefs, and those of our characters. We must become minor experts in quantum physics, neuroscience, credit-default swaps — you name it. We learn the difference between gamagrass and crab apple, elm and poplar, and alexandrine and slug lines; between Barthes's texts of pleasure and texts of bliss (*Pleasure* 21). Objective correlatives emerge from our once *matte* texts. "The making and exchange of literary talents and gifts is, of course, a highly civilized and humane act; and appropriately, academe has accepted the practice and making of the literary arts along with study and scholarship in the literary arts" (Fenza). Karen explained that "the post-secondary setting creates a different kind of incentive and more 'real' deadlines for writing projects. Also, feedback from a university professor tends to be more objective (and therefore useful) than feedback from a writing group member." The study of creative writing puts students in direct contact with literary masters. For example, in what other context would Hubert "Cubby" Selby Jr. (*Last Exit to Brooklyn, Requiem for a Dream*, etc.) have pointed out to me that I was alternating between fourteen- and sixteen-syllable lines in my writing? It took a master to notice this raw, organic formalism emerging.

Poet and critic R.M. Vaughan advised me, "Perhaps in the larger sense, even if most of the students will never end up getting published or have careers as writers, they will be more literate, more media savvy, and more prone to think independently, and thus be better consumers. On the other hand, I think knowledge sharing ought to be assessed for its innate value, not on an economic level. A more creative populace makes for a more creative world, and that obviously includes economic prosperity." We North Americans are "well aware that something is seriously amiss" (Judt 29). It is inspiring to see that so many of us have taken up our pens quietly and doggedly to earn our keep but also to contribute to the collective good. The architectures of empathy that we create allow readers to have their own experiences of themselves and the rest of us. We hunger for the textured intermittences of a Proust or an Alice Munro. There, in the drawing rooms of *fin de siècle* Paris or the fox farms of southwestern Ontario, we are recalled and revived in the symbolic world that literature erects. The author's skill at crafting these structures and qualities can be practised in class so that we can then deploy them publicly in our writing. As we have seen, these contributions benefit civil society, the economy, and our own well-being enormously. In an era where neo-liberal policies have decimated savings, eliminated jobs, and grossly exaggerated the income gap, creative writing offers the means to contribute our suffering, losses, and triumphs to the public good.

WORKS CITED

Ariel. "Public Good Student Responses." Message to the author. 14 Jan. 2011. Email.

Bal, P. Matthias, and Martijn Veltkamp. "How Does Fiction Reading Influence Empathy? An Experimental Investigation on the Role of Emotional Transportation." *PLOS ONE* 8.1 (2013): 1–12. Print.

Barlett, Bruce. "Health Care: Costs and Reform." *Forbes*. Forbes.com, July 2009. Web. 8 Jan. 2011.

Barthes, Roland. *The Grain of the Voice: Interviews 1962–1980*. New York: Hill and Wang, 1985. Print.

———. *The Pleasure of the Text*. New York: Hill and Wang, 1975. Print.

Baudoin, P. "Boring." New Media Blog, 2011. Web. 12 Dec. 2011.

Benjamin, Walter. "On the Concept of History." *Walter Benjamin: Selected Writings, Vol. 4, 1938–1940*. Ed. Howard Eiland. Cambridge, MA: Belknap, 2003. 389–400. Print.

———. "On Some Motifs in Baudelaire." *Walter Benjamin: Selected Writings, Volume 4, 1938–1940*. 313–55.

———. "The Work of Art in the Age of Reproducibility." *Walter Benjamin: Selected Writings, Volume 4, 1938–1940*. 251–83.

Bradley, Larry. *Chaos and Fractals*. Seminar Website, Department of Physics and Astronomy, Johns Hopkins U, 2010. Web. 2 Jan. 2011, www.stsci.edu/~lbradley/seminar/.

Brownlee, J. *Ruling Canada: Corporate Cohesion and Democracy*. Halifax: Fernwood, 2005. Print.

Centers for Disease Control and Prevention. "Healthy Youth! Student Health and Academic Achievement." Centers for Disease Control, 2010. Web. 18 Apr. 2011.

Chatman, Seymour. "What Novels Can Do That Films Can't (and Vice Versa)." *Film Theory and Criticism*. Eds. G. Mast, M. Cohen, and L. Braudy. Oxford: Oxford UP, 1992. 405–19. Print.

Clabaugh, Gary K. "The Educational Legacy of Ronald Reagan." *Educational Horizons* 82.4 (2004): 256–59.

Conference Board of Canada. "Valuing Culture: Measuring and Understanding Canada's Creative Economy." Conference Board of Canada, 2008. Web. 18 Apr. 2011.

Defense Talk. "Global Military Spending Soars Despite Crisis: Report." Defense Talk, 2009. Web. 9 Jan. 2011.

Duménil, Gérard, and Dominique Lévy. *Costs and Benefits of Neoliberalism: A Class Analysis*. 2002. Web. 31 Oct. 2013.

Eagleton, Terry. "Reappraisals: What Is the Worth of Social Democracy?" *Harper's Magazine* Oct. 2010: 77–80. Print.

———. *Walter Benjamin, or Towards a Revolutionary Criticism*. Brooklyn: Verso, 1981. Print.

Evans, Richard. *The Coming of the Third Reich*. New York: Penguin, 2005. Print.

Fenza, David. "About AWP." Association of Writers and Writing Programs, 2010. Web. 12 Dec. 2010.

Ferguson, Charles. *Inside Job*. Representational Pictures and Sony Classics, 2010. Film.

Freud, Sigmund. *The Interpretation of Dreams*. Trans. Joyce Crick. New York: Oxford UP, 1999. Print.

Gramm-Leach-Bliley Act 1999. U.S. Congress. Senate. S-900. 106th Cong. Rec. (12 Nov. 1999): 113 Stat. 1338. Washington, DC: Library of Congress. Web. 18 Apr. 2011.

Hill Strategies Research. "Culture Goods Trade (2008)." *Arts Research Monitor* 8.8 (2010). Web. 4 Sep. 2012.

Hussain, Ghaffar. "No Such Thing as Society." *The Commentator*, 17 Apr. 2013. Web. 31 Oct. 2013. www.thecommentator.com/article/3276/no_such_thing_as_society.

Judt, Tony. *Ill Fares the Land*. New York: Penguin, 2010. Print.

Kid, David C., and Emanuele Castano. "Reading Literary Fiction Improves Theory of Mind." *Science* 342 (2013). Web. 11 Nov. 2013.

Klee, Paul. *Angelus Novus*. 1920. Watercolour. Israel Museum, Jerusalem.

Koch, Cynthia. "The Contest for American Culture: A Leadership Case Study on the NEA and NEH Funding Crisis." *Public Talk*. Penn National Commission on Society, Culture and Community, 1998. Web. 31 Oct. 2013.

Kristeva, Julia. *Time and Sense*. New York: Columbia UP, 1995. Print.

Lapajne, Branka. "The Other Side of the Arts Funding Issue." *Canada Free Press*, 6 Oct. 2008. Web. 31 Oct. 2013.

McD, Karen. "Public Good Student Responses." Email to the author. 2010.

Milliot, Jim. "Units Had Modest Decline in 2010." *Publishers Weekly* 10 Jan. 2011. Web. 11 Jan. 2011.

Moran, Mark. "Brain Fingerprinting: Is the Science There?" *Neurology Today Online* 4.11 (2004). Web. 2 May 2011.

Munt, G. "Financial and Funding Trends in Canadian Universities." Presentation document, University of Winnipeg. Strategic and Budgetary Priorities, 2010. Web. 11 Jan. 2011.

National Endowment for the Arts. "How the United States Funds the Arts." Washington, DC: Office of Research and Analysis, NEA, 2007. Web. 5 Sep. 2012.

———. "To Read or Not to Read: A Question of National Consequence." NEA Report #47. Washington, DC: Office of Research and Analysis, NEA, 2007. Web. 5 Sep. 2012.

Proust, Marcel. *Finding Time Again*. Trans. Ian Patterson. New York: Penguin, 2002. Print.

———. *Swann's Way*. Trans. Lydia Davis. New York: Penguin, 2003. Print.

Pytka Productions. "It's Morning in America." Television commercial. 1984. Web. 6 Apr. 2011.

Rawls, John. *Justice as Fairness*. Cambridge: Belknap, 2003. Print.

"Rob, Doug Ford Taunt Anti-Ford Crowd as Council Debates Mayor's Powers." *Global News*, 18 Nov. 2013. Online broadcast.

Robinson, Bill, and Peter Ibbot. "Canadian Military Spending: How Does the Current Level Compare to Historical Levels? … To Allied Spending? … To Potential Threats?" Project Ploughshares Working Papers 2003. Web. 15 Dec. 2010.

Rogers, Joel, and Thomas Ferguson. *Right Turn*. Northern Illinois UP, 1986. Web. 25 Nov. 2010.

Ross, Bob. "Charter Schools on the Rise: What You Need to Know." Education.com. Web. 12 Jan. 2011.

Rudolph, Thomas J., and Jillian Evans. "Political Trust, Ideology, and Public Support for Government Spending." *American Journal of Political Science* 49.3 (2005): 661.

Rushdie, Salman. *The Satanic Verses*. London: Penguin, 1989. Print.

Serrano, Andres. *Piss Christ*. 1987. Photograph. Artist original, New York.

Simpson, Jeffrey. "Whistlin' Past the Graveyard of Conservative Vows." *Globe and Mail*, 14 Jan. 2011. Web. 14 Jan. 2011.

Statistics Canada. "Culture Goods Trade: Data Tables." Catalogue no. 87-007-X, Service Bulletin, 2008. Web. 18 Apr. 2011.

———. "Perspectives on Labour and Income." Catalogue no. 75-001-XPE. Periodical Publication, 2006. Web. 11 Nov. 2013.

Stilson, Larry. *Quaternion Julia Sets.* 1995. Web. 24 Nov. 2010.

Taylor, Charles. *Multiculturalism and "the Politics of Recognition."* Ed. A. Gutmann. Princeton, NJ: Princeton UP, 1994. Print.

Tea Party. "Core Beliefs." TeaParty.org, 2010. Web. 5 Jan. 2010.

UNESCO. "International Flows of Selected Cultural Goods and Services, 1994–2003." Montreal: UNESCO Institute for Statistics, 2005. Print.

U.S. Congress. House. Personal Responsibility and Work Opportunity Reconciliation Act of 1996. H.R.3734. 104th Cong. Rec. (3 Jan. 1996). Washington, DC: Library of Congress, Web. 18 Apr. 2011.

U.S. Department of Justice. "Correctional Populations in the United States 2009." Washington, DC: Bureau of Justice Statistics, 2010. Web. 3 Jan. 2010.

Vaughan, Richard. Message to the author. 2010. Email.

Vernon, Thom. "The Angel at Our Table." *Food and Appetites: The Hunger Artist and the Arts.* Cambridge, MA: Cambridge Scholars Press, 2012. Print.

———. *The Drifts.* Toronto: Coach House, 2010. Print.

———. "Selling It: Creative Writing & the Public Good." *The Creativity Market: Creative Writing in the 21st Century.* Ed. Dominique Hecq. Bristol, U.K.: Multilingual Matters, 2012. Print.

Vobejda, Barbara. "Clinton Signs Welfare Bill amid Division." *Washington Post*, 23 Aug. 1996. Web. 10 Jan. 2011.

Watson, Stephen H. "Heidegger, Paul Klee, and the Origin of the Work of Art." Review of Metaphysics 60.2 (2006): 327–57. Print.

Wolff, Edward N. "Recent Trends in Household Wealth in the United States: Rising Debt and the Middle-Class Squeeze — an Update to 2007." Levy Economics Institute of Bard College, 2012. Web. 11 Nov. 2013.

Wilcox, Alana. Message to the author. 2010. Email.

Acknowledgements

Thank you to the Canadian Creative Writers and Writing Programs Association (CCWWP) for championing this project among our members and beyond. We are delighted to donate our royalties to this organization in Memory of Rishma Dunlop, who helped build a culture of creative writing pedagogy and research exchange in Canada. We are also grateful to all members of CCWWP and to Canadian writers everywhere for continuing to contribute to this exciting and vital field during a time in history when words and beauty and stories are perhaps more important than ever. Thank you as well to our international counterparts.

We would like to thank all our generous contributors to this anthology and all supporters of the project. Also, thanks to York University for funding support; Christopher Doda for initial editorial work; and to all our partners and families for encouragement, patience, and indulgence.

Thank you to everyone at Dundurn Press for welcoming this project with open arms and open minds, especially Margaret Bryant, Sheila Douglas, Dominic Farrell, Kathryn Lane, Kendra Martin, Jenny McWha, Elena Radic, and Laura Boyle.

Contributor Biographies

Christian Bök is the author of *Eunoia* (Coach House, 2001) — a bestselling work of experimental literature, which has gone on to win the Griffin Poetry Prize. Bök is one of the earliest founders of Conceptual Literature (the poetic school of avant-garde writing made famous, in part, by the performance of its ringleader, Kenneth Goldsmith, at the White House in 2011). Bök has created artificial languages for two television shows: Gene Roddenberry's *Earth: Final Conflict* and Peter Benchley's *Amazon*. Bök has earned many accolades for his virtuoso recitals of "sound-poems" (particularly *Die Ursonate* by Kurt Schwitters), and he has performed lectures and readings at more than two hundred venues around the world in the last four years. Bök is on the verge of finishing his current project, entitled *The Xenotext* — a work that requires him to engineer the genome of an unkillable bacterium so that the DNA of such an organism might become not only a durable archive that stores a poem for eternity, but also an operant machine that writes a poem in response. Bök teaches in the Department of Literary Studies at Charles Darwin University.

Stephanie Bolster is the author of four books of poetry, the most recent of which, *A Page from the Wonders of Life on Earth*, was a finalist for the Pat Lowther Award; an excerpt from her current manuscript, *Long Exposure*, was a finalist for the 2012 CBC Poetry Prize. Her first book, *White Stone: The Alice Poems*, which began as her MFA thesis at UBC, won the Governor General's and the Gerald Lampert Awards in 1998. Editor of *The Best Canadian Poetry in English 2008* and co-editor of *Penned: Zoo Poems*, she teaches in the creative writing program at Concordia University in Montreal.

Catherine Bush is the author of four novels, *Accusation* (2013), *Claire's Head* (2004), *The Rules of Engagement* (2000), and *Minus Time* (1993). Her novels have been published internationally and short-listed for literary awards. Bush's non-fiction has appeared in publications including the *Globe and Mail*, the *New York Times Magazine*, the literary magazine *Brick*, and the anthology *The Heart Does Break*. Bush has a degree in comparative literature from Yale University, has held a variety of writer-in-residence positions, and has taught creative writing at universities including Concordia, the University of Florida, the University of Guelph, and in the University of British Columbia's low-residency MFA. She lives in Toronto and is the coordinator of the creative writing MFA at the University of Guelph. More info is available at www.catherinebush.com.

Louis Cabri is anti-author of the anti-poetry books *Posh Lust* (New Star), *Poetryworld* (CUE), and *The Mood Embosser* (Coach House). He is currently writing two anti-translation projects based on poetry by Marc-Antoine Girard, Sieur de Saint-Amant, and Théodore de Banville. Editing projects include *The False Laws of Narrative: The Poetry of Fred Wah* (Wilfrid Laurier UP); a feature on poetry and sound for *ESC: English Studies in Canada*, with Peter Quartermain; *PhillyTalks*, a poets' dialogue series, with Aaron Levy; *hole* magazine and various books, with Rob Manery; and two *Open Letter* double issues of letters to/from poets, with Nicole Markotić. He writes on modern and contemporary poetry, recently completing longish essays on the work of Ted Greenwald and Catriona Strang. He teaches poetry (and anti-poetry) at the University of Windsor.

Wanda Campbell teaches creative writing and women's literature at Acadia University in Wolfville, Nova Scotia. She has published a novel, *Hat Girl*, and five collections of poetry, *Sky Fishing*, *Looking for Lucy*, *Grace*, *Daedalus Had a Daughter*, and *Kalamkari and Cordillera*. She has also edited *Literature: A Pocket Anthology* and *Hidden Rooms: Early Canadian Women Poets*, and her articles have appeared in several of the Reappraisals of Canadian Writers Series (U of Ottawa P) and in academic journals, including *Canadian Literature*, *Canadian Poetry*, *Essays in Canadian Writing*, *Mosaic*, and *Studies in Canadian Literature*.

Jennifer Duncan is the author of *Sanctuary & Other Stories* and *Frontier Spirit: Brave Women of the Klondike*. She was one of the two key designers of the original Yukon School of Art curriculum and has been teaching writing for twenty years, for the last decade in the York University creative writing program. She has a BA in English and creative writing from York University, a BEd from OISE/University of Toronto, and an MA in English/creative writing from Concordia University. Currently, she is completing her dissertation on creative writing pedagogy for York's language, culture and teaching doctoral program while in the final stages of revising her first novel.

Lorri Neilsen Glenn is the author and editor of fourteen collections of poetry, scholarly research, and creative non-fiction, including *Following the River: Traces of Red River Women* (2017), the acclaimed bricolage memoir *Threading Light* (2011), and the anthology *Untying the Apron: Daughters Remember Mothers of the 50s* (2013). Her poetry and essays have been widely anthologized and have earned several national and international awards. A former Halifax Poet Laureate, she is the recipient of Halifax's Woman of Excellence Award for her work in the arts and a Research Excellence Award from Mount Saint Vincent University (where she is professor emerita). She has taught creative writing for thirty years across Canada and in Europe, Chile, and Australia. She serves as a mentor in the MFA program in creative non-fiction at the University of King's College in Halifax.

David B. Goldstein is a critic, poet, and food writer, and an associate professor at York University. He has published two poetry collections, *Lost Originals* (2016) and *Laws of Rest* (2013), and several chapbooks. His first scholarly monograph, *Eating and Ethics in Shakespeare's England*, shared the 2014 biennial Shakespeare's Globe Book Award. He has co-edited two essay collections devoted to Shakespeare, and writes essays on early modern literature, Emmanuel Levinas, food studies, ecology, and contemporary poetry.

Gülayşe Koçak is a Turkish writer living in Istanbul who grew up in the U.S., Ethiopia, Denmark, Germany, and Turkey. She has been conducting creative writing workshops since 2004. Apart from translations, book reviews, and essays, she has four novels: *Beyond the Double Doors* (YKY, 1993), *How Can I Cure the Sadness in her Eyes?* (YKY, 1997), *Top* (YKY, 2002), and *Black Scent*

(YKY, 2012), the last two of which are dystopian. She also has a book of personal essays, *Don't Say She Didn't* (Alfa, 2017). Her experiences teaching participants varying from university students to prison guards moved her to write *The Pleasures of Creative Writing* (Alfa, 2013), which is about the challenges of teaching creative writing to participants with an educational background of rote learning, who were raised with taboos, and who haven't internalized freedom of expression. In it she shares the methods that were successful in overcoming these and other cultural barriers. Since 2006, Koçak has been travelling to underprivileged parts of Turkey to encourage creative and critical thinking and writing and to raise gender awareness in schools and with local decision-makers.

Kathryn Kuitenbrouwer is a PhD candidate in the English department at the University of Toronto. She has taught creative writing at Colorado College, the University of Toronto's School of Continuing Studies, the New York Times Knowledge Network, and Ryerson University's Chang School. She is the bestselling author of the novels *All the Broken Things, Perfecting, The Nettle Spinner,* as well as the short story collection, *Way Up.* Her books have been nominated for the First Novel Award, the Toronto Book Award, the ReLit Prize, and Canada Reads, and have won a Danuta Gleed Award. Her fiction and non-fiction have appeared in *Granta Magazine,* the *Walrus,* the *Lifted Brow, Maclean's* magazine, *7X7,* and *Storyville,* where she won the inaugural Sidney Prize. Kathryn has been awarded residencies at Yaddo Corporation and the Virginia Center for the Creative Arts. She is associate faculty with the creative writing MFA at the University of Guelph. For more information please visit www.kathrynkuitenbrouwer.com.

Kathy Mac (a.k.a. Dr. Kathleen McConnell) has published a book of poetic essays (or perhaps didactic poems), *Pain, Porn and Complicity: Women Heroes from Pygmalion to Twilight* (Wolsak and Wynn, 2013), and three books of poems: *Human Misunderstanding* (Roseway, 2017), *The Hundefräulein Papers* (Roseway, 2009), and *Nail Builders Plan for Strength and Growth* (Roseway, 2002, a finalist for the Governor General's Award and winner of the Gerald Lampert Award). She teaches at St. Thomas University in Fredericton, New Brunswick.

Nicole Markotić is a novelist, critic, and poet published in literary journals in Canada, the United States, Australia, and Europe. Her books include four of poetry (including the latest, *Whelmed*, with Coach House), three novels (including the latest, *Rough Patch*, a YA novel with Arsenal Pulp Press), a critical collection of essays (*Disability in Film and Literature*, with McFarland & Co.), and several edited books (including the latest, *Robert Kroetsch: Essays on His Works*, with Guernica). She edits the chapbook series Wrinkle Press, and has worked as a book editor for various presses, currently on the NeWest literary board as one of its fiction editors. She teaches creative writing, Canadian literature, children's literature, and disability studies at the University of Windsor.

Lori A. May is the author of several books, including *The Write Crowd: Literary Citizenship & the Writing Life* (Bloomsbury, 2014). She is a frequent guest speaker at writing conferences and teaches in the creative non-fiction MFA program at the University of King's College in Halifax. May writes across the genres, and her work has appeared in the *Atlantic, Writer's Digest, Midwestern Gothic*, and elsewhere. More information is available online at www.loriamay.com.

Suzette Mayr is the author of four novels, including her most recent book, *Monoceros*, which won the ReLit and W.O. Mitchell Awards, and was nominated for the 2011 Giller Prize, the Ferro-Grumley Award for LGBT Fiction, and the Georges Bugnet Award for Fiction. Her novel *The Widows* was a finalist for the Commonwealth Prize for Best Book in the Canada-Caribbean region. She is a former president of the Writers' Guild of Alberta, and she teaches creative writing at the University of Calgary.

Yvette Nolan is a playwright, dramaturge, and director. Her plays include *Annie Mae's Movement, BLADE, Job's Wife, Ham and the Ram, Scattering Jake, The Birds* (a modern adaptation of Aristophanes' comedy), and *The Unplugging*, which won the 2012 Jessie Richardson Award for Outstanding Original Script. From 2003 to 2011 she served as the artistic director of Native Earth Performing Arts in Toronto. *Medicine Shows*, a book about Native theatre in Canada, was published in 2015.

Mary Schendlinger is a writer, illustrator, editor, publisher, and retired teacher and author of *Prepare To Be Amazed: The Geniuses of Modern Magic, Power Parenting Your Teenager*, and many shorter articles. Writing as Eve Corbel, she is the author of more than fifty comics published in periodicals and anthologies. She taught writing for graphic forms at the University of British Columbia and was a member of the faculty for the Master of Publishing program at Simon Fraser University. She is also co-founder and former senior editor of *Geist* magazine, a literary and cultural quarterly.

Andrea Thompson is a writer, spoken word artist, and educator who has performed her poetry across the country for over twenty years. In 1995 she was featured in the documentary *Slamnation* as a member of the country's first national slam team, and in 2005, her CD *One* was nominated for a Canadian Urban Music Award. She is the author of the novel *Over Our Heads* and co-editor of the anthology *Other Tongues: Mixed Race Women Speak Out.* A graduate of the University of Guelph's MFA creative writing program, Thompson currently teaches fiction at Brock University and spoken word in the continuing studies departments of the Ontario College of Art and Design University and the University of Toronto. More information is available at andreathompson.ca.

Judith Thompson has written numerous plays and screenplays, including *The Crackwalker, I Am Yours, Lion in the Street, Sled, Habitat, Lost and Delirious*, and *The Thrill.* She won the Governor General's Award for Drama in 1985 for *White Biting Dog*, and in 1989 for a collection of her plays, *The Other Side of the Dark.* She is proud to have won the Amnesty International Freedom of Expression Award for *Palace of the End*, and has also won a Toronto Arts Award and the Canadian Authors Association Award, as well as a Floyd S. Chalmers Canadian Play Award and a Dora Mavor Moore Award. In 2005 she was made an Officer of the Order of Canada, and in 2007 she was awarded the Walter Carsen Prize for Excellence in the Performing Arts by the Canada Council for the Arts. In 2008 she became the first Canadian to be awarded the Susan Smith Blackburn Prize, recognizing outstanding women playwrights each year. She is also the artistic director of RARE theatre, which has produced theatre pieces such as *Rare* (Soulpepper, 2012), created with nine performers with Down Syndrome, *Borne* (Soulpepper, 2014), created with nine wheelchair users, and *Wildfire* (Soulpepper, 2016) with seven members of the *Rare* cast. She is currently in the process of developing her newest play, *After the Blackout*, which will be performed at Soulpepper in May 2018 by six actors with exceptionalities.

Peggy Thompson is a screenwriter, film producer, story editor, and author. She was the screenwriter for the feature films *The Lotus Eaters* and *Better than Chocolate* and has also written extensively for television. She was recently executive producer on Sharon McGowan's documentary *Bearded Ladies: The Photography of Rosamond Norbury*. She was an associate professor at UBC for many years, where she taught screenwriting in the creative writing program. She serves on the advocacy committee of Women in Film + Television Vancouver.

Aritha van Herk is the author of five novels, four works of non-fiction, and two works (with photographer George Webber) of place-writing, as well as hundreds of articles, reviews, and essays. Her irreverent but relevant history of Alberta, *Mavericks: An Incorrigible History of Alberta,* frames the *MAVERICKS* exhibition at the Glenbow Museum. Her latest work of prose poetry is *Stampede and the Westness of West*. She teaches creative writing and Canadian literature at the University of Calgary.

thom vernon is a writer, educator, and performer living in Toronto.

Darryl Whetter has published three books of fiction and two collections of poetry. His debut collection of stories was a *Globe and Mail* Top 100 Book of 2003. His bicycle novel, *The Push & the Pull*, followed in 2008. In 2012 he released *Origins*, a SSHRC-funded book of poems which examines evolution, energy, and extinction. Whetter has taught creative writing and English at the University of New Brunswick, the University of Windsor, Dalhousie University, Université Sainte-Anne, and at the first creative writing MA program in Southeast Asia at Singapore's Lasalle College of the Arts. He has published or presented papers on contemporary literature in France, Sweden, Canada, Germany, the United States, India, and Iceland and has read internationally in Singapore, Bali, Malaysia, Wales, and Australia. His book reviews appear regularly in papers such as the *Globe and Mail,* the *National Post,* and the *Toronto Star*. Between 2005 and 2008 he was a regular reviewer on the national CBC Radio show *Talking Books*. His latest books are the pot-smuggling novel *Keeping Things Whole* and the poetry collection *Search Box Bed*. See darrylwhetter.ca.

Editor Biographies

Rishma Dunlop published five books of poetry: *Lover Through Departure, White Album, Metropolis, Reading Like a Girl,* and *The Body of My Garden.* CBC Radio produced her radio drama, *The Raj Kumari's Lullaby,* about an immigrant daughter's coming of age in Quebec. She won the Emily Dickinson Prize for Poetry and has been a finalist for the CBC Poetry Prize and Non-Fiction Prize. Her publications as editor are *Red Silk: An Anthology of South Asian Canadian Women Poets; White Ink: Poems on Mothers and Motherhood;* and *Art, Literature and Place: An Ecopoetics Reader.* In 2009 she was awarded the Canada-U.S. Fulbright Research Chair in Creative Writing, and in 2011 she was elected a Fellow of the Royal Society of Canada. Dunlop was professor of English and education at York University, Toronto. She was coordinator of the creative writing program from 2007 to 2011. Further information can be found at rishmadunlop.com.

Daniel Scott Tysdal is the author of three books of poetry: *Fauxccasional Poems* (Goose Lane, 2015), *The Mourner's Book of Albums* (Tightrope, 2010), and *Predicting the Next Big Advertising Breakthrough Using a Potentially Dangerous Method* (Coteau, 2006). *Predicting* received the ReLit Award for Poetry (2007) and the Anne Szumigalski Poetry Award (2006). His poetry textbook, *The Writing Moment: A Practical Guide to Creating Poems* (2014), was published by Oxford University Press. He currently teaches creative writing and English literature at the University of Toronto Scarborough.

Priscila Uppal is an internationally acclaimed poet, a fiction writer, memoirist, essayist, playwright, and a professor of English at York University, where for nearly a decade she was coordinator of the creative writing program. Among her publications are ten collections of poetry, including *Sabotage* (2015), *Ontological Necessities* (2006; shortlisted for the Griffin Poetry Prize), *Traumatology* (2010), *Successful Tragedies: Poems 1998–2010* (Bloodaxe Books, U.K.), *Winter Sport: Poems*, and *Summer Sport: Poems*; the critically acclaimed novels *The Divine Economy of Salvation* (2002) and *To Whom It May Concern* (2009); and the study *We Are What We Mourn: The Contemporary English-Canadian Elegy* (2009). Her work has been published internationally and translated into Croatian, Dutch, French, Greek, Italian, Korean, and Latvian. She was the first-ever poet-in-residence for Canadian Athletes Now during the 2010 Vancouver and 2012 London Olympic and Paralympic games as well as the Rogers Cup Tennis Tournament in 2011. Her first play, *6 Essential Questions*, had its world premiere as part of the Factory Theatre 2013–14 season and was published by Playwrights Canada Press in 2015. Her memoir, *Projection: Encounters with My Runaway Mother* (2013), was a finalist for the Hilary Weston Writer's Trust Prize for non-fiction and the Governor General's Award for non-fiction. She has edited numerous anthologies, including *Barry Callaghan: Essays on His Works*, *Best Canadian Poetry*, *The Exile Book of Canadian Sports Stories*, *The Exile Book of Poetry in Translation*, and *Red Silk: An Anthology of South-Asian Canadian Women Poets*. *Time Out London* dubbed her "Canada's coolest poet." For more information visit priscilauppal.ca.